# too close for comfort

## ALSO BY MAUDE BARLOW

*Profit Is Not the Cure: A Citizen's Guide to Saving Medicare* (2002)

*Blue Gold: The Battle Against Corporate Theft of the World's Water* (with Tony Clarke, 2002)

*Global Showdown: How the New Activists Are Fighting Global Corporate Rule* (with Tony Clarke, 2001)

*Frederick Street: Life and Death on Canada's Love Canal* (with Elizabeth May, 2000)

*MAI: The Multilateral Agreement on Investment Round 2; New Global and Internal Threats to Canadian Sovereignty* (with Tony Clarke, 1998)

*The Fight of My Life: Confessions of an Unrepentant Canadian* (1998)

*MAI: The Multilateral Agreement on Investment and the Threat to American Freedom* (with Tony Clarke, 1998)

*MAI: The Multilateral Agreement on Investment and the Threat to Canadian Sovereignty* (with Tony Clarke, 1997)

*The Big Black Book: The Essential Views of Conrad and Barbara Amiel Black* (with Jim Winter, 1997)

*Straight through the Heart: How the Liberals Abandoned the Just Society* (with Bruce Campbell, 1995)

*Class Warfare: The Assault on Canada's Schools* (with Heather-jane Robertson, 1994)

*Take Back the Nation 2* (with Bruce Campbell, 1993)

*Take Back the Nation* (with Bruce Campbell, 1992)

*Parcel of Rogues: How Free Trade Is Failing Canada* (1990)

# too close for comfort

## Canada's Future within Fortress North America

# Maude Barlow

Copyright © 2005 by Maude Barlow

**Library and Archives Canada Cataloguing in Publication**

Barlow, Maude
    Too close for comfort : Canada's future within fortress North America / Maude Barlow.

ISBN 0-7710-1088-5

    1. Canada – Relations – United States.    2. United States – Relations – Canada.    3. Canada – Economic policy – 1991-.
4. Canada – Social Policy.    I. Title.

FC249.B368 2005    971.07'1    C2005-903393-2

We acknowledge the financial support of the Government of Canada through the Book Publishing Industry Development Program and that of the Government of Ontario through the Ontario Media Development Corporation's Ontario Book Initiative. We further acknowledge the support of the Canada Council for the Arts and the Ontario Arts Council for our publishing program.

Typeset in Bembo by M&S, Toronto
Printed and bound in Canada

This book is printed on acid-free paper that is 100% recycled, ancient-forest friendly (100% post-consumer recycled).

McClelland & Stewart Ltd.
*The Canadian Publishers*
75 Sherbourne Street
Toronto, Ontario
M5A 2P9
www.mcclelland.com

2  3  4  5    09 08 07 06 05

To my grandchildren, Maddy, Ellie, and Baby Angus

# contents

# about this book

In many ways, this book is a culmination of several years of reflection and action. Along with colleagues in the Council of Canadians and other civil-society groups in Canada and around the world, I have been fighting the forces of powerful corporations and institutions for many years. John Ralston Saul called it a "*coup d'état* in slow motion" – a bid systematically launched thirty years ago by the wealthy and powerful to roll back decades of democratic progress. There have been wins and losses. The FTA and NAFTA are deeply entrenched, with the results we predicted. Canada has adopted the class system of our neighbours to the South and has its own entrenched underclass. Low taxes for the rich have reinforced a sense of entitlement enjoyed by those in the upper reaches of our social structure. Social security has been gutted, and Canada is slowly sliding to a two-tiered health-care system. If this development is not checked, Canada will soon have American health-care corporations and their investors selling their services here.

We have given away control of our energy supplies. Canada now imports oil to provide for the needs of its own citizens in order to honour export commitments made under NAFTA to supply an energy-hungry United States. Water may go the same route as a thirsty America eyes water resources totally unprotected by the Canadian government. And environmental deregulation now underway is further damaging an ecosystem still reeling from deep cuts made over the course of the last decade.

There have been many victories, of course. Canadians led the successful global fight against the Multilateral Agreement on

Investment and civil-society groups have worked to support Third World governments in their firm resolve to stand up to the powerful North in international trade negotiations. As a result, World Trade Organization meetings have failed twice in recent years and NAFTA's successor, the Free Trade Area of the Americas, is fighting for survival. Canadians continue to cherish and fight for the social legacy that was the triumphant achievement of a generation shaped by the Depression and war. And Canadians were successful again in forcing the Martin government to say no to George Bush's Ballistic Missile Defense plan.

These battles have been fought, and won or lost, over a period of years. But now the push is on to make them happen all at once. Deep integration – the effective erasure of the border between Canada and the United States – will affect everything: the economy, the social structure, social programs, the environment. Even democracy itself will be compromised, because the terms of integration call for many aspects of Canadians' lives to be governed, not by their elected representatives, but by a distant, secretive, and unaccountable secretariat. In the pages that follow, I have tried to trace the ramifications of integration in a number of spheres: defence and foreign policy, social programs, the intelligence and security apparatus, and the environment. In some ways, this exploration makes bleak reading.

But even as the business elites gather their forces for the push to eliminate all meaningful distinctions between life in Canada and in neo-conservative America, there is something else happening. In Canada and around the world, a civil society is emerging. It is challenging the juggernaut of free-market fundamentalism that has broken the social fabric in countries around the world. It is reclaiming public places, renewing civic discourse, renegotiating its relationship to government. It is creating what American education scholar Henry Giroux calls the "language of possibility." George W. Bush and the hawks surrounding him have one vision for the world. Most of the world's people have another. Where will Canada stand?

# acknowledgements

I am deeply grateful to many people for their assistance, wise advice, and moral support in the writing of this book. First and foremost I want to express my delight in working once again with Jonathan Webb, my terrific editor, and with Susan Renouf, and the team at M&S, including Jenny Bradshaw. My Council of Canadians family came through as always, providing background information, guidance, and encouragement. Special thanks to Cathy Holtslander, Sara Ehrhardt, Brent Patterson, Guy Caron, Ariel Troster, and my assistant, Melanie O'Dell. I also consulted many colleagues and want to express my deepest gratitude to Steven Staples, Roch Tasse, Mike McBane, Elizabeth May, Alice Slater, John Cavanagh, Heather-jane Robertson, Tony Clarke, Larry Kuehn, Fred Wilson, Colleen Fuller, Gordon Laxer, Pat Mooney, Bonnie Diamond, Jim Stanford, Shiv Chopra, Dennis Howlett, Janice Harvey, David Coon, and Steven Shrybman. I wish to acknowledge with gratitude the support of the Lannan Foundation for its generous assistance and the honour of its fellowship award. Finally, I am, as always, so grateful for the support of my family, and, in particular, my husband, Andrew.

# fortress
# north america

*Corporate Canada and the Rise of the Christian Right*

In April 2003, just seventeen months after the terrorist attacks on New York and the Pentagon, Thomas d'Aquino, president and chief executive officer of the Canadian Council of Chief Executives (CCCE), hosted several dozen Canadian business leaders at an exclusive meeting in Washington that included Tom Ridge, then secretary of homeland security, Spencer Abraham, then secretary of energy, and Richard Perle, one of the key authors of the Bush doctrine on national security. The Canadian business community had come to express its grave concern about the effect of U.S. security measures on the flow of traffic and goods across the Canada–U.S. border. The delays and disruptions caused by intensified security measures brought home to the CCCE its vulnerability in the event that Canada should find itself outside of Fortress North America. Eighty-seven per cent of all Canadian exports go to the United States and some 40 per cent of Canada's GNP is tied to Canada–U.S. trade. This dependence is a direct result of the two trade agreements, the Canada–U.S. Free Trade Agreement (FTA) and its successor, the North American Free Trade Agreement (NAFTA), for which d'Aquino and his friends had lobbied furiously in the 1980s. No major country in the world is as dependent on a single trading partner as Canada, post-NAFTA.

But now d'Aquino and his colleagues had come to Washington to convey their dismay. They were shocked to realize that NAFTA was not enough to keep the border open and keenly aware that the Bush administration was prepared to rewrite unilaterally the terms and conditions of entry into its markets, regardless of any previous agreement. They were worried that their historically privileged relationship with Wall Street and Washington would be eroded as the United States forged ties and bilateral trade agreements with other states, such as Mexico and China. And they understood that, following the invasion of Iraq, Britain and Australia were seen as closer and more loyal military allies than the northern neighbour, which had withheld its support for the war. So Canada's business leaders were anxious when they walked into the Washington meeting.

They got an earful. One badly shaken CEO said later that Richard Perle told the group that Canada had better figure out where its interests lie. The message was clear: security trumped all other concerns. If Canadian business leaders wanted the border to stay open, they would have to help build a security perimeter around North America and support America's military, energy, and economic interests abroad.

## THE POLITICS OF DIVISION

Nine eleven changed everything. It gave a directionless U.S. president new energy and a cause. It drastically altered the context of international politics and set the stage for an aggressive new U.S. foreign policy. It led to the erosion of civil liberties everywhere. On the home front, in the period leading up to the 2004 election campaign, post-9/11 manoeuvring saw the entrenchment of a powerful alliance of big-business interests, neo-conservative politicians, and Christian evangelicals that appears set to dominate United States politics for years to come.

American political culture is deeply divided: gone is the broad liberal consensus that defined political competition in the years after the Second World War. (The nature of this revolution is explored more fully in Chapter 2.) The Canadian political scene is marginally less partisan. Evangelical Christians have not yet challenged the separation of Church and state in Canada as they have in the United States. And other differences remain, notably the Canadian public's attachment to certain social values that are largely absent from the American political scene. But these Canadian values are under attack as never before and the business community continues to play a leading role in the assault. Deep integration with the United States would serve the interests of big business very nicely. If it happens – and the process is much further advanced than most Canadians realize – then the nature of Canadian politics and society is likely to be altered profoundly and irrevocably.

## THE CCCE TAKES CHARGE

A striking similarity between Canadian and American political structures at present is the extraordinary influence both in the Prime Minister's Office and in the White House of the heads of the continent's most powerful corporations. No one embodies that influence in Canada more completely than Thomas d'Aquino, head of the CCCE, Canada's foremost corporate lobby. D'Aquino has been a driving force behind Fortress North America for almost thirty years. He claims, and would like to believe, that North American economic integration is "irreversible." The CCCE is made up of the CEOs of the 150 largest corporations in Canada, many of them branch plants of U.S. transnationals. D'Aquino founded the predecessor to the CCCE, the Business Council on National Issues (BCNI), in 1976 and it became the private-sector leader in the development and promotion of both the FTA and NAFTA. The BCNI spent millions of dollars to sell these deals to the Canadian people. (In his memoir, *Wrestling with the Elephant: The Inside Story of the Canada–U.S. Trade Wars*, Gordon Ritchie, deputy chief trade negotiator for the FTA, boasted that "in a radical departure from past practice," he brought the BCNI into the negotiation process as a partner to government. Needless to say, no labour, environmental, or human-rights groups had similar access to power.)

Member chief executives of the CCCE head companies that collectively have annual revenues of more than $600 billion and control a majority of Canada's private-sector investments and exports. In addition to d'Aquino, the CCCE Executive Committee includes a who's who of the corporate elite in Canada, among them: Chairman Richard L. George, president and CEO of Suncor Energy Inc.; Honorary Chairman A. Charles Baillie, CEO of Toronto Dominion Bank; Vice-Chairman Dominic D'Alessandro, CEO of Manulife Financial; Paul Desmarais, Jr., head of Power Corporation of Canada; Jacques Lamarre, CEO of SNC-Lavalin Group; Gwyn Morgan, CEO of EnCana Corporation; and Gordon Nixon, of the Royal Bank of Canada. Members of the CCCE enjoy easy and regular access to the halls of power in Ottawa and Washington. D'Aquino is a good friend of many influential Republicans, including George Bush, Sr. On a fishing trip they took together in Labrador in the summer of 2002, Bush convinced d'Aquino that his concerns about delays at the border would not be taken seriously in Washington until Canada was prepared to meet U.S. security demands.

Member companies of the CCCE have done very well under NAFTA. While the rest of Canadian society, apart from the very rich, has seen its standard of living stagnate or decline in the years following the implementation of the two trade agreements, the big-business community has prospered. In 1988, the 150 members of the BCNI claimed collective assets of $1 trillion. Today these same companies have collective assets of $2.5 trillion. Between 1988 and 2002, thirty-nine BCNI/CCCE member corporations increased their revenues by 105 per cent, while at the same time, decreasing their workforce by almost 15 per cent. Their promises of "jobs, jobs, jobs" did not materialize.

Following the traumatic meeting in Washington, d'Aquino raised $2 million from his private-sector friends to launch the North American Security and Prosperity Initiative. A year later, under the auspices of the CCCE, he released a forty-three-page manifesto entitled "New Frontiers: Building a 21st Century Canada–United States Partnership in North America." "New Frontiers" called on the Canadian government to seek a special relationship with the United States to protect Canadian trade from being disrupted by American security concerns by placing Canadian goods and companies beyond the ambit of normal U.S. trade law.

"Economic and physical security are inseparable," declared the CCCE. "Canada must integrate our plans for achieving economic advantage with a strategy for assuring the security both of our own borders and the continent as a whole." Allan Gotlieb, former Canadian ambassador to the United States, agreed: "The Canadian political agenda is economic security; for Americans, it is homeland security. Therein lies the potential element of a grand negotiation." Wendy Dobson, of the influential right-wing think-tank the C.D. Howe Institute, which has published no fewer than thirteen reports promoting deep integration in the last two years, called it the "Big Idea." She added, "Canadian concerns about economic security need to be linked with U.S. domestic priorities. . . . Since homeland security is the single overriding U.S. goal . . . what's needed is a strategic framework that links security and defence with economic goals."

D'Aquino was delighted with the December 2004 Ottawa meeting between President George W. Bush and Prime Minister Paul Martin. D'Aquino reported that more than "meets the eye" was accomplished between the two men (he would know) and noted that a "new spirit, new mood, and new chemistry" had broken the status quo that had existed between former prime minister Jean Chrétien and the Bush administration. In a speech to a January 2005 meeting of the CCCE, d'Aquino took credit for the Canada-Mexico Partnership Agreement signed by President Vicente Fox and Prime Minister Martin earlier that year during a meeting co-convened by the CCCE and its Mexican counterpart, the Consejo Mexicano de Hombres de Negocios. "We had a direct hand in the drafting of this agreement, and we have offered to convene a working group on competitiveness within this process."

D'Aquino said that the re-election of President Bush "opens an 18-month window for building political support in the U.S." To that end, "we continue to seize every opportunity to expand our relationships with key players in government, business, and academia . . . and will explore the possibility of joint activities with our United States counterparts in the Business Roundtable as well as other means to recruiting key business leaders in the United States to the cause."

## TAKEN TO TASK

A significant step was taken toward furthering the CCCE's deep-integration campaign with the release in May 2005 of the final report of the Independent Task Force on the Future of North America. The task force was organized under the auspices of the U.S. Council on Foreign Relations, a body that functions as a quasi-official foreign-policy think-tank of the U.S. government and publishes the influential conservative journal *Foreign Affairs*. Task force co-chairs were William Weld, former Republican governor of Massachusetts, ex-Mexican finance minister Pedro Aspe Armella, and former Liberal deputy prime minister John Manley. Thomas d'Aquino served as one of Canada's vice-chairs, and was joined by former Conservative finance minister Michael Wilson and former Alberta Conservative treasurer and current TransAlta executive James Dinning.

The choice of John Manley as the Canadian chair should come as no surprise to anyone who has watched his political career. When he replaced Lloyd Axworthy as foreign minister in the summer of 2000, he became a welcome and frequent guest in Washington, where his deferential style was well received by the

Bush administration. Manley became the chairman of an ad hoc cabinet committee on terrorism and the government's post-9/11 point man on security. He negotiated the "Smart Border" Accord with then U.S. attorney general John Ashcroft and Homeland Security Secretary Tom Ridge, with whom Manley proclaims he has a "strong personal relationship." He was a pro-U.S. hawk in the Chrétien cabinet and led the faction that supported the American invasion of Iraq. In a 2003 meeting with the editorial board of the Montreal *Gazette*, Manley said that Canada couldn't expect to sit at the G8 table and then, when the waiter presents the bill, excuse itself and go to the bathroom. In his book, *Uncle Sam and Us*, political scientist Stephen Clarkson writes that by making Manley deputy prime minister in 2002, Chrétien "gave maximum authority to the politician in whom the Bush Administration had the greatest trust."

A bitter rival of Paul Martin, Manley, since leaving politics, has been quick to criticize anything that might be interpreted as anti-Bush sentiment in the Liberal Party. His absence from active politics is probably temporary: he is widely assumed to have leadership ambitions when Martin's job opens up.

As co-chair of the Task Force on the Future of North America, John Manley called on the leaders of Canada, the United States, and Mexico to "think big and show some vision . . . be the architects of the future, rather than the custodians of the past." He wrote in the diplomatic magazine *Embassy*, "I think we've had 11 years of incrementalism, and during that time we have seen the EU expand its borders, eliminate borders among member countries, and launch a common currency. We're going to have to provide a vision that is more bold than incrementalism. What's the choice? Europe has made enormous steps in the years since NAFTA was signed. China has been going through a transformative process. In Canada, our only leverage is access to the U.S. market."

It should be noted that John Manley serves on the board of directors of a number of corporations that benefit from cross-border trade, including Nortel; Obvious Solutions Inc., whose flagship product, Abrica, is a software program that automates supply-chain transactions between trading companies; and Comnetix Inc., a leading provider of biometric security programs. One of the key recommendations of the task force is that all airports and border crossings in North America be equipped with state-of-the-art biometric security devices of the kind that Comnetix manufactures. Manley will "advise and counsel the Company on various matters, including matters related to homeland security both in Canada and the United States," according to the company's public announcement of his appointment.

The *National Post*, a tireless promoter of deeper integration, welcomed the creation of the task force with enthusiasm and this description of its mandate: "Senior business and political leaders from Canada, the United States, and Mexico are joining forces to establish a blueprint for a powerhouse North American trading bloc to take on the world, shielded by a Fortress-America style defence perimeter." When the task force issued an interim report in March 2005, the *Toronto Star* called it a "new vision of a Fortress North America in which the continent is wrapped in a security perimeter from the Arctic all the way to the Guatemalan border."

The CCCE was delighted with the final task-force report, which essentially reiterated the lobby group's own major demands: a "common security perimeter by 2010" that would require changes to unnamed policies and statutes; a "unified North American border action plan" that would harmonize visa and refugee regulations; increased shared military and security intelligence; a "North American energy strategy" that would further harmonize a deregulated North American energy market; a "common external tariff" that would require North America to negotiate international trade agreements as a bloc; a "tested once" policy for pharmaceuticals that would harmonize the "regulatory burden" so that drugs approved in the United States would now have to be accepted into Canada; and a review of "some sectors" of NAFTA that were excluded from the original agreement.

While the final report does not specify what these sectors might be, they were laid out, along with an even more ambitious agenda for deep integration, in the confidential minutes of the Toronto, October 2004, meeting of the task force obtained by the Council of Canadians. While a number of these ideas and recommendations appeared in the final report, some are conspicuously absent. However, the minutes, which the scribe says represented a "consensus" among the three countries, clearly catalogue the larger agenda of the members of the task force and describe what they are really planning when their deliberations are behind closed doors. The minutes offer insight into the breathtaking plans the business community has for a North American Union, one in which Canada would supply resources and political acquiescence, Mexico would provide cheap migrant labour for the continent, and the peoples of all three countries would see their environmental and social security standards weakened in order to promote the interests of an increasingly integrated and powerful business sector.

All agreed, the minutes recorded, that North American economic integration is so advanced that any return to the status quo would be extremely costly to all three countries. Task-force members favoured "a bold vision for regional integration, even if elements of that vision could not immediately be put into practice."

Proposals included a North American "brand name" – a "discourse and set of symbols designed to distinguish the region from the rest of the world . . . portraying North America as a sort of club of privileged members"; a North American security perimeter incorporating air, land, and sea; common exclusion lists for people from Third World countries; joint legal responses to terrorist organizations; parallel bureaucratic structures in all three countries to facilitate security collaboration and crisis response; deployment of new aerial radar systems around the North American perimeter; joint planning for terrorist attacks; biometric identification at the borders; a North American passport; common powers for customs and immigration agents; trilateral customs and immigration systems; joint visa requirements for people outside the continent; a one-inspection, one-test, one-certification system for North America; elimination of NAFTA rules of origin and a common tariff; recognition of all North American citizens as domestic investors in each country; a North American currency union; elimination of current exemptions for culture and agriculture; an integrated North American electrical grid; and a "North American resource pact that would allow for greater intra-regional trade and invest-ment in certain non-renewable natural resources, such as oil, gas, and fresh water."

To underline that Canada's water supplies are very much part of future negotiations, the task-force members agreed that "con-tentious or intractable issues will simply require more time to ripen politically." But, say the minutes, "no item − not Canadian water, not Mexican oil, not American anti-dumping laws − is 'off the table.'"

(Canadian task-force member Thomas Axworthy issued a dis-senting opinion to the final report. He wrote: "I am not persuaded that the benefits of a common security perimeter are worth the risks in harmonizing visa and asylum regulations. Problems in the [Maher] Arar case, for example, show the dangers. On the environ-ment, the North Dakota water diversion project threatens its Manitoba neighbour and ignores the 1909 Water Boundaries Treaty. The commitment to a cleaner North American environment must be stronger, and certainly cannot wait until 2010. Finally, I do not agree with reviewing those sections of NAFTA that were initially excluded: cultural protection and a prohibition for bulk water exports should remain within national not joint jurisdiction.")

Both the task-force final report and the CCCE's "New Frontiers" manifesto embody a radical vision for the future of North America. It is little wonder that d'Aquino was ecstatic to see these ideas almost instantly embraced by the politicians. When Paul Martin, George Bush, and Vicente Fox met in Waco, Texas, on March 23, 2005, they signed the Security and Prosperity Partnership of North America, an almost word-for-word replica of the CCCE's North American

Security and Prosperity Initiative. All the CCCE's central demands had been included in the Waco pact, said d'Aquino, who pronounced the agreement "an ambitious vision for the future of our continent."

## THE ELITES AND THE CANADIAN PUBLIC

It would be a mistake to imagine that these reports and agreements are mere words and without significance. Already, a plethora of bureaucratic panels, workgroups, and task forces are working tirelessly to harmonize regulatory systems, border policies, defence and emergency programs, and immigration and refugee procedures between Canada and the United States. What is so shocking about these developments is that most Canadians are completely unaware of them. At no point have they been asked what they think. With the exception of ballistic missile defence, which generated considerable debate, all other aspects of the deep-integration agenda are unfolding in something close to secrecy. The only sector in Canada substantively influencing the Canadian government on the future of North America is the big-business lobby and its backers in the mainstream press.

The voices of opposition to this agenda are regularly belittled even though they represent the majority opinion in Canada. Indeed, polls show that Canadians do not like George Bush and his beliefs, and do not want to adopt either his foreign policy or his domestic social security agenda. An Ekos Research poll taken for the Department of National Defence in early June 2005 found that Canadians believe that President Bush is almost as great a threat to Canada's national security as Osama bin Laden (CanWest, June 13, 2005). And an international survey of attitudes about the United States, commissioned for the Pew Center in the United States and released at the end of June 2005, reported that Canadians' opinion of the United States has eroded so far that they now view China as favourably as they do their neighbour to the south. Canadians told the pollsters that they now see Americans as rude, greedy, and violent (*Globe and Mail*, June 24, 2005). While negative views of the United States have grown everywhere, the Pew Center reported, it is in Canada where approval has declined the most markedly. As Bruce Campbell of the Canadian Centre for Policy Alternatives points out, polls also show a deep and growing divide in attitudes and values between the business elite in Canada and the Canadian public. Yet d'Aquino calls anyone who disagrees with his campaign to promote deeper ties to the Bush administration, even those who work on international development, "extremist nationalists." Hugh Segal of the Institute for Research on Public Policy calls opponents of deep integration "proponents of 'Little Canada,' merchants of insecurity and polarization." He says the business community must "begin the inoculation process against the 'Canadian Disease' by advancing the prospects, issues, challenges, and opportunities of a North American community."

This deep divide between the Canadian public and the business community became starkly evident in the reaction to Paul Martin's decision not to join Bush's ballistic missile defence plan. According to a March 2005 Decima poll, almost 60 per cent of Canadians supported his decision, and only one-quarter of Canadians opposed it. However, a COMPAS poll taken the same week found that 85 per cent of Canadian CEOs strongly opposed the decision and saw it as a "serious barrier to good relations with the United States," more harmful, in fact, than any other recent government decision or action. So upset was the Chamber of Commerce that chief executive Nancy Hughes met with her American counterparts to smooth the waters. "We can't leave this relationship to the politicians," she told the press.

The same issue highlighted a similar gap between the Canadian media and the public. The overwhelming majority of media pundits, commentators, and editorial writers fiercely criticized the Martin government for the BMD decision, leading the *Globe and Mail's* Lawrence Martin to write that the mainstream media in this country no longer represent the views of the majority of Canadians. Martin traced the change of the journalism culture in Canada to the mid-1990s, when Southam, the country's biggest newspaper chain with a history of hewing to a mainstream political course, was taken over first by Conrad Black's Hollinger Inc., and then by CanWest Global, which makes no secret of its pro-American, conservative bias. As well, the conservative tabloid Sun chain became Canada's second largest newspaper group in the last decade. The result was the establishment of two major newspaper chains to the right of the political spectrum, and none on the left or in the centre. Further, Martin pointed out, the two national newspapers are major agenda-setters: the *National Post* is decidedly right-wing, the *Globe and Mail* conservative. At *Maclean's* magazine, Kenneth Whyte, former editor of the *Post*, runs the show, and L. Ian MacDonald, a Mulroney devotee, now edits *Policy Options*, once a liberal magazine. Even the publicly owned CBC gives prominence to right-wing voices. On Peter Mansbridge's "At Issue" panel on *The National*, regulars include Gordon Gibson of the Fraser Institute, Andrew Coyne of the *National Post*, and former Conservative pollster Allan Gregg; only Chantal Hébert, national affairs writer for the *Toronto Star* and a columnist for *Le Devoir*, represents a more liberal point of view.

"Today's press, most strikingly on the question of U.S. relations – BMD, Iraq, defence spending, taxation, etc. – has become concertedly conservative, moving to the right of the population," wrote Martin. "The conservative media tends to favour a closer embrace of the United States and its values. Canadians themselves show little inclination to go that route. It is a story line – the press vs. the people – that runs right to the heart of the debate over the future of the country." Martin added that as a result of the corporate takeover of the Canadian print media, the largest segment of the population, centre-left Canadians, were at risk of losing their voice.

This situation will be exacerbated if the Canadian and U.S. chambers of commerce are successful in their campaign to have the Canadian government remove its foreign-ownership restrictions in the telecommunications industry, one of the many recommendations put forward by cross-border business lobbyists. The Canadian government is currently reviewing these restrictions and has indicated a willingness to abandon regulatory control. The Communications, Energy and Paperworkers Union of Canada warns that deregulating telecommunications would mean that Canadian content controls in radio, television, and newspapers would have to be abandoned as many telecommunications companies, such as Quebecor, Rogers, Bell Canada, and CanWest Global, have cross-ownership interests in these other forms of media.

## LIBERALS TOE THE LINE

How has it come to pass that a small handful of corporate executives are setting a particular course for Canada and North America in the future when the polls consistently show that Canadians would choose a different one? Undoubtedly, the big-business lobby in Canada has become increasingly powerful in recent years, as it has all over the world. (Many transnational corporations now have assets greater than those of most nation states.) Economic globalization has freed corporations from many nation-state laws, giving them enormous bargaining leverage with governments who vie for their business with tax breaks and other incentives. Thomas d'Aquino regularly cites the need for more tax breaks for Canadian companies in order to be competitive with emerging economies like China, even though corporate tax rates in Canada are among the lowest in the Organization for Economic Co-operation and Development (OECD).

In the last twenty years, the corporate lobby in Canada has succeeded in influencing policy at every level. It has funded powerful think-tanks, such as the C.D. Howe and the Fraser institutes, that publish policy papers serving the interests of the business community. It has influenced academia by being heavily represented on university boards. It has bought newspapers whose pages are more and more closed to dissenting opinion. And it is increasingly tied to politicians in the two major political parties.

For instance, Rx&D, the Canadian lobby group of the giant brand-name drug companies (most of whom are foreign-based), has formed very close ties with the federal Liberal Party. In an in-depth investigative story, *Ottawa Citizen* writer Glen McGregor documented the intimate relationship that has been built up between the Liberal Party and the drug companies over the years, including the hiring of senior Liberal backroom strategists and former aides to cabinet ministers to lobby the government that was their previous employer. As a result, the drug companies have successfully lobbied the Liberals to abandon an earlier promise to end their twenty-year patent protection that has caused drug prices to rise so dramatically in recent years.

The CCCE can take a lot of credit for the steady rightward drift of the two major mainstream political parties over the last two decades, a development that mirrors the entrenchment of neo-Liberal market policies in Washington and deep inside international institutions such as the World Bank and the World Trade Organization (WTO). Jean Chrétien's Liberals fought Brian Mulroney's Progressive Conservatives and their pro-American policies for the entire time they were in Opposition and adopted every single plank of the Mulroney agenda when they took office, including NAFTA, leading d'Aquino to welcome the party "back from the wilderness."

Years of harmonization under NAFTA have imposed policy constraints on Canada as power has shifted from government to the market and corporations have become more influential in dictating policy. The dramatic increase in Canada's reliance on U.S. markets for economic survival has also subjected all Canadian laws, practices, and regulations, including government spending, to the test of whether they violate American business interests. This in turn has limited Canada's ability to maintain social, cultural, and environmental policies that are in the interest of Canadian citizens.

Savage cuts to social spending started in the Mulroney era with the elimination of child benefits, the "clawing back" of family allowances and old-age pensions, and the elimination of government support for unemployment insurance. They were followed in the Chrétien years with the 1995 federal budget of Finance Minister Paul Martin, which cut an unprecedented 40 per cent from federal cash payments to the provinces for health care, social assistance, and post-secondary education, and ended the Canada Assistance Plan, which provided a universal standard for Canadians in need.

It cannot be a surprise then that Prime Minister Martin signed the Waco pact, thereby advancing the deep-integration agenda of the CCCE. Martin, after all, was a wealthy businessman and has strong ties with the corporate community. His cabinet includes Finance Minister Ralph Goodale, whose first public pronouncement was to defend $4.4 billion in corporate tax cuts; Deputy Prime Minister Anne McLellan, who as the minister of natural resources was a favourite of the big energy companies for her further deregulation of the energy sector; and Foreign Minister Pierre Pettigrew, who as minister of international trade was a hardline proponent of free trade with the United States and helped establish WTO negotiations on the trade in services, including health care.

Martin's first major policy initiatives all focused on Canada–U.S. relations. He set up a powerful new Ministry of Public Safety and Emergency Preparedness, chaired by Deputy Prime Minister Anne McLellan, which oversees intelligence and border security and is linked to the U.S. Department of Homeland Security. He appointed Rob Wright, former commissioner of the Canada Customs and Revenue Agency as the first Canadian national security adviser, and situated him in the PMO for easy access. He appointed Scott Brison, a former Tory leadership candidate who advocates a "seamless border" between Canada and the United States as his parliamentary secretary with special responsibility for Canada–U.S. relations. And to signal the weight he gives to the issue,

Paul Martin himself chairs the cabinet committee on Canada–U.S. relations.

Martin also established a comprehensive foreign-policy review, which was tabled in the House of Commons on April 19, 2005. The review received very little attention because it was overshadowed by the Gomery inquiry's revelations of corruption and the showdown over passage of the budget. The report, "Canada's International Policy Statement – A Role of Pride and Influence in the World," mirrors the foreign-policy position of both the Canadian Council of Chief Executives and the Task Force on the Future of North America. Touted the "first integrated plan designed to strengthen Canada's role in the world," it recommends "revitalizing Canada's North America partnership with the U.S. and Mexico by enhancing security and promoting prosperity," and "marks the beginning of a long-time process to strengthen our military . . . to meet the increasingly complex needs of a new security environment." The review calls for strengthening coordination and cross-border law enforcement and counterterrorism programs with the United States; strengthening the border and harmonizing and bolstering security systems at points of entry to North America; expanding harmonized pre-clearance trade systems across the border; strengthening the link between Canada's new Integrated Threat Assessment Centre and its U.S. counterpart, the U.S. National Counterterrorism Center; building twenty-first century borders by countering threats with the imposition of electronic visas; collaborating with the United States to share critical infrastructure, including cybernetic and communication networks; and a unique Canada–U.S. passport using biometric identifiers. The report also says it will work with the United States to push for the full implementation of international conventions to combat terrorism.

The fact that this long-awaited foreign-policy review concentrates so much on Canada's relationship with the United States, as well as on combating terrorism when Canada has not been the subject of a terrorist attack, shows the disposition of the Martin government to satisfy the demands from both Washington and Canada's big-business community for deeper continental integration.

Perhaps most telling was Paul Martin's choice of Frank McKenna, lawyer, businessman, and former premier of New Brunswick, as ambassador to the United States. Steven Staples of the Polaris Institute has followed Frank McKenna's career closely and warns that he will serve the interests of the CCCE almost exclusively in Washington. McKenna was always in the "business" wing of the Liberal Party, rather than its "social" wing. He supported free trade even when the federal party did not. After stepping down in 1997, McKenna made an easy transition from legislature to boardroom, Staples writes, and now serves on many corporate boards, including Noranda, General Motors of Canada, and CanWest Global Communications Corp. However, it is his involvement with one company in particular that gives cause for concern to those worried about big business setting the agenda.

The Washington-based Carlyle Group is a huge private equity firm with assets of almost $19 billion. It has been called the "ex-presidents' club" because of the firm's success in recruiting former politicians such as former Conservative British prime minister John Major; James A. Baker III, George Bush, Sr.'s secretary of state; and Frank Carlucci, Ronald Reagan's defense secretary and a former deputy director of the CIA. George Bush, Sr., served on the company's Asia advisory board until 2004. McKenna serves on the Carlyle Canada Advisory Board along with Power Corp's Paul Desmarais, Bombardier's Laurent Beaudoin, and Allan Gotlieb.

The company's most high-profile investment has been with United Defense, a U.S. arms manufacturer that builds combat vehicles, artillery, naval guns, and missile launchers for the U.S. government. Carlyle also owns Vought Aircraft Industries, which makes the B2 stealth bomber, and WCI Cable, which built the undersea fibre-optic cable that connects Alaska to the continental United States to carry secure data for the U.S. national missile defence system. The Carlyle Group's connections to senior officials of the White House has led to charges of insider influence. The company has also gained notoriety for its long-time financial relationship with the Saudi Binladen Group, the US$5-billion construction firm run by Osama bin Laden's estranged family. (Carlyle severed its ties with the family in the wake of the September 11, 2001, attacks.)

In 2001, McKenna hosted a meeting between the Carlyle Group and Canadian powerbrokers, including Paul Martin, at his home in Moncton. The next year, he organized a second meeting, this time with over two hundred members of the Canadian business elite and featured speaker, George Bush, Sr., who stayed on at the McKenna home as a guest. That year, the Canada Pension Plan Investment Board invested US$60 million in Carlyle, provoking criticism that the Canadian government was profiting from the enormous expansion of military spending in the United States. However, Frank McKenna continues to defend closer military ties with the United States. In a February 2002 speech to the Canadian Bar Association, he said, "The United States wants to create a continental defence structure. To cut to the chase, I am not troubled by that concept. I personally don't believe that our sovereignty is at risk in participating in such an exercise."

## "RED-MEAT" CONSERVATIVES

If the Martin Liberals are dangerously open to the overtures of big business to create Fortress North America, Stephen Harper's Conservatives would represent a whole new threat to Canadian sovereignty if elected. This is because Stephen Harper is in very many ways, the Canadian George W. Bush. He is a fiscal and social conservative who would be at home with the American religious right that put Bush in the White House and that dominates the political landscape in the United States today.

Harper is a pro-American hawk. In a May 2003 speech to the Institute for Research on Public Policy, he said that Canada's traditional support for multilateralism is a "weak nation strategy" and called for Canada to replace the "soft power" of persuasive diplomacy and peacekeeping with the "hard power capabilities" of intelligence and military power in the service of continental security. A Stephen Harper government, he said (he was then leader of the Canadian Alliance) would root its foreign policy in respect for the United States. Canada shares the same fundamental values in a dangerous world, he asserted, with a country that just "happens" to be the world's sole superpower.

In this speech and others, Stephen Harper supported American military aggression around the world. "The time has come to recognize that the U.S. will continue to exercise unprecedented power in a world where international rules are unreliable and where the security and advancing of the free democratic order still depend significantly on the possession and use of military might." To ensure that Canada is "never again" perceived as a potential source of threats, Harper called for a "long-overdue" reform of our refugee programs.

He dismissed the Canadian government's decision not to participate in the U.S. invasion of Iraq as "abrasively neutral," and (incorrectly) said that Canadians supported the war. As leader of the Alliance, Harper called for active participation in George Bush's continental ballistic missile defence program and the massive "hard-power" buildup of Canada's military capacity. As Conservative Party leader, however, he vacillated on the issue when polls showed BMD to be unpopular, even with Conservative Party supporters, earning a stern rebuke from President Bush when he made his first visit to Canada. And now, the party has adopted resolutions in favour of BMD, in keeping with Stephen Harper's natural inclination.

Stephen Harper promotes "continental economic and security integration" with the United States, which would pave the way for a customs union between the two countries. Under a Harper government, Canada would lose the right to set its own labour, environmental, and security standards. He proposes to negotiate international trade agreements in partnership with the very superpower whose corporations want to come to Canada and deliver our public services on a for-profit basis. Stephen Harper has also called for a continental energy strategy that would be broadened to "a range of other natural resources." (This sounds like code for Canada's water.)

Stephen Harper is also deeply conservative in the George Bush tradition on domestic and social issues. No matter how much he tries to re-brand himself with a new party and a more moderate image, the fact remains that he hails from the far right and his values are not the values of most Canadians. His gurus are the right-wing ideologues at the University of Calgary, men like Tom Flanagan, David Bercuson, and Barry Cooper. Cooper told *Maclean's* magazine that Harper hasn't changed his views since becoming leader of the Conservative Party. He has simply "repackaged" himself to appeal to Ontario.

In January 1997, Harper resigned his seat as Reform MP for Calgary West to head up the National Citizens Coalition (NCC), in order, as he said at the time, to be able to be more forthright on his views than he had been under Preston Manning's leadership. The NCC and Stephen Harper had already forged deep bonds: both considered Brian Mulroney's Conservatives to be "too pink" and the NCC poured thousands of dollars into attack ads in the 1993 election against Harper's opponent, incumbent Progressive Conservative Jim Hawkes. The newly minted Reform MP Harper thanked the NCC for "a great victory for freedom in Canada" in Parliament while then NCC president David Somerville boasted that Reform "cribbed probably two-thirds of our policy book."

The National Citizens Coalition is a right-wing movement founded in 1967 by Colin M. Brown, a health-insurance salesman who hated medicare. In a 1984 newsletter to its members, the NCC claimed Canadians would "die" as a result of the Canada Health Act. The organization is currently run by Colin T. Brown, son of the founder. The NCC website contains no information about its "members," its funding, or its board of directors. However, the NCC has an advisory board, which consists of a who's who of the corporate world, and takes a pro-big-business perspective on all issues.

Over the years, the NCC has been a highly funded opponent of unions, official bilingualism, multiculturalism, universal social programs, public schools, the post office, equity programs for women and minorities, the Wheat Board, and government grants to the arts. An article in the May 1995 newsletter claimed that democracy is an Anglo-Saxon institution. When he was head of the NCC, Harper said that bilingualism is now a "religion" in Canada – but a "God that failed." Somerville wrote in the March 1996 newsletter that Canada should abandon attempts to keep Quebec in the Confederation. "If you want red meat for breakfast then you want to get involved in something like the National Citizens Coalition," he said.

Stephen Harper holds his own share of "red-meat" views. Several years ago, he slammed Atlantic Canada as a "can't do" culture and called Canada a "second-tier socialistic country" (*National Post*, December 8, 2000). He also signed the infamous "Firewall Manifesto" after the 2000 election, calling on Alberta to withdraw from the Canada Pension Plan and medicare, collect its own taxes, and kick out the RCMP. Harper told a journalist with the *BC Report* on January 11, 1999, that human-rights commissions are an attack on our fundamental freedoms – "totalitarianism, in fact." He wrote about the need to oppose "new projects costing billions of dollars for 'child poverty'" when he worked for the NCC and told the *National Post* on March 6, 2004, that "I'm very libertarian in the sense that I believe in small government." He has dismissed the Kyoto accord on climate change as a "boondoggle."

Harper takes credit for the assault on universal social programs in Canada. In a 1994 speech to the NCC annual dinner in Ancaster, Ontario, Harper cited the achievements that the Reform Party and the NCC had made in the five years since he last addressed the gathering: "What has happened in the past five years? Let me start with a positive side. . . . Universality has been severely reduced; it is virtually dead as a concept in most areas of public policy. The family allowance program has been eliminated and unemployment insurance has been seriously cut back. . . . These achievements are due in part to the Reform Party of Canada and in part to groups like the National Citizens Coalition."

Anyone studying the conservative right in the United States will immediately see all the hallmarks of this movement in the words and actions of Stephen Harper. He would fit very nicely in the Bush White House. But to really get the flavour of the similarities between the Harper Conservatives and the Christian right in the United States, one has to look to Harper and his party's positions on "the family." While his views are not perhaps as extreme as those expressed by some Conservative Party members – Randy White has said that gays have a "deviant lifestyle" – Stephen Harper is decidedly against rights for gays and lesbians. On January 20, 2005, he told the CBC, "I hate to say this but I think you have to draw the line somewhere . . . I believe we have to recognize the traditional definition of marriage in law. Otherwise we will continue to be presented with demands that just get more radical . . . I fear if we do this, the next thing on the Liberal agenda will be polygamy, and who knows what else."

Harper created a storm of protest when on February 16, 2005, he said that Liberals are hardly "lily-white" when it comes to protecting human rights and cited the anti-Jewish immigration policies of the Canadian government during the Second World War and the internment of Japanese-Canadians at that time. Human-rights groups from both communities reacted with outrage, saying that Harper was using past human-rights abuses as a measuring stick for today's situation and called on Harper to retract his statement. "I don't think that the memory of six million should be exploited to political advantage today," said Harold Troper, an historian at the University of Toronto.

Harper triggered similar concerns when his party placed ads in ethnic community newspapers opposing same-sex marriage on the assumption that ethnic communities are more traditional than mainstream Canadian society. This backfired for many minorities, however, because they understand that if a party can discriminate against one minority – gays and lesbians – it can discriminate against others. Stephen Harper reached a personal low point on October 23, 2002, in the House of Commons when he shouted at gay MP Svend Robinson, "I am sure the picture of the Honourable Member of the NDP is posted in much more wonderful places than just police stations."

## NORTHWARD CHRISTIAN SOLDIERS

Sincerely held religious beliefs accompanied by strict morality are obviously not a bad thing, and any Church is entitled to make its own rules about who, for example, it will choose to marry under Church auspices. (Some may deplore a lack of tolerance for alternative lifestyles displayed by particular denominations, but the freedom of religion means that people are free to make such choices.) Civil rights are another matter. Increasingly, however, the sometimes narrow convictions of Christian sects are being exploited by politicians in both Canada and the United States (where the tendency is highly developed) to introduce into the political realm a degree of inflexibility, passion, and rancour that tend to undermine the spirit of accommodation and tolerance that is essential to the functioning of a democratic society. Our civil liberties are threatened as a result. The point is that people are free to believe what they want privately, but if they enter politics to inflict those beliefs on others, then their religious concerns become fair game.

Intolerance for gays, passionate opposition to abortion, and a handful of other "hot-button" issues are pushing a growing number of born-again Canadians to identify with the evangelical, right-wing views of American fundamentalist groups such as Focus on the Family and the Christian Coalition, two of the groups that helped put George W. Bush in the White House. These groups and others from the far right share many of the same values and world view of both the NCC and its political wing, the Reform/Alliance/Conservative party of Stephen Harper. Many evangelical Christians share not only Harper's views on gays and lesbians, and abortion, but also on small government, privatized health care, environmental regulation, and an aggressive foreign policy backed up by force. These groups, so powerful in the United States, are now moving into Canada.

The Ottawa-based Campaign Life Coalition calls itself the "political wing of the pro-life movement in Canada" and lobbies politicians to outlaw abortion. Also in Ottawa is the Evangelical Fellowship of Canada, a "national movement that purposes to engage an increasingly inclusive participation of evangelicals" in Canadian life and believes that God will judge the living and the dead – the saved into "the resurrection of life," those who are lost into "the resurrection of damnation." The Christian right has launched a new social-policy think-tank called the Institute for Canadian Values to push for "greater representation of religious and moral consideration in government policy." Its founders liken the new institute to the Fraser Institute but with a decidedly religious tinge and count among their members Stephen Harper, Stockwell Day, and independent backbencher Pat O'Brien, who quit the Liberal Party because of its support for same-sex marriage.

While Focus on the Family, a right-wing, evangelical U.S. powerhouse with 2.5 million members, has been in Canada since 1983 (originally operating out of an office in Langley, B.C.), it is only in the last several years that money and resources have been pouring across the border. Armed now with an annual budget of $11 million, the Canadian office of Focus on the Family has been on a hiring spree in the last year and has opened a nine-person Ottawa office to advance its public-policy agenda with federal politicians. The reason is Bill C-38. The Civil Marriage Act, which allows same-sex marriage, received Royal assent on July 23, 2005. With the aid of funding from south of the border, the Canadian office mailed letters to hundreds of thousands of potential right-wing voters and fundamentalist Christians, who in turn, inundated the offices of members of Parliament. The *Globe and Mail*'s Jill Mahoney reported on January 29, 2005, that James Dobson, the founder of Colorado-based Focus on the Family (who has said that homosexuality will destroy the earth and is the prime architect of the anti-gay marriage bans passed in eleven U.S. states), has set his sights on Canada. Dobson used his media empire – his radio broadcasts are heard by more than 200 million listeners in 164 countries and in twenty-five languages – to influence the vote in Parliament. During the winter of 2004 and into the spring of 2005, he told his followers that the struggle for traditional marriage had "turned ugly" in Canada and asked for their prayers and money to support the fight.

Some seem to have heard the message literally. Members of Parliament in favour of the bill received dozens of calls from Americans who seemed to be very organized and who said, when asked who they represented, that they "work for Jesus." A secretive group called Concerned Canadian Parents, whose only traceable address was a post office box at a 7-Eleven store on Weston Road in Toronto, ran a very expensive ad campaign in major Canadian newspapers in spring 2005 urging Canadians to vote against Bill C-38 because it would be the "thin edge of the wedge that will destroy our Canadian way of life and damage our families." Concerned Canadian Parents has since been outed. On July 15, 2005, the *Vancouver Sun* ended the mystery and identified them as a Canadian wing of the Exclusive Brethren, a highly secretive sect of evangelical Christians with larger followings in Britain and the United States. The Exclusive Brethren practise a very strict moral code, believe deeply in the sanctity of marriage, and are utterly opposed to homosexuality. They require their women to wear headscarves and normally shun all political activity, including voting. But in the last U.S. presidential election, the Exclusive Brethren broke with tradition and donated US$500,000 to the Bush campaign. Now they have become involved in Canadian politics as well.

Focus on the Family Canada insists that it is an independent organization in spite of the millions of dollars in services and direct funding it receives from its U.S. parent. However, two of its thirteen directors, Tom Mason and Jim Daly, live in Colorado Springs and are directly affiliated with the U.S. organization. Days before C-38 was passed in the House of Commons, knowing they were going to lose the vote, the religious conservative groups said that the debate had awakened a "sleeping giant" in Canadian politics and vowed to escalate the fight. "Things might look dark to some people today," David Krayden of the Defend Marriage Coalition told the *Ottawa Citizen* (June 26, 2005), "but we do have the beginning of a new broader-based political coalition in Canada."

A number of former and current Conservative MPs are members of right-wing evangelical churches and share the world view of the Christian conservatives so powerful in the Bush White House. Christian News Ottawa is a website devoted to following (and promoting) the evangelical affiliations of Canadian politicians. "The fact is there are linkages everywhere you look between some sectors of evangelical Christianity and the Canadian Alliance" it states. Sharon Hayes, who sits on the board of Focus on the Family, was a Reform MP from 1993 to 1997. Stockwell Day, the Conservative Party's foreign affairs critic, is a lay Pentecostal minister who has publicly professed his belief that the world is only six thousand years old, that Adam and Eve were real, and that humans and dinosaurs coexisted.

Stephen Harper is a member of the Christian and Missionary Alliance church, which adopts a literal interpretation of the Bible and sounds very much like the teachings of the hard religious right in the United States. "The Old and New Testaments, inerrant [sic] as originally given, were verbally inspired by God and are a complete revelation of His will," says the mission statement. This church believes that salvation and redemption are provided only through Jesus Christ and the "Second Coming of Lord Jesus Christ is imminent and will be personal and visible." In an interview with the now-defunct *Conservative Times*, Harper characterized himself as a "Conservative Christian."

There are also links between Focus on the Family Canada and current candidates for the Conservative Party. Darrell Reid is the former president of the group's Canadian arm and the current nominated candidate for the party in Richmond, British Columbia. He was also chief of staff to former Reform leader Preston Manning and ran as a Reform candidate in 1997. Reid told the *Globe and Mail* (May 28, 2005): "I'm going to talk about the big issues and marriage is one big issue out there." Cindy Silver, the candidate in North Vancouver, was Focus on the Family's legal counsel until recently and is a past executive director of the Christian Legal Fellowship. John Weston, the candidate for West Vancouver–Sunshine Coast, writes for the Christian Legal Fellowship website and holds weekly office devotionals at his law firm. And Marc Dalton, Conservative candidate for Burnaby–New Westminster was a pastor of a community church and says he is concerned about the "erosion of religious liberties in the past number of years."

In Ontario, David Sweet is the candidate for Ancaster-Dundas-Flamborough-Westdale. Sweet is the past president of the Canadian chapter of Promise Keepers, whose mission is to "challenge Canadian men to discover the incredible life quest that God has for them as revealed by Christ and the Holy scriptures." Rondo Thomas beat former Conservative MP Rene Soetens for the nomination in Ajax. Dr. Thomas is a top official with the Canada Christian College, which is run by Charles McVety, a senior director of the Defend Marriage Coalition. On its website, the Coalition describes itself as a "rapidly growing" grass-roots movement out to defend the traditional Canada. Its mission statement resembles those of the far right in the United States that combine a narrow view of "family" with conservative views on small government and low taxes. "Canada is a nation that builds upon its Christian-Judeo heritage, embraces our freedoms, including our freedom of religion, and promotes marriage as the ideal situation for raising the next generation. It is a country that upholds decency and virtue and promotes individual responsibility, and insists on fair taxation and a limited government."

One of the Coalition members, the Calgary-based Canadian Conservative Union, goes even further in merging the beliefs of evangelicals with the politics of free enterprise. "Through the use of news media, the Canadian Conservative Union seeks to unite supporters of conservative principles, including: freedom of religion; freedom of speech; capitalism and free-enterprise; traditional moral values; commitment to a strong national defence; and provincial utilization of existing constitutional powers."

Three candidates in Nova Scotia – Andrew House in Halifax, Rakesh Khosla in Halifax West, and Paul Francis in Sackville–Eastern Shore – are evangelical Christians. All three were encouraged and endorsed by Tristan Emmanuel, a Presbyterian minister who calls himself a "Christian cultural apologist" and runs a political training program for evangelicals named Equipping Christians for the Public Square Centre. Emmanuel also calls himself the "motivational speaker" of Canada's Defend Marriage Coalition and ran for the far-right Christian Heritage Party in Ontario. "Our culture is hell-bent on cultural destruction and is dragging freedom-loving Christians along with it," he writes on his website. Emmanuel wrote a book entitled *Christophobia: The Real Reason Behind Hate Crime Legislation*, to fight Bill C-250, which would have added sexual orientation to the hate-crimes section of the Criminal Code. He endorsed U.S. evangelist Franklin Graham's definition of Islam as "evil" and organized a 2003 "Canadians for Bush" rally in support of the invasion of Iraq. Link Byfield, publisher of the now-defunct far-right gay-bashing *Alberta Report*, said of Emmanuel's book, "Clearly, calmly, and boldly, he explains why Christians must stop apologizing, stop hiding, and stop pretending they can peacefully coexist with the perverse new faith that has seized control of North American culture."

Emmanuel is also strongly endorsed by P. Andrew Sandlin, president of the California-based Center for Cultural Leadership. The Center believes that a "ravenously anti-Christian culture, which mocks and attacks the Bible" has taken over in America. He trains and equips young evangelicals to go into politics and law to lead a "Christian Transformation" of the culture. Sandlin cannot say enough about his counterpart in Canada: "Tristan Emmanuel is perhaps the most pivotal figure in Canada's future living today. Devout, intelligent, energetic, savvy and visionary, Tristan is spearheading a new Reformation, calling Canada back to its historic roots, one committed to changing Canadian culture. He is a cultural leader to whom Canada's Christians should look for guidance in rebuilding on new, Christian foundations." Emmanuel told the *Globe and Mail* (June 13, 2005), "It's time we stopped apologizing and started defending who we are. The evangelical community in Canada, by and large, as well as socially conservative Catholics, are saying we have been far too heavenly minded and thus we have been of no earthly value for far too long on too many fronts." He told the *Globe*'s Gloria Galloway that there is intensive recruiting of evangelical Christians to the party in Ontario: "Even in Toronto we have incredible people from the immigrant community who are stepping up to the plate who are just awesome candidates and sincere Christians."

Adds Defend Marriage Coalition's McVety: "There is a desire to see pro-marriage candidates become nominated right across the country. We know that we have 141 pro-marriage MPs now and our hope is to achieve a pro-marriage Parliament. The distortion of the separation of church and state has driven people of faith out of leadership and this is very wrong."

This is an important moment for Canada. Well below the radar screen and unknown to most Canadians, a serious commitment has now been undertaken by their government to create a North American fortress with a common economic, security, resource, regulatory, and foreign-policy framework. It is being driven by the mutual interests of big business on both sides of the border, and the foreign policy and security hawks in the White House who want a compliant and well-behaved Canada. While obviously sensitive to the growing antipathy in Canada toward the Bush administration, the Martin government, in its heart, is supportive of the call for deeper integration. Steadily and incrementally, it is advancing the agenda of the Canadian Council of Chief Executives. Waiting in the wings is Stephen Harper and his Conservatives, who embrace a pro-Republican, pro–George Bush, pro-military future for North America. Harper and his Conservatives also represent a departure from the separation of church and state that has so long characterized Canadian politics. With them comes U.S.–style evangelical Christianity, and the intolerance it represents.

Together with the massive regulatory harmonization now taking place between the two countries and the assault by right-wing groups on Canada's public health system, it is not hard to imagine a very different Canada emerging within a decade if other voices are not listened to now. While deep integration with the United States may be good for big business, it will be bad for most Canadians. That is not to say that security issues are unimportant or that Canada shouldn't do its part. Canadians understand the security fears of Americans and want to be good neighbours. However, what Thomas d'Aquino and John Manley have in mind would bring Canada dramatically closer to the Bush administration and everything it represents.

# the wreckage
# is breathtaking

*The Neo-Con Revolution*

James Inhofe, the Republican senator from Oklahoma who jokes that his 1994 campaign slogan was "God, Guns, and Gays," embodies as well as anyone the combination of big-business bias, foreign-policy neo-conservatism, and fundamentalist Christian belief that make up the essential elements of the Bush revolution.

A big oil backer who once characterized the U.S. Environmental Protection Agency as "the Gestapo bureaucracy," Inhofe was recently appointed to head the powerful Senate Committee on Environment and Public Works. This is bad news for environmentalists, whom he calls "snake oil salesmen," and great news for the industry, which has rewarded him with almost US$600,000 in donations since 1999. Inhofe has said that global warming is the second-largest hoax ever played on the American people – the first being the separation of Church and state. In 2004, he helped to defeat a mild bipartisan bill on climate change, years after destroying the trailblazing study on the impact of climate change on the United States during the Clinton administration. The Natural Resources Defense Council says he is "as menacing as they come." He has received a score of 0 out of 100 by the League of Conservation Voters every year since 1997.

James Inhofe is a neo-conservative hawk. He sits on the Senate Armed Services Committee. When a special session of the committee was convened on May 11, 2004, to take testimony regarding the horrific abuses by American soldiers at the Abu Ghraib prison in Iraq, he stunned those in attendance by launching into a passionate defence of the American perpetrators – some of them are now serving time in jail – and a vitriolic condemnation of the victims. "They're terrorists, murderers, insurgents," he said of the abused prisoners, many of whom were innocent citizens caught up in random military roundups. Inhofe further expressed his outrage at the "humanitarian do-gooders crawling all over these prisons looking for human rights violations." Inhofe is a solid supporter of George Bush's Middle East policy and has consistently supported an enlarged military.

And James Inhofe is an evangelical who has warned that children of gay marriage will become "a whole new class" that could end up dependent on "the American people." He has received a 100 per cent approval rating from the Christian Coalition for his voting record since his first election. He supported the 1999 "Religious Freedom Amendment," which would have required accommodation of religion in all government actions, especially in schools, but was defeated by the then Democratic majority. Inhofe is also a Zionist Christian who has told the Senate that the West Bank belongs to Israel because it says in Genesis that it is the place where God appeared to Abram. "This is not a political battle at all. It is a contest over whether or not the word of God is true."

The intersection of his religious beliefs with his neo-conservative views and his support of big business is very important in understanding not only this senator but also the Bush White House in general. "I trust God with my legislative goals and the issues that are important to my constituents," he told a reporter for *Pentecostal Evangel* magazine. "I don't believe there is a single issue we deal with in government that hasn't been dealt with in the Scriptures." A literal interpretation of the Bible dictates policy for Inhofe and many other Republican leaders. Inhofe's foreign-policy views are based upon an End-Time belief system (that is, a belief that the world will soon end) that requires not only support of Israeli expansion in the West Bank, but in significant other parts of the Middle East as well. The invasion of Iraq is part of that plan. Similarly, the End-Time philosophy makes long-term considerations like environmental stewardship immaterial.

## THE WORLD AFTER 9/11

George W. Bush is perhaps the most right-wing ideologue ever to occupy the Oval Office. A social and fiscal conservative, Bush and the team that surrounds him have set out to permanently transform America. They have done this by forming a powerful coalition of big business (particularly those industries engaged in the war on terror, such as defence, security, and energy), the evangelical Christian right, and neo-conservative foreign-policy hawks. While these three groups do not always share a world view, they have learned to work with one another to consolidate their power and to achieve their separate objectives. The face of American politics has been drastically changed as a result.

In the wake of 9/11, George W. Bush fashioned a new foreign policy for his nation: The world, as he (inspired by the neo-cons) sees it, is divided into those who are friends of the United States and those who stand with the terrorists. This tidy division, coupled with Bush's obsession with the possibility of weapons of mass destruction falling into the hands of a rogue state, set the stage for the new doctrine of pre-emptive attack. In the name of opposing tyranny and fostering freedom, an aggressive new foreign policy has been launched. Enforcing freedom through world domination is expensive. The American people are spending more than US$445 billion a year on the Department of Defense and US$7 billion per month on the occupation of Iraq.

Robert F. Kennedy, Jr., notes in the epilogue of his 2004 book *Crimes Against Nature* that Bush has transformed a projected US$5.6

trillion ten-year surplus inherited from the Clinton administration into a US$1.4 trillion deficit – a massive transfer of funds to the military and the wealthiest Americans, in particular the president's friends. As Kennedy notes, this policy has mired the Bush administration in a war that has killed more than fifteen hundred Americans and maimed another twelve thousand. (As of mid-August 2005, the number of American dead had risen to more than 1,840.) "He has made America the target of Islamic hatred, caused thousands of new terrorists to be recruited into al-Qaeda, isolated us in the world, and drained our treasury of the funds necessary to rebuild Afghanistan and to finance our own vital homeland security needs," Kennedy wrote in the May 2005 issue of *Vanity Fair*.

At the same time, the Bush team has set out to gut social security and environmental law in its second term. Chicago *Tribune* columnist and former CBS News correspondent Jerry Landay took stock of the list of federal programs due to be slashed in the Bush budget of 2006 and listed them in a scathing column on March 28, 2005. "The wreckage is breathtaking," he wrote, "a blot on our collective soul." It includes termination of a program that tests bio-engineered food safety; conservation programs for American forests and energy; flood prevention plans; funds for studies in advanced technologies; vital telecommunications facilities for schools and libraries; drug-free school programs; workers' job retraining; vocational rehabilitation; enhanced teaching quality; adult education; community service; child emergency medical services; disease control and prevention; water conservation; rural fire-fighting facilities; hiring of police; protection of national parks; education of migrant workers; the Hubble space telescope; high-speed rail; and vocational assistance for veterans.

Deep cuts are slated for medical care; watershed rehabilitation; environmental quality controls; research in non-fossil-fuel alternatives; and programs for the disabled and children's hospitals. The Bush administration, says Landay, intends to "drown government." The middle and blue-collar classes are victims of declining wages, historic levels of personal debt, ever-higher health-care costs, and runaway energy prices. "Behind the smokescreen of a glorious 'patriotic war,' fear of terrorism, and pumped-up religious fervor lies a home-front war against the blue-collar classes: a conservative counter-revolution which aims at a colossal redistribution of wealth upward, to the New Aristocracy – supported by a self-serving rewriting of the law based not on legal principle but on 'free-market' theory." The intended result is the creation of a poverty class driven to the bottom by the need to compete against China and India, working for bargain-basement wages.

John R. MacArthur, the distinguished publisher of *Harper's Magazine*, agrees. On the sixtieth anniversary of the death of Franklin Delano Roosevelt (April 11, 2005), he wrote that Roosevelt's New Deal is threatened on every front: public programs for the poor and the aged; strong labour laws and the protection of collective bargaining; the United Nations; adherence to international law; and the strict regulation of an out-of-control and arrogant Wall Street finance system – all are threatened. "The Bush brothers," writes MacArthur, "George W. and Florida Governor Jeb, have more in mind than mere civil devolution. They aim to wipe out the very ideal of government that formed the core of the Roosevelt Administration."

## THE NEO-CON REVOLUTION

Like all successful revolutions, this one took many years of preparation. Its foreign-policy component was created by a core group of neo-conservatives who have been working together since the Nixon years.

The neo-conservatism of the Bush administration is a philosophy that combines the laissez-faire free-market ideology of neo-liberalism (but not its attendant philosophy of individual social freedom), the social conservatism of evangelical Christianity, and an aggressive foreign policy to ward off communism and other anti-American political and religious systems. With the end of the Cold

War, neo-conservatives in America changed their focus to redefine both the practice of democracy at home and America's place in the world. The *Christian Science Monitor* summarized the new world view of the Bush neo-conservatives on its website: "Neocons believe that the United States should not be ashamed to use its unrivalled power – forcefully if necessary – to promote its values around the world. Neoconservatives believe modern threats facing the U.S. can no longer be reliably contained and therefore must be prevented, sometimes through pre-emptive military action. . . . Neocons envision a world in which the United States is the unchallenged superpower, immune to threats. They believe that the U.S. has a responsibility to act as a 'benevolent global hegemon.'"

This movement can be traced back to the University of Chicago, where teachers and writers such as Leo Strauss promoted the notion of militant nationalism and Allan Bloom railed against the "cultural relativism" of 1960s youth culture. Albert Wohlstetter, a mathematician at Chicago was also an influential neo-con figure. He later became a senior policy analyst with the Rand Corporation and a key figure in nuclear-warfare strategy and the redesign of American foreign policy. Students of these men include current powerbrokers such as Richard Perle, former chair of the Defense Policy Board and a key adviser to the Pentagon; Paul Wolfowitz, Middle East hawk, now head of the World Bank; Ahmed Chalabi, the man the Bush administration favoured to succeed Saddam Hussein; and James Woolsey, ex-CIA director who recently declared that the invasion of Syria and Iran are inevitable and that the United States is fighting the Fourth World War. (The Third World War, according to Woolsey, was the Cold War. Now, there is a "new enemy on the march," a combination of rogue states, terrorist networks, and the hidden threat of weapons of mass destruction.)

These men first rose to prominence in Republican Party circles in the aftermath of Watergate. On November 1, 1975, just weeks after Gerald Ford was sworn in as the thirty-eighth president of the United States, his cabinet was significantly shuffled. Gone were James Schlesinger, secretary of Defense, and William Colby, director of the CIA, to be replaced by Donald Rumsfeld and George H. Bush, respectively. They were joined by Henry Kissinger as secretary of state and Dick Cheney, chief of staff.

These changes set the stage for the challenge to American foreign policy that had moved from neutrality to containment after the Second World War and then to détente, which sought to assert American power but under conditions that minimized confrontation. The neo-cons, who called themselves "Team B," and whose members also included Richard Perle and Paul Wolfowitz, were opposed to détente and advocated a more aggressive and confrontational American foreign policy. They started to assert their power in the Reagan years and were able to take credit for Reagan's characterization of the Soviet Union as an "evil empire," a phrase echoed years later by George W. Bush when he referred to Iraq, Iran, and North Korea as an "axis of evil." The neo-con hawks were also responsible for the "Star Wars" project so beloved of Ronald Reagan.

A major concern of those in power in the 1970s was the rise of popular democracy in America and other Western societies in the form of rights for women, minorities, and the poor. This democracy movement challenged the growing power of private corporations and the influence they had on governments in the West. In 1973, David Rockefeller of the Chase Manhattan Bank founded the Trilateral Commission to consolidate the power blocs of North America, Europe, and the newly emerged power, Japan. Rockefeller was deeply influenced by Zbigniew Brzezinski, academic and adviser to Jimmy Carter, who wrote, "The American system is compelled gradually to accommodate itself to this emerging international context, with the U.S. government called upon to negotiate, guarantee, and to protect the various arrangements that have been contrived, even by private business." Senator Barry Goldwater, no fan of the Trilateral Commission, called it "a vehicle for multinational consolidation of commercial and banking interests."

In one of its first publications, *The Crisis of Democracy*, its American author, Cold War scholar and neo-con Samuel P.

Huntington, deplored an "excess of democracy" in the United States and called for a "greater degree of moderation in democracy." Huntington, then coordinator of security planning for the National Security Council, had some pretty scathing thoughts about governance: "Truman had been able to govern the country with the co-operation of a relatively small number of Wall Street lawyers and bankers," he wrote. By the early 1970s, that era was past and the public now questioned the "legitimacy of hierarchy, coercion, discipline, secrecy, and deception – all of which are in some measure inescapable attributes to the process of government." Stating that a "governable democracy" requires "apathy and non-involvement" on the part of the populace, Huntington bemoaned the political awakening of "previously passive and unorganized groups in the population – blacks, Indians, Chicanos, white ethnic groups, students, and women."

(Lest one thinks that Huntington went the way of the dinosaurs, he is today a tenured Harvard professor, and a famous neo-con author whose books, including *The Clash of Civilizations and the Remaking of World Order* [1996] and *Who Are We?: The Challenges to America's National Identity* [2004], have ignited international debate and charges of racism. In *The Clash of Civilizations*, Huntington articulated a theory of a multi-civilizational world headed for conflict. *Le Monde diplomatique* called this book a covert way to legitimize U.S. aggression against the Third World in order to prevent it from developing economically. In *Who Are We?*, Huntington argued that the Anglo-American heritage of the United States is under threat by the influx of Latinos who will not abandon their culture. "While Muslims pose the immediate problem in Europe," he wrote, "Mexicans pose the problem for the United States. . . . There is no Americano dream. There is only the American dream by an Anglo-Protestant society. Mexican Americans will share in that dream only if they dream in English.")

The neo-cons went underground to an extent during the Clinton years, sitting on right-wing think-tanks and producing materials for neo-conservative publications such as the *National*

*Review*. In 1997, they created the Project for the New American Century (PNAC) to promote increases in military spending and to challenge foreign regimes hostile to American interests. Founding members include Vice President Dick Cheney, Defense Secretary Donald Rumsfeld, Bruce Jackson, a former Pentagon official and vice-president for weapons manufacturer Lockheed Martin, and Perle and Wolfowitz among others. PNAC is staffed by men who previously served with groups like Friends of the Democratic Center in Central America (PRODEMCA), which supported the dictatorships in Nicaragua and El Salvador, and the Committee on the Present Danger, which spent years advocating that a nuclear war with the Soviet Union was "winnable." In 1998, a group of PNAC members signed a letter urging President Clinton to invade Iraq. Ten of those signatories are now part of the Bush administration.

In 1999, the Project for the New American Century produced a now infamous report, "Rebuilding America's Defenses: Strategy, Forces and Resources for a New Century." The ninety-page report called for a foreign policy that "boldly and purposefully promotes American interests abroad," and that would shape a century favourable to America's principles. The authors called for a leader who will accept the "global responsibilities" of the United States, warning "if we shirk our responsibilities, we invite challenges to our fundamental interests." The report also demanded global political leadership from the United States rather than the United Nations, which it criticized for its "stance of neutrality." This sentiment was hardly surprising, coming from authors like Richard Perle, who wrote a guest column for the *Guardian* newspaper on March 21, 2003, called "Thank God for the Death of the UN."

## THE CANDIDATE

George W. Bush was the perfect candidate for the neo-cons and their project. He was born into a family of enormous wealth, political influence, and impeccable conservative credentials. His grandfather,

Prescott Bush, made his fortune by managing Nazi companies after Hitler seized power. In 1942, his companies were confiscated for collaborating with the enemy. His father, George Bush, Sr., president from 1988 to 1992, armed and financed Saddam Hussein. A French documentary film, *The World According to Bush*, which aired on the CBC on July 3, 2005, alleged that Bush, Sr., approved the shipping of germ warfare strains to Iraq, enabling the country to launch a chemical attack against Iranian troops and the Kurdish population. George W. attended a prestigious prep school and then Yale and Harvard. He used his six years in the governor's mansion in Texas to build an "outsider's" challenge for the White House, as ridiculous as that was for the son of a former president. He selected Richard Cheney to be his running mate, as a signal of solidarity with his neo-conservatives allies.

George W. also let it be known that he was a friend of big business, having been rescued from a wild youth by his father's buddies in the oil patch. The now-disgraced Ken Lay, who was then CEO of Enron, gave him US$114,000 for his presidential campaign, a figure matched by Lay in earlier contributions to Bush's gubernatorial campaigns. (One of Bush's first acts as president was to convene a series of meetings with high-level energy industry leaders, including Ken Lay, to get their input on a new national energy policy.) Bush was also a favourite with the big pharmaceutical lobby, which spent an unprecedented US$197 million in 2000 to elect him and other friendly Republicans, making it the biggest and costliest corporate campaign in American history, according to the *New York Times*.

Bush spent his first months in office initiating legislation friendly to the very rich and his corporate allies. But then his presidency seemed suddenly somewhat aimless – as if he had no other goal. The terrorist attacks of September 11, 2001, gave him – and the neo-cons – a new opportunity and orientation. Shortly after the attacks, Bush unveiled his new foreign policy in a report on national security. The United States possessed unprecedented and unequalled strength and influence in the world, Bush declared, and would not hesitate to act alone, "if necessary, to exercise our right of self-defense by acting pre-emptively." Once a threat has been identified, he affirmed, "America will act against such emerging threats before they are fully formed."

George Bush had a new mandate. Together with his homeland-security crackdown and massive tax cuts, his war on terror internationally came to define his first term in office. His new foreign policy was widely supported by Democrats as well as Republicans in both Congress and the Senate, even though it represented a radical departure from past policy. The invasions of Afghanistan and Iraq followed in quick succession. And even when it became clear that there were no weapons of mass destruction to be found in Iraq, which had been presented to the world as the reason for war, the American people continued to support their president. In the 2004 election, George W. Bush won the highest popular vote in American history.

## KARL ROVE AND THE RELIGIOUS RIGHT

How has so far-reaching a revolution been cemented in such a short time? There are a number of factors, besides the power, money, and influence of the neo-conservative bloc. Much of the credit must go to Karl Rove.

Karl Rove – sometimes referred to as "Bush's brain" – is arguably the most powerful insider in Washington. He has been much in the news as these words are being written, after having been directly linked to a media leak that revealed the name of a CIA agent (Valerie Plame) whose husband, former ambassador Joseph Wilson, angered the Bush administration by disputing the claim that Iraq had weapons of mass destruction. In spite of the "Turd Blossom" (a Texas term referring to the flower that emerges from a pile of cow dung) scent that surrounds Rove, Bush is standing by his man.

As deputy chief of staff, Karl Rove coordinates the National Security Council, the National Economic Council, and other

advisory panels, to ensure that the ideas they develop are "comple-
mentary" to the Bush plan. In other words, Karl Rove's job is to
oversee all policy in Washington. "It's hard to overstate his power,"
says Lou Dubose, a Texan journalist and Rove biographer. "He is
unique in the modern presidency." John Dilulio, the former head
of the White House Office of Faith-based and Community Initiatives, has been critical of how Rove screens "real-world" news
from the president lest it might counter Rove's own extreme conservative views. He says: "Karl is enormously powerful, maybe the
most powerful person in the modern, post-Hoover era ever to
occupy a political adviser post near the Oval Office." *Vanity Fair*
(July 2005) says that Rove is straight out of Ayn Rand – "an all
powerful creator, designer, mastermind, and, if he chooses, or if his
mind wanders, destroyer. . . . He's a curse. A terrifying spectre.
Something alive in the night."

Rove knew that George W. Bush could speak the language of
the religious right and he set out to connect his candidate to this
constituency on such issues as birth control, family planning,
homosexuality, and stem-cell research. During a 1999 campaign
appearance in New Orleans, Bush expressed doubts about teaching
evolution in schools: "I believe children ought to be exposed to
different theories about how the world started . . . the jury is still
out on this question," he said. Soon after, he told *George* magazine,
"I've heard the call. I believe God wants me to run for President."
(As governor of Texas, Bush proclaimed June 10 "Jesus Day.") To
an Amish group in Pennsylvania, he said, "I trust God speaks
through me. Without that, I couldn't do my job." After 9/11, Bush
started to use his personal relationship with God even more explicitly in defending his aggressive new foreign policy. "God told me
to strike at al-Qaeda," he was quoted saying in the Israeli newspaper *Ha'aretz* in June 2003, "and I struck them. Then He instructed
me to strike at Saddam which I did. And now I am determined to
solve the problem in the Middle East."

Bush's faith has helped keep things simple for him – good and
evil, friends and enemies. This is how Karl Rove would have it. In

an October 2004 cover story in the *New York Times Magazine*, journalist Ron Suskind reported that Bush's faith-based governance had led to a "disastrous" crusade in the Middle East and laid the groundwork for a "battle between modernists and fundamentalists, pragmatists and true believers, reason and religion."

At least 75 million Americans identify themselves as born-again Christians. There are more than 1,600 evangelical Christian radio stations in the United States and 250 television stations. Most evangelical Christians are also social conservatives and political right-wingers. Eighty per cent of the 26.5 million evangelicals who voted in the 2004 election, according to the *Washington Post*, cast their ballot for the Republicans. As a result, evangelical Christians dominate the White House, the Senate, and the House of Representatives, and may soon dominate the Supreme Court. They have become a powerful presence in the military. *Time* magazine (June 27, 2005) reported on a controversy at the U.S. Air Force Academy in Colorado Springs (the headquarters of Focus on the Family), where the academy is rife with an officially encouraged religious evangelization. Students are made to submit to mandatory Bible classes, aggressive recruitment to evangelical Christianity, opening prayers at official gatherings, and chants during training where the senior officer yells "Airpower!" and is greeted with the reply yell, "Rock Sir!" – a reference to Jesus' words being built on rock.

Evangelicals are also creating a social revolution in the United States. In a May 22, 2005, investigative piece, the *New York Times* reported that evangelical Christianity, once seen as the "religion of the disinherited," is forming a beachhead in the American elite. Over the last forty years, evangelicals have pulled steadily closer in income and education to mainline Protestants in the historically affluent establishment denominations. In the process, they have overturned the old social pecking order in which *fundamentalist* or *evangelical* were code words for "lower class." Evangelicals, according to the *New York Times*, are now increasingly likely to be college graduates and in the top income brackets. "Evangelical CEOs pray together on monthly conference calls, evangelical investment bankers study the Bible over lunch on Wall Street, and deep-pocketed evangelical donors gather at golf courses for conferences restricted to those who give more than US$200,000 to Christian causes." Their growing wealth and education help explain the new influence of evangelicals in American culture and politics. Their buying power fuels the booming market for Christian books, music, and films. They build vast mega-churches in the suburbs across America and their charitable contributions finance dozens of religious broadcasters and service groups. Last year, the Campus Crusade for Christ raised more from private donors than the Boy Scouts of America, the Public Broadcasting Service, or the Easter Seals campaign.

Evangelical Christians tend to be small "c" conservatives who fear government and its institutions, reject government-run social programs and social security, and believe in tax relief and free markets. In his bestselling book about child-rearing, *Dare to Discipline*, James Dobson of Focus on the Family wrote that all functioning Christian families have a strict know-it-all father who calls the shots and never asks for permission. Respected Berkeley professor of linguistics George Lakoff says that the Dobson model of the family serves as a manifesto when translated by the religious right into the political arena. The strict father is the president. Good and evil are absolute. Social programs are immoral and deserve to be starved out of existence. People who prosper are virtuous; those who fail are sinful. Therefore the unregulated market is the perfect vehicle for rewarding virtue. "The Strict Father model links morality to prosperity," Lakoff wrote in the bestselling *Don't Think of an Elephant* (2004). "James Dobson is very clear about the connection between the Strict Father worldview and free market capitalism."

(In his book *What's the Matter With Kansas? How Conservatives Won the Heart of America*, journalist Thomas Frank described this world view as "evangelical economic doctrine," and wrote that it helped explain the coalition between evangelical Christians and members of the big-business community who may not share each other's values. Sophisticated business leaders will hold their noses when "family values" are front and centre during an election, he noted, because they know that family values always take a back seat to the needs of big money once elections are won. Vote to stop abortions, wrote Frank, and receive a rollback in capital gains tax. Vote to get government off your back and receive electricity deregulation. Vote to stand tall against terrorism and receive social security privatization. "The leaders of the backlash may talk 'Christ,' but they walk 'corporate,'" he added.)

Many of these Christians, including those among the elite and politicians, take the Bible literally and it instructs all their political decisions. Pennsylvanian senator Rick Santorum, a Catholic evangelical whom *Time* magazine named in its list of America's "25 Most Influential Evangelicals," told *Christian Today* magazine (March 28, 2003): "I draw no line between my faith and my decisions." Santorum has said that the Supreme Court should not overturn state anti-sodomy laws because it would provide a justification for bigamy, polygamy, incest, and bestiality. The *New York Times Magazine* (May 22, 2005) profiled Santorum in a lengthy piece titled "The Senator from a Place Called Faith." He told the magazine that Americans of faith have, until recently, felt constrained from expressing their views on public policy where God's "moral code" is flouted. "To have faith in God but to reject moral absolutes? How is it possible that there exists so little space in the public square for expressions of faith and the standards that follow from belief in a transcendent God?"

A *Time*/CNN poll found that 59 per cent of Americans believe that the prophecies found in the Book of Revelation are going to come true. Nearly one-quarter think the Bible predicted the 9/11 attacks. And about 50 million Americans believe in The Rapture, the literal end of the earth. The Rapture is an End-Time event when born-again Christians (and only born-again Christians, except embryos, who will be assumed to be pure and removed from their unsaved mothers' wombs) will be "caught up" into the air and meet Christ in the sky. They will literally rise from their cars, offices, and kitchens and ascend to heaven. This will signify a thousand-year reign of Christ, which will result in the end of history and a "new heaven and earth." Most of humanity will remain on earth and God will visit terrible tribulation on those left behind.

Israel is central to believers in The Rapture. They anticipate that once Israelis have occupied all the rest of the "Biblical lands," legions of the anti-Christ will attack it, triggering a formal show-down in the valley of Armageddon. As the Jews who have not been converted are burned, the Messiah will return for The Rapture. This is why the religious right in the United States supports Israel and the Jewish settlements and gives millions of dollars every year to Israel. (In the last eight years, more than four hundred thousand born-again evangelicals have sent Rabbi Yechiel Eckstein's International Fellowship of Christians and Jews, one of the more prominent Christian Zionist groups, about a quarter of a billion dollars to support Israel.) Iraq was a warm-up act predicted in the Book of Revelation, where four angels "which are bound in the great river Euphrates will be released to slay the third part of man." A war with Islam in the Middle East is not something to be feared, but welcomed, as the only way to final redemption.

The Rapture is based on twelve books called the *Left Behind* series written by Tim LaHaye and Jerry Jenkins. These books, in adult and children's editions, have sold more than 75 million copies and generated more than US$650 million in sales, making them among the most successful publishing projects of all time. Christ's final return to earth is portrayed in the last book in the series, *Glorious Appearing: The End of Days*. Here is how believers in the Rapture predict Christ will dispose of non-believers: "Jesus merely raised one hand a few inches and a yawning chasm opened in the earth, stretching far and wide enough to swallow all of them. They tumbled in, howling and screeching, but their wailing was soon quashed and all was silent when the earth closed itself again." The surviving Christians had to drive their cars with care, "to avoid hitting splayed and filleted bodies of men and women and horses." Evangelical Christians with these views have regular access to the White House. The Apostolic Congress, a fundamentalist Pentecostal movement, claims on its website that it meets regularly with senior White House officials on Mideast policy. There, they find a president who speaks their language.

While other presidents since Franklin Roosevelt have seen themselves as petitioners of God, seeking blessings and guidance, George W. Bush positions himself as a prophet, directly in touch with God and therefore able to issue declarations of divine desires for the nation and the world. David Domke is a professor in the Department of Communications at the University of Washington and has studied the president's use of language to better understand his assumption of a prophetic relationship to God. For instance, in his September 2, 2004, address to the nation, Bush tells his audience that they have a divine mission to take freedom and liberty to the world: "I believe that America is called to lead the cause of freedom in a new century. I believe that millions in the Middle East plead in silence for their liberty. I believe that given the chance, they will embrace the most honourable form of government ever devised by man. I believe all these things because freedom is not America's gift to the world, it is the Almighty God's gift to every man and woman in the world."

Domke surveyed the Inaugural and State of the Union addresses of all the presidents from Roosevelt to Bush and found that, for presidents other than Reagan and Bush, only 7 per cent contained claims linking the wishes of God with freedom or liberty. Such claims were present, however, in almost half of the addresses by Ronald Reagan and George W. Bush. The certitude of a president/prophet is a dangerous development, argues Domke, because U.S. presidents have the ability to act upon their beliefs in a way that affects the lives of billions.

## GOD'S BUSINESS

The relationship between the Republican Party and the religious right started in earnest in 1981 with the creation of the powerful insider club known as the Council for National Policy (CNP). Excited by Reagan's election, Tim LaHaye of the *Left Behind* series, Paul Weyrich of the Free Congress Foundation, Richard Viguerie, a wealthy Republican fundraiser, and other far-right conservatives decided to bring together the religious right, the small government/anti-tax right, and several extremely wealthy, like-minded businessmen such as Joseph Coors (whose company recently bought Molson) and Herbert and Nelson Bunker Hunt, rabid anti-Communists affiliated with the John Birch Society. Their mandate was to influence White House policy and elect far-right and social conservative candidates to office. They initiated the Moral Majority Coalition and recruited Jerry Falwell to run it (Tim LaHaye recently gave US$4.5 million to Falwell for his Liberty University) and later welcomed other religious leaders such as Focus on the Family's James Dobson and the current "small government" crowd like Grover Norquist of Americans for Tax Reform. (In later years, the CNP reached out to the foreign-policy neo-conservative crowd as well. The organization has hosted speeches recently by UN ambassador John Bolton, Defense Secretary Donald Rumsfeld, and both Vice President Cheney and President Bush.)

The relationship between the evangelical right and the Republican Party started by the Council for National Policy has not wavered since it was established more than twenty-five years ago. Joan Bokaer, a professor at the Center for Religion, Ethics, and Social Policy at Cornell University, has studied the fundamentalist movement in the United States. Working through fundamentalist Pentecostal and charismatic churches, she reports, the Christian Coalition has promoted right-wing Republican candidates by mailing voters' guides to their constituents – telling them how to vote. Seventy million guides were sent out in the 2000 election alone. Reverend Rick Scarborough, an evangelical Baptist from Texas, has used his pulpit and his organization, Vision America, to help elect conservative politicians and judges for more than a decade. Vision America has recruited and trained close to four thousand "patriot pastors" in the southern and midwestern

United States to get out the evangelical Christian vote. "Christians have a moral responsibility in this country to be involved in politics" Scarborough told *Time* magazine (May 23, 2005). Reverend Richard Land, of the powerful Southern Baptist Convention, says, "Our job is to reclaim America for Christ, no matter what the cost," and claims to meet with Karl Rove and other senior White House officials every week. The result of this open relationship between evangelical Christians and politicians is a more openly religious and socially conservative White House than would have been tolerated in former decades.

(The same is true for state governments. The current Republican Party platform in Bush's home state of Texas "reaffirms the United States of America as a Christian Nation," and seeks to nullify the separation of Church and state. It would abolish the Environmental Protection Agency, and the federal Departments of Energy and Education. It dismisses global warming as myth and promotes public-school education "based upon Biblical principles," not upon secular humanism, which teaches Darwinian evolutionary theory and a scientific world view.)

## REPUBLICANS FOR CHRIST

Former attorney general and author of the Patriot Act John Ashcroft is a practising member of the Assembly of God, which has 2.5 million adherents in the United States. This evangelical sect teaches that homosexuality is evil; Christians should not make friends with non-Christians; speaking in tongues is a necessary component of salvation; and government and laws should be predicated on the teachings of the Christian life. Ashcroft often compares himself to Christ: his autobiography is called *Lessons From a Father to His Son*. He refers to his political defeats as "crucifixions" and his political successes as "resurrections." The day before George W. Bush was sworn in for his first term as president, seventeen hundred religious and political leaders attended a prayer luncheon for Bush.

Soon-to-be Attorney General Ashcroft "brought down the house with a tale of amazing grace," reported the *Washington Times*. Ashcroft was an early advocate of "charitable choice," the practice of taking public funds from government-sponsored social-assistance programs and giving them to Christian groups to administer, and an avowed opponent of homosexuality and abortion. During his tenure, he held daily prayer breakfasts that were understood by staff in the Homeland Security Office to be mandatory.

Senate Majority Leader Bill Frist and House Majority Leader Tom DeLay are two other powerful right-wing evangelical Christians in the Republican Party. Tom DeLay is a Christian fundamentalist who believes that the earth is only a few thousand years old. He displays the Ten Commandments on his office wall and once suggested that the Columbine, Colorado, school shootings happened "because our school systems teach our children that they are nothing but glorified apes who have evolutionized out of some primordial mud." The *Washington Post* magazine reports that DeLay sees himself "marching forward with a Biblical worldview," and wants to convert America into a "God centered" nation whose government promotes prayer, worship, and the teaching of Christian values. DeLay called the 2000 election an apocalyptic "battle for souls," a fight to the death against the forces of liberalism, feminism, and environmentalism that are corrupting America.

Tom DeLay is also a Christian Zionist, an "End-Time" subset of the Christian right numbering about 20 million. Christian Zionists, many of them Rapture believers, support the state of Israel because its existence (and subsequent destruction) is a necessary step toward the Second coming of Christ. (The *National Review* reports that a group of ultra-Christian Texas ranchers are helping fundamentalist Israeli Jews breed a pure red heifer, a genetically rare beast that must be sacrificed to fulfill an apocalyptic prophecy found in the Book of Numbers.) In 2002, DeLay visited Cornerstone Church in San Antonio, Texas, run by pastor John Hagee, who believes in The Rapture, the second coming of Christ, and has written bestselling books with such titles as *Final Dawn Over Jerusalem* and *God's Two-Minute Warning*. Hagee gave a horrifying sermon that day that was broadcast over his Global Evangelism Television network, which he claims reaches 92 million Americans. "The war between America and Iraq is the gateway to the Apocalypse," he thundered. Tom DeLay jumped to his feet and told the crowd, "What has been spoken here tonight is the truth from God."

Senator Frist, the choice of Karl Rove to succeed former Senate majority leader Trent Lott, inherited, with his brother Thomas, HCA, America's biggest for-profit hospital chain. In 2002, charges were laid against the company for defrauding government health programs, leading to the largest fraud settlement in modern history. The company is still in business, thanks to the Bush administration, and the giant Frist fortune is untouched. Senator Frist is a wealthy businessman who is also a social and religious conservative. In 2003, he backed a controversial proposed constitutional ban on gay marriage, citing his fears that "criminal activity" – meaning homosexual sex – would now be allowed within the home.

On April 25, 2005, against the advice of moderate church leaders, among others, Frist joined prominent Christian conservatives in a taped telecast portraying Democrats as "against people of faith" for blocking President Bush's judicial nominees. The Family Research Council, which organized the broadcast, claimed it reached 61 million homes. Almost half a million conservative Christians support this well-funded group that lobbies for prayer in school and the right to discriminate openly against gays and lesbians. (Tom Coburn, the newly elected senator from Oklahoma, has said that lesbianism is so rampant in public schools that girls should not be allowed to go to the bathroom in pairs.) The organization is also opposed to reproductive freedom, the National Endowment for the Arts, and the federal Department of Education. It calls for a "Conservative Christian standard of morals in all of America's domestic and foreign policy." Also on the program of the six-thousand-member Baptist church in Louisville, Kentucky, were James Dobson, founder of the stridently anti-gay Focus on the

Family (who has been known to back political candidates who have called for the execution of abortion providers); Chuck Colson, the born-again Watergate criminal (taped from his prison cell); and Dr. Al Mohler, president of the Southern Baptist Theological Seminary.

The Christian right, egged on by social conservatives in the Republican Party, are now gearing up for the battle to control the Supreme Court. This is the culmination of a thirty-year culture war seen by the right as a way to reverse decades of decisions about abortion, prayer in the schools, religion in public life, gay rights, and marriage. Already, Republican judges are in the majority in ten of the nation's thirteen federal appellate courts. By the end of George W. Bush's second term the count will likely be twelve out of thirteen. About 85 per cent of circuit court judges will be Republican appointees by then according to a March 2005 report of the *National Law Journal*. As well, seven of the nine sitting members of the Supreme Court (and sixteen out of twenty-two appointments in the last fifty years) are Republican appointments. However, these Republican justices on the Supreme Court are not all radical enough for the evangelical Christian movement. The retirement of Justice Sandra Day O'Connor and the expected retirement of Chief Justice William H. Rehnquist is setting the stage for a ferocious battle in Washington. Bush's nominee to replace O'Connor is the perfect candidate for the far right. Judge John Roberts has ruled against the Clean Air Act and the Endangered Species Act, helped coal companies strip-mine mountaintops, and, as a lawyer, argued and won a case to stop some doctors from even talking about abortion.

"As the liberal, anti-Christian dogma of the left has been repudiated in almost every recent election," says Tony Perkins of the Family Research Council, "the courts have become the last great bastion for liberalism. For years, activist courts aided by groups like the American Civil Liberties Union, have been quietly working under the veil of the judiciary, like thieves in the night, to rob us of our Christian heritage and our religious freedoms." Perkins has compared judges "in black robes" who threaten religious liberties to white-robed members of the Ku Klux Klan.

The May 2005 showdown in the Senate over the use of the filibuster to block hardline right-wing nominees was just a skirmish. "This is a procedural fight that is part of the larger cultural war," Marshall Wittmann, a senior fellow at the Democratic Leadership Council, told the *Globe and Mail*. "Republicans want to change the balance of the court in order to overturn Roe v. Wade, which protects abortion rights. This may seem like a boring fight over procedure but it's actually a build-up to a huge confrontation over the most sensitive issues that are part of the cultural war that has been going on for the past thirty years."

The filibuster fight centred around two particularly sensitive nominees for the federal appeals court, Priscilla Owen and Janice Rogers Brown. Priscilla Owen is a former corporate lawyer and protegé of Karl Rove who raised US$1 million to help her get elected to the Texas Supreme Court in 1994. Owen is an anti-abortion hardliner and a darling of corporations such as Enron and Halliburton (Vice President Dick Cheney's firm), both of which contributed to her judicial campaign. California judge Janice Rogers Brown is a black woman whose pro-corporate, anti-government right-wing views are notorious. She has described the 1937 Supreme Court decision allowing government regulation of the economy as a "triumph of our own socialist revolution" and is deeply opposed to separation of Church and state. "Some things are apparent," she said in an April 2000 speech to the Federalist Society. "Where government moves in, community retreats, civil society disintegrates, and our own ability to control our destiny atrophies. The result is families under siege; war in the streets; unapologetic expropriation of property; the precipitous decline of the rule of law; the rapid rise of corruption; the loss of civility; and the triumph of deceit. The result is a debased, debauched culture, which finds moral depravity entertaining and virtue contemptible."

At the April rally, Focus on the Family's Dobson railed against current members of the Supreme Court who are, he said, "unelected and unaccountable and arrogant and imperious and determined to redesign the culture according to their own biases and values, and out of control." He singled out the half dozen "squishy" Republicans in the Senate, such as John McCain, who do not share the radical view of Bill Frist, and as he named them their photos and phone numbers scrolled across a giant screen. He urged viewers to call the senators to get them to change their moderate positions.

## GOD SETS THE LEGISLATIVE AGENDA

Environmental journalist Glenn Scherer has written extensively about the connection between the religious right in the White House and the headlong reversal of environmental laws and infrastructure by the Bush administration. It is true, Scherer points out, that George Bush and Dick Cheney are former oil men who have been rewarded with huge contributions from the industry for their pro-business policies. However, it is more complicated than that for End-Time believers. While differences exist between the various sects, all have a reason to fight environmental regulation. "Reconstructionists" believe that Christ will return only when a righteous nation applies Biblical law to its people, thereby ending the separation of Church and state and abolishing regulatory agencies like the EPA. "Dispensationalists," like Pat Robertson and Jerry Falwell, believe that environmental disasters such as hurricanes and floods are God's punishment for a "debauched" society that has allowed the breakdown of the family. Followers of The Rapture believe that environmental degradation is a sign that Armageddon is near and actually rejoice in it. (They feel the same about war, particularly nuclear war, which is part of "God's plan" according to the *Left Behind* series.)

Environmental organizations have studied the voting record of the Republicans and found that those politicians who align themselves with the religious right are also rabidly anti-environmental. According to the Washington-based Americans United for Separation of Church and State, 186 House members in the last Congress who allied themselves with the religious right earned barely a 15 per cent average approval rating with the League of Conservation Voters. Of forty-five senators given an 80 to 100 per cent approval rating by the Christian Coalition, the average League of Conservation Voters' approval rating fell below 10 per cent. In this Congress, Republican leadership hails almost exclusively from the religious right, scoring a perfect 100 per cent from the Christian Coalition, but getting barely 4 per cent approval rating from environmental groups.

Says Scherer, "Many Christian fundamentalists feel that concern for the future of our planet is irrelevant, because it has no future. . . . Why care about the earth when the droughts, floods, and pestilence brought by ecological collapse are signs of the Apocalypse foretold in the Bible? Why care about global climate change when you and yours will be rescued in The Rapture? . . . Like it or not, faith in the Apocalypse is a powerful driving force in modern American politics. Because of its power as a voting bloc, the Christian right has the ear, if not the souls, of much of the nation's leadership. . . . That, in turn, is sobering news for those who hope for the protection of the earth, not its destruction."

While many in the big-business community do not buy into End-Time religion, there are some who are willing to take advantage of believers to further their own interests. This is the key to the success of the Bush coalition. For instance, ExxonMobil, the world's largest oil company, has spent over US$12 million since 1998, reports the April 2005 edition of *Mother Jones* magazine, on groups and foundations that debunk the theory of climate change. Right-wing think-tanks regularly quoted in Washington and Ottawa that got funding included the Competitive Enterprise Institute, US$1,380,000; the Cato Institute, US$75,000; and Canada's Fraser Institute, which received US$60,000 in 2003 alone. (The next year the Fraser Institute reported that 2004 had been one of the coolest years in recent history; a month later, the United Nations' World Meteorological Organization pronounced 2004 to be the fourth warmest year since 1861.)

A number of the groups ExxonMobil funds are right-wing

Christian organizations with ties to the Bush administration. The Acton Institute for the Study of Religion and Liberty, often quoted by Senator James Inhofe, received US$110,000 between 2000 and 2003. It is closely aligned to the Interfaith Council for Environmental Stewardship, a radical right-wing Christian group founded by none other than Focus on the Family's James Dobson. Their message of hatred against gays and women who have abortions, and their desire to hasten the end of the world so they can be personally saved may not sit well with the sophisticates who populate the boardrooms of ExxonMobil and who fund *Masterpiece Theatre*, but theirs is a marriage of convenience. Last year, ExxonMobil made net earnings of over US$25 billion in George Bush's deregulated America. And the company received a letter of thanks from President Bush for its "active involvement" in helping the administration to determine its policy on climate change. The *Guardian* newspaper (June 8, 2005) reported that ExxonMobil had been influential in getting the president to water down reports containing warnings from government scientists about global warming at the same time that the British prime minister was trying to get world support for an action plan.

## GETTING THE MEDIA ON MESSAGE

No examination of the revolution underway in the United States would be complete without an acknowledgement of the role of the media. American media is consolidating into the hands of a very few, very powerful corporations. The U.S. Consumers' Union reports that just six corporations control the vast majority of what Americans see on television. One company owns more than one thousand radio stations. Since 1975, two-thirds of all independently owned newspapers have disappeared. The control of American news by these powerful for-profit companies has dramatically narrowed public discourse in the United States, says the Consumers' Union, affecting both the diversity and quality of information available to

Americans. Even more insidiously, the Bush White House is infil-
trating local news broadcasts with taxpayer-funded propaganda.
On March 13, 2005, the *New York Times* published a major exposé
on the production and distribution of Video News Releases, or
VNRs, government-sponsored "news" stories distributed to the
American people by the so-called independent media.

"Under the Bush Administration, the federal government has
aggressively used a well-established tool of public relations: the
pre-packaged, ready-to-serve news report that major corporations
have long distributed to TV stations to pitch everything from
headache remedies to auto insurance. In all, at least twenty federal
agencies have made and distributed hundreds of television news
segments in the past four years, research and interviews show. Many
were subsequently broadcast on local stations across the country
without any acknowledgement of the government's role," said the
*Times*. VNRs are produced for the government by private contractors and the State Department's Office of Broadcasting Services,
the Agriculture Department's Broadcast, Media and Technology
Center, and the Defense Department's Pentagon Channel. The
Center for Media and Democracy, a media watchdog group, claims
that the use of VNRs helped sell the first Gulf War to the American
people when George Bush, Sr., was in the White House.

Robert Kennedy, Jr., in the May 2005 edition of *Vanity Fair*,
reports that talking points are developed at weekly meetings convened by Grover Norquist for a wide assortment of right-wing
legislators, lobbyists, and evangelical leaders. These points are then
sent to the conservative media via a sophisticated fax tree. "Soon,"
says Kennedy, "millions of Americans are hearing the same message
from cable news commentators and thousands of talk jocks across
America. Their precisely crafted message and language then perco-
late through the mainstream media to form the underlying assump-
tions of our national debate."

News outlets such as talk radio – the vast majority of which is
rabidly right-wing – and FOX News eagerly embrace these government stories and spin more than a few of their own. FOX News

continued to claim, for instance, that Saddam Hussein was con-
cealing weapons of mass destruction long after most other outlets,
even those openly supporting the Bush administration, were
reporting that this claim was false. As late as July 2004, FOX anchor
Brit Hume was claiming that WMD had been found and other
FOX reporters falsely claimed that they had been moved to Syria.
Many Americans get their news from FOX; according to Neilson
Media Research, FOX is the cable-news leader with a viewership
almost two and a half times that of CNN. Small wonder then that
so many Americans believed the lies that George Bush and company
told about the war. According to an October 2004 survey by the
Program on International Attitudes at the University of Maryland,
72 per cent of Bush supporters believed Iraq had weapons of mass
destruction; 75 per cent believed that Iraq was providing substantial support to al-Qaeda; and 82 per cent thought that the rest of
the world, even in the Islamic world, supported the U.S. position
in Iraq. The survey also found that most Bush supporters favoured
the Kyoto Protocol on climate change, the Land Mines Treaty, and
strong labour and environmental standards in trade agreements –
and wrongly believed that Bush supported these policies too.

The relationship between the major media corporations and
the White House is disturbingly close. The *New York Times* exposé
also reported that the major networks, which help distribute the
VNRs, collect fees from both the government agencies that produce
segments and the affiliates that air them. More importantly, the Bush
administration has been very supportive of the industry demand for
a loosening of the rules governing media concentration and cross-
ownership. In 2003, the Federal Communications Commission,
which has traditionally been charged with enforcing rules to
prevent media concentration and control, brought forward a proposal to radically revise the rules of ownership that would let one
company own the local newspaper, cable service, eight radio stations, and three television stations in each community. A coalition
of community groups fought the FCC all the way to the Supreme
Court, claiming that the new rules would put almost all media into

the hands of a few right-wing corporations. On June 13, 2005, the Supreme Court ruled in agreement with the community groups, and sent the FCC back to the drawing board. This is just one more reason why the far right wants to consolidate conservative control of the Supreme Court. The court decision would likely be different now, after the replacement of Justice O'Connor with Judge John Roberts, who served as legal counsel to many corporations when he was practising law.

Now, undeterred, the industry is counting on the deregulation of cross-ownership through a review of the Telecom Act of 1996, for which it has been largely responsible. The Center for Public Integrity, a national organization that monitors government ethics, reports that between 1998 and 2004, the media industry spent US$1.1 billion lobbying for deregulation and other corporate-friendly policies. Meanwhile, the Bush administration has set its sights on PBS, charging it with "liberal" bias. In June 2005, the House Appropriations Committee approved a bill that will cut funding for PBS by 25 per cent. George Bush appointed Ken Tomlinson, a right-wing Republican who ran Voice of America (an international broadcasting service funded by the U.S. government) in the Reagan era, to be chairman of the Corporation for Public Broadcasting and Patricia Harrison, co-chair of the Republican National Committee and a bitter public opponent of Hillary Clinton, as its president. Bill Moyers is now gone; a new era is dawning for public broadcasting in America, one of the few liberal voices left.

What has happened in the United States is a virtual *coup d'état*. The Bush administration is dominated by unelected business interests and a narrow-minded theocracy that has taken over almost every branch of government and done everything in its power to subvert the democratic checks and balances envisioned by the nation's founders. Now, through its military buildup, unprecedented since the Second World War, the hawks in the White House are intent upon imposing their revolution on the world and creating an enemy out of anyone who dares to dissent.

# we have it, we like it, and we're going to keep it

*The Aggressive Assertion of American Power*

Prime Minister Paul Martin was in a jam. Members of his government, in private consultation with their counterparts in the United States, had as good as promised that Canada would participate in the Bush version of Ronald Reagan's Star Wars, now revived and renamed the Ballistic Missile Defense plan, or BMD. The Department of National Defence was already deep in negotiations with the Pentagon to formulate Canadian co-operation with the plan. The Canadian Council of Chief Executives was in favour of Canadian participation, of course, and so were its members. In fact, 85 per cent of the CEOs of major Canadian corporations said that a decision to opt out of BMD would be "bad for business." There was just one problem. Ordinary Canadians disagreed. Two out of three Canadians, including members of the Liberal Party, were opposed to the plan.

Perhaps in their hearts, Canadians knew they were not intended to be real partners with the Americans, but rather were meant simply to offer up their wide-open spaces for a dubious system. The Center for Strategic and International Studies, a conservative Washington-based think-tank that promotes Canada–U.S. military harmonization, was very clear in a December 3, 2003, briefing on Capitol Hill about the need for Canadian participation: "Having missiles intercepted overhead is something Canadians will simply have to live with. Missile debris will hit Canada. . . . It's Canadians who will have to deal with the debris from destroyed enemy rockets raining down on them. The Pentagon needs little from Canada for its proposed missile shield – except the air space in which to blast apart incoming missiles. . . . Canada might want to request extra funding for hardhats, but there's not much else that can be done about it."

Canadians apparently agreed with critics who pointed out that the missile defence plan, which employs an aggressive new breed of space-based missile interceptors, would be a mighty drain on Canada's military budget. They knew their acquiescence would lend support to a program that has been described as "trying to hit a bullet with a bullet." They may have read in newspapers that the technology has repeatedly failed in tests, that it would lead to the weaponization of space (which Canada is treaty-bound to oppose), and that it would dramatically escalate the global arms race. American strategy called for inserting nuclear weapons into space, a step that would effectively put an end to nuclear non-proliferation, a key component of Canada's foreign policy since the end of the Second World War. Proponents argued that the plan is needed to protect North America from terrorism. But as international affairs analyst Jillian Skeet told the Citizens' Inquiry on Canada–U.S. Relations in Victoria in December 2004, it would likely do the opposite: "Rather, if missile defence is seen by the world's poor and powerless as yet another effort to increase U.S. global domination and to use the nuclear threat to coerce other states, then missile defence may, in fact, increase – not decrease – the incidence of global terrorism."

There were many persuasive reasons to object to BMD and Canadians made their opposition to it known to their representatives in Parliament. The vulnerable Martin minority government gave into popular pressure and announced in spring 2005 that Canada would not participate in the program. President George W. Bush was not pleased. Neither was Thomas d'Aquino who went on a ten-city tour of the United States apologizing for Canada's "mistake" and promising to continue to work to change the government's mind.

## FUTURE PROBABILITIES

Canada's opting out of BMD did nothing to slow it down. In this initiative, as in virtually all others, the United States is more than ready to take unilateral action. In any case, what it really wanted from Canada was the appearance of political co-operation in the international community. The mechanics of the plan can be done without placing any missiles on Canadian soil. And BMD is just one aspect of the aggressive projection of American power that typifies the Bush administration.

The respected New Mexico–based International Relations Center, a policy studies institute devoted to making the United States a more responsible member of the global community, tracks foreign-policy trends through the media, academic studies, and the analyses of the political parties themselves. Authors Tom Barry, Laura Carlsen, and John Gershman published a wide-ranging report after Bush's 2004 victory with predictions of his second-term foreign-policy priorities. The Bush priorities are clear: a continued assault on multilateral institutions and treaties the United States does not control; an accelerated attack on all vestiges of political liberalism in American foreign-policy institutions; and an intensified determination to act forcefully in a unipolar world.

The U.S. grand strategy to restructure the Middle East will remain central to U.S. foreign policy, and will be pursued at a more rapid rate. The occupation of Iraq will not lead to the democracy and freedom the White House predicts, but the administration will not admit its mistakes. Intelligence reform will not improve U.S. intelligence operations that track the real threats to American security. The president and his close advisers are less interested in the accuracy of intelligence information than in its conformity to U.S.

national security doctrine, the needs of the military-industrial complex, and the administration's political and military agenda.

Barry, Carlsen, and Gershman are not alone in thinking that the United States will remain preoccupied by the Middle East. In the January 24–31, 2005, issue of the *New Yorker*, Seymour Hersh, the acclaimed investigative journalist who broke both the My Lai massacre story and news of the abuses by American soldiers at the Abu Ghraib prison in Iraq, warned that the second-term Bush White House sees the Middle East as a "huge war zone" and is taking extraordinary measures to give the Pentagon free rein in the area. The hawks surrounding Bush have consolidated control of all military intelligence in the Pentagon and the role of the CIA has already been dramatically downgraded to allow the United States to carry out covert operations without the oversight of Congress. (The CIA is required by law to report all covert activities to the House and Senate Intelligence committees.) The Pentagon now controls 80 per cent of intelligence spending, giving Defense Secretary Donald Rumsfeld enormous power to expand the war on terror and to beef up covert operations against terrorist suspects in at least ten countries. Already, Hersh charged, the United States has "action teams" operating in the Middle East authorized to find and destroy terrorists – "pseudo gangs" reminiscent of the right-wing execution squads that operated in El Salvador in the 1980s.

Hersh also claimed that the Bush administration has plans for an attack on Iran. Europe has been negotiating with Iran to get that country to abandon its nuclear weapons in exchange for an end to sanctions, but the United States is refusing to join the negotiations, opting instead for the threat of a military strike. While an attack on key nuclear weapons sites is the preferred option, the United States is also preparing for a full-scale invasion, according to Hersh, and could now launch it from land through Iraq or Afghanistan, instead of by sea, as it would have had to do previously. A target strike would have its problems of course: how would they know all the sites had been hit? What would be the likelihood of an Iranian counterattack that could be both military and terrorist in scope?

Iran has long-range missiles and ties to the radical Lebanese organization Hezbollah. A full-scale invasion would require troops the United States does not have, and any notion that it would lead to a popular uprising against the Mullahs is pure fantasy, says Hersh. Nevertheless, he quoted inside sources who told him the Bush team was moving ahead on this agenda.

Echoing Hersh, the three authors of the International Relations Center report predicted that the State Department and the CIA will become yet more subservient to both the Pentagon and the vice-president's office. Dissenting voices will be ignored or suppressed.

They go on to say that, as the U.S. budget crisis deepens, the administration will reduce funding for development and humanitarian assistance abroad unless it directly furthers U.S. foreign- and military-policy goals. This has already happened. In December 2004, the Bush administration announced cuts of US$100 million to charities delivering food aid overseas (*New York Times*, December 22, 2004). Charities such as Save the Children and Catholic Relief Services warned that between 5 and 7 million people would be affected by the cuts at a time when global hunger is on the rise again. "The global divide between the U.S. government and other nations will deepen in this term and the coalitions that the United States builds will be with nations that are either ideologically aligned (such as Italy), are driven primarily by economic opportunism (such as Japan), share a sense of an Anglo-American world (Great Britain, Australia), can be counted on to promote the U.S. agenda regionally (Colombia), are repressive nations that have become new dependencies in the war on terror (Pakistan and Uzbekistan), or are countries that appeal to imperial or hegemonic prerogatives in their regions (such as Israel and Russia)."

It is likely that a number of other nations will confront a U.S. agenda that constantly undermines international law and multilateral rules. Gradually, we can expect a more unified and clearly articulated counter-agenda by blocs of nations that insist on the importance of international treaties, reassert the primacy of diplomacy in settling security issues, and forge a policy consensus around solutions that address the precarious state of the international economy and the growing impoverishment of many nations and communities. Countries targeted by the Bush administration and the neo-conservatives as existing or potential threats to U.S. supremacy – Iran, North Korea, and China – will likely take active steps to develop an effective deterrent capacity against military strikes, thus leading to increased weapons proliferation and a reduced willingness by nations to enter into arms-control agreements. The administration will remain committed to a foreign policy of regime change effected by a combination of military, political, and economic interventionism in such countries as Cuba and Syria.

U.S. trade and budget deficits will remain problems that will undermine the U.S. global superpower status and will increasingly threaten the fragile state of the international economy. Pressure from Europe and international financial institutions for the United States to restructure its economic policies will trigger intensifying friction internationally, leading to new pressure for the U.S. government to restructure its domestic economic policies by raising taxes, cutting military spending, and increasing interest rates – all measures it opposes in principle. The three authors conclude that the second Bush term will be forced to recognize how dependent the U.S. economy actually is on the capital flows of foreign investors to sustain the unprecedented debt burden accumulated by Washington.

## PRESENT REALITIES

The Bush administration is already massively retooling its military. This has entailed an enhanced use of advanced military technology, especially space systems, new nuclear weapons systems, and a continental missile defence system. The administration's post-9/11 war on terror and the militarized response to the terrorist attacks are a replication of the plans for U.S. global domination laid out by the neo-conservatives in their Project for the New American Century back in 1999. The National Security Strategy, announced in 2002, opened the door to the use of pre-emptive military intervention to defend U.S. security and commercial interests, including the maintenance of the global free-market system. (George Bush is no classic free trader in the Clinton mould, however. He uses free trade as an instrument to advance American corporate power; when it fails in this purpose, he distances himself from international trade-agreement obligations.)

To pay for this retooling, military spending soared from US$315 billion in 2001 to US$445 billion in 2005, and according to the World Policy Institute, will swell to US$500 billion in 2006. (These figures do not include the cost of the Iraq occupation, which is slated to be US$220 billion for the 2005/2006 year. In a May 27, 2005, speech to a conference of the Canadian Centre for Policy Alternatives, filmmaker Avi Lewis pointed out that this appropriation for Iraq could have been used to pay for health insurance for over 100 million American children, hire 3 million new teachers, or build 1.5 million new units of housing in the United States. If it had been used globally, it could have almost single-handedly met the UN Millennium Development goal of cutting world hunger in half by 2015 or filled the Global AIDS Fund for fifteen years.) The United States now spends more on its military than the next thirty countries combined. Military spending is so widely distributed that it turns up everywhere: the Center for Defense Information reports that 60 per cent of all federal research funding for universities is military related. In fact, as the *Korean Times* pointed out in a May 25, 2005, editorial, the United States outspends the "rogue" regimes of Iran, Iraq, Syria, North Korea, Libya, and Cuba on weapons of mass destruction (nuclear weapons) by a ratio of 22-1.

The Pentagon has shifted its strategy to fight against much weaker adversaries in the Third World using advanced weapons such as smart bombs, nuclear-tipped "bunker busters," unmanned aerial vehicles, and rapidly deployable special forces. And a whole new generation of fighter-bombers, warships, submarines, and missile-defence systems is being developed too.

Although the United States is a signatory to the 1970 Nuclear Non-proliferation Treaty, it has never met its obligations to begin the process of eliminating its nuclear arsenal. Under the terms of the treaty, the five countries that admitted publicly to owning nuclear weapons at that time – the United States, China, Britain, France, and Russia – made a commitment to destroy their arsenals in exchange for an agreement by the other signatories not to pursue nuclear weapons. (Since the treaty was signed, India, Pakistan, China, and possibly North Korea have acquired nuclear capability. Israel is thought to have possessed nuclear weapons since the 1950s but admitted it publicly only comparatively recently.) Not only has the United States not lived up to its obligations at all, under the Bush administration, it has entered a dangerous new phase of nuclear proliferation. The centrepiece of the White House nuclear policy is counterproliferation. This policy includes the potential pre-emptive use of nuclear weapons by the United States to meet the supposed threat of nuclear, biological, and chemical weapons wielded by America's enemies.

Physicians for Social Responsibility estimates that there are close to thirty thousand nuclear weapons on earth – 95 per cent of them belong either to Russia or the United States. There are 10,350 nuclear warheads deployed in the United States today. Fifty-two hundred are "operational" and two thousand of them are on "hair-trigger" alert, meaning they are ready to be deployed at any time. This generation of nuclear warheads is very powerful: the surface of a modern-day nuclear fireball irradiates as much as three times the light and heat as the surface of the sun. Yet under George W. Bush, the United States is spending billions of dollars more developing thermonuclear bombs and mini-nukes. The hawks in the White House are also seeking a resumption of nuclear testing. Not surprisingly, the Bush administration abandoned the U.S. commitment to the Anti-Ballistic Missile Treaty in 2001 and is opposed to the nuclear-testing ban.

Former U.S. defense secretary Robert McNamara was one of many observers disappointed that a month-long United Nations review of the Non-proliferation Treaty in May 2005 did not stop the escalation of nuclear weapons. In a press conference held at the United Nations, the man who oversaw the huge nuclear buildup during the Cold War condemned the refusal of the United States to renounce the first-strike option and its failure to reduce its nuclear arsenal. He said the nuclear policies of the Bush White House are "immoral, illegal, militarily unnecessary, very, very dangerous in terms of accidental or inadvertent use and destructive of the non-proliferation regime." Sadly, while that UN review was still meeting, military analyst William Arkin of the *Washington Post* exposed a terrifying new development. In the summer of 2004, Donald Rumsfeld approved a top secret "Interim Global Strike Order" directing the military to assume and maintain readiness to attack hostile countries on short notice. Two months later, Lt. Gen. Bruce Carlson, Commander, 8th Air Force, said it had been put in place. "We have the capacity to plan and execute global strikes anywhere in the world in a half day or less," he told the *Post*. The strike could be nuclear if needed, he added.

As the controversy over BMD demonstrated, the Bush White House is also planning for war in space. President Bush ordered a review of space policy in 2002 after a commission chaired by Donald Rumsfeld concluded that the United States could face a "Space Pearl Harbor." Under Clinton, space policy was based on the need for "space control," a way of defending America's billions of dollars worth of public and private investment in navigation, communications, and spy satellites. But it was implemented in such a way, according to Theresa Hitchens of the Center for Defense Information, that any kind of space weapon would be used only as a last resort. The Bush administration is placing much more emphasis on using space as a proactive domain for military operations. The critical policy document laying out these plans is the U.S. Air Force Transformation Flight Plan, a 176-page report that MSNBC called a "sweeping look at how best to expand America's military space tool kit" (February 22, 2005). The use of space is highlighted throughout the report, with emphasis on three capabilities: protecting space assets; denying adversaries' access to space; and quickly launching vehicles and payloads into space to replace space assets that fail or are destroyed. "From space global laser engagement, air-launched anti-missile satellites, to space-based radio frequency energy weapons and hypervelocity rod bundles heaved down to Earth from space – the U.S. Air Force flight plan portrays how valued space operations have become for the warfighter and in protecting the nation from chemical, biological, radiological, nuclear, and high explosive attack," said MSNBC. Says former commander-in-chief of Pentagon Space Command General Joseph Ashby, "It's politically sensitive, but it's going to happen. Some people don't want to hear this, and it sure isn't in vogue, but absolutely, we're going to fight into space. That's why the U.S. has developed programs in directed energy and hit-to-kill mechanisms. We will engage in directed targets someday – ships, airplanes, land targets, from space. We will engage targets in space, from space."

The United States is now spending billions of dollars in its so-called black budget, researching and testing offensive space weapons, including miniature satellites that could attack other satellites, high-powered lasers, and even space planes that could drop weapons from space, says pre-eminent U.S. weapons scientist Dr. Richard Garwin, physicist, author, and senior fellow with the Council on Foreign Relations. One that has been funded is the common aero vehicle (CAV), a hypersonic spacecraft that the air force in its 2003 Transformation Flight Plan says would "guide and dispense conventional weapons – from and through space – within one hour of tasking." Others under consideration are hypervelocity rod bundles – nicknamed "Rods from God" – and space-based radio frequency energy weapons. The Rods from God, tungsten metal rods dropped from satellites in space, "would provide the capability to strike ground targets anywhere in the world," according to the air force. Energy weapons would use high-power radio-frequency transmitters to destroy a military's command and control system.

Everett Dolman, professor at the air force's School of Advanced Air and Space Studies, told the *International Herald Tribune* (May 20, 2005) that the United States is close to being able to deploy space weapons: "With only the proven technology the U.S. has developed to date, the U.S. could adapt and field a comprehensive space weapons capability that includes space-to-space and space-to-ground weapons." Dr. Garwin warns that if the Bush administration persists in going in this direction, it will have profoundly negative implications for the global balance of power. China and Russia would feel bound to follow suit, he warns, with dire consequences. Never mind, says Gen. Lance Lord, Chief of the Air Force Space Command: "Space superiority is essential to our vision of controlling and fully exploiting space to provide our military with an asymmetric advantage over our adversaries. . . . Space superiority is not our birthright, but it is our destiny. Simply put, it is the American way of fighting." Adds Keith Hall, air force assistant secretary for space, "With regard to space dominance, we have it, we like it, and we're going to keep it."


## IRAQ, INC.


Even as it prepares for new military adventures abroad and in space, the United States becomes ever more deeply mired in the Iraq war. The death toll there continues to climb. By late summer 2005, more than 1,800 American soldiers and civilian contractors to the military have lost their lives since the outbreak of war and many more – estimates vary from 12,000 to 38,000 – have been wounded. Estimates of Iraqi casualties are disputed but unquestionably high. The CBC uses a source called Iraq Body Count because it lists civilians actually reported killed by U.S. military personnel. As of June 2005, this site listed over 25,000 Iraqi casualties. All observers (with the possible exception of General Tommy Franks, former top officer at U.S. Central Command in Iraq, who says the United States doesn't "do body counts") agree that this is just the tip of the iceberg. In its fall 2004 edition, *The Lancet*, a highly respected British medical journal, published a report by Johns Hopkins University that put the Iraqi civilian death toll at close to 100,000. This analysis used Iraqi death-rate reports from before and after the start of the war. But these terrible casualties – American and Iraqi – are being deliberately kept from the consciousness of the American public. A six-month survey of six major newspapers as well as *Time* and *Newsweek* magazines conducted by the *Los Angeles Times* and reported on May 21, 2005, found that in a period in which 559 Americans and other Westerners had been killed in Iraq, there were "almost no" photos of dead Americans and only forty-four pictures of the thousands of soldiers wounded during that period.

Conditions inside Iraq are terrible. According to War on Want, a British international development agency fighting global poverty, the unemployment rate stands at nearly 70 per cent and the country's debt has reached US$310 billion. Acute malnutrition among Iraqi children between the ages of six months and five years has doubled since the war and the risk of death from violence is 58 per cent higher. The risk of death from all causes is two-and-a-half-times greater now than before the war.

But these awful numbers have not stopped American corporations from reaping a bonanza of profits in Iraq. When Paul Wolfowitz (who now heads the World Bank) was deputy defense secretary, he oversaw the redesign of Iraq. In direct contravention of U.S. government obligations under international law (the Geneva Convention requires that an occupying force must respect the laws in force in the invaded country), the Bush administration has deliberately altered the entire economy of Iraq, massively privatizing public services, allowing American corporations to take over state assets, and forcing farmers to stop growing food for Iraqis and instead grow genetically engineered luxury crops for export. The goal, as stated in the contract with BearingPoint Inc., the Virginia-based corporation that is overseeing this transformation, is to "transition Iraq from a centrally planned economy to a market force . . . and implement private-sector involvement including asset sales, concessions, leases and management contracts" in every major sector of the Iraqi economy, including public services, media, banking, investment, taxes, agriculture, oil, electricity, and water.

In 2003, L. Paul Bremer, then administrator of the U.S. Coalition Provisional Authority, spelled out the key elements of a conversion to a market economy in Iraq: privatization of state-owned assets; "national treatment" of foreign firms, meaning that American corporations can own every business, control the construction, do all the work, and not employ a single Iraqi; unrestricted tax-free remittance of investment, meaning that American corporations can transfer all profits out of the country without rebuilding the local economy or reinvesting in communities; and forty-year foreign ownership licenses with options of unlimited renewal, giving American corporations years of control and profit in Iraq. As well, the Bremer orders give American corporations the right to sue for financial compensation any future government of Iraq that tries to reassert any control over these services and government assets.

The purpose (and benefits) of this plan for the Bush administration are threefold. The first is control of key resources in Iraq. As Stephen C. Pelletière, a former CIA senior political analyst on Iraq wrote in the *New York Times* on the eve of the Iraq war, "America could alter the destiny of the Middle East in a way that could not be challenged for decades, not solely by controlling Iraq's oil, but by controlling its water as well." The second is to use Iraq as the entry point to transform the whole Middle East into a market-style "democracy" friendly to U.S. policies and interests. Within months of the start of the war, President Bush announced plans for a Middle East Free Trade Zone by 2013. As George Wolfe, director of Economic Policy for the former Coalition Provisional Administration, told the *New York Times*, "In the long run, the United States hopes that Iraq will become an economic model for the Middle East." This was put more bluntly by Neil King, a journalist with the *Wall Street Journal*: "For many conservatives, Iraq is now the test case for whether the U.S. can engender American-style free-market capitalism within the Arab world."

But always, of course, this is also about making money for U.S. corporations. Several months after the new market-friendly orders came into effect, the U.S. Commerce Department held a "Doing Business in Iraq" conference attended by some five hundred U.S. corporations, including Boeing, Caterpillar, DaimlerChrysler, Microsoft, IBM, and Motorola. Hundreds of American corporations are now "doing business" in Iraq. JPMorgan was awarded a contract to run a consortium of thirteen banks that constitutes the Trade Bank of Iraq. A giant San Diego engineering company, Science Applications International Corporation, was given a US$90 million contract to rebuild Iraq's media. (The company, which supplies surveillance for U.S. spy agencies, came under so much criticism for using the U.S. government-run Voice of America to patch together nightly news shows made up entirely of dubbed stories from U.S. television programs, that its contract was not renewed in 2004.)

The demand for security services to protect foreign corporations operating in Iraq and the growing trend for outsourcing of military service to contractors have provided a bonanza for private military companies. United Kingdom–based private military companies' annual revenue increased from just under US$400 million a year before the war to almost US$2 billion in 2005. CorporateWatch, a research institute out of San Francisco, says that Iraq is the new Wild West where fortunes are being made as easily as lives are being lost. "While the country's resources and infrastructure are being carved up by large multinationals, private security firms, armed to the teeth and controlled by no-one, are stepping up to protect their operations as well as the activities of foreign governments." Aegis Defence Systems Ltd, a U.K.–registered company whose mercenaries have operated in Sierra Leone, Chile, and Papua New Guinea, got a US$293 million contract from the Pentagon to coordinate all security operations for VIPs in Iraq. But by far, the lion's share of contracts has gone to two companies: Bechtel, the San Francisco–based engineering giant; and Halliburton, the oil-services company with links to Vice President Cheney.

Halliburton's engineering and construction arm, Kellogg, Brown and Root, was in Iraq within seventy-two hours of the invasion and is the biggest contractor to the military there, handling most support services for the troops, from mail delivery to providing gasoline for military vehicles. Halliburton, with contracts worth more than US$17 billion, saw its revenues increase 80 per cent in 2004 and is poised to make an even greater profit in 2005. The company is currently the subject of multiple criminal investigations into kickbacks and overcharging for items as diverse as embroidered towels and gasoline. On April 22, 2005, Inter Press Service reported that Henry Waxman, a top Democrat on the U.S. House of Representatives subcommittee on government reform, said that Pentagon audits showing additional overcharges totalling US$212 million had been concealed by U.S. officials. "The evidence suggests that the U.S. used Iraqi oil proceeds to overpay Halliburton and then sought to hide the evidence of these overcharges from the international auditors," said Waxman.

Bechtel is another company that has profited on a grand scale from the war. With US$3 billion in contracts, the company saw its non-U.S.-generated revenues increase by a whopping 158 per cent in 2004. Bechtel, too, has been dogged by controversy. From schools and hospitals to electrical and water services, Bechtel is failing to meet its commitments.

Antonia Juhasz of the International Forum on Globalization has researched the legacy of Bechtel inside Iraq. Sewage plants are not working, allowing the waste water from 4 million people to run into the Tigris River. Electricity is totally unreliable. Retired air force colonel Sam Gardiner told the *Village Voice* that giving Iraqi electricians bailing wire and a little time would have solved the problem in six months. Reinforcing this theme, an Iraqi blogger excerpted in the *Guardian Weekly* (July 14–18, 2005) wrote that an Iraqi engineering firm estimated the cost of rebuilding a bridge at US$300,000. An American firm that quoted US$50 million got the job instead. Reports of shoddy work on schools and hospitals come out of Iraq on a weekly basis. *Public Citizen* reports that drinking water throughout the country is in a crisis state. Some villages have no access to water while larger cities get water only 50 per cent of the time, at best. This has led to vast outbreaks of cholera, diarrhea, nausea, and kidney stones. On April 10, 2005, the *Los Angeles Times* reported that at least forty water, sewage, and electrical plants refurbished by Bechtel are no longer working properly. One U.S. official was quoted as saying that "hundreds of millions had been squandered." As a result, schoolchildren have to step over rancid brown puddles on their way to school. Families swim in, fish, and get their drinking water from the polluted Tigris and Euphrates rivers, "leading to high rates of child mortality and water-borne illnesses."

Bestselling author and journalist Naomi Klein calls the trend to cash in on the crises in Iraq and other countries "Disaster Capitalism." She reported in the April 14, 2005, edition of *The Nation* that the White House created the Office of the Coordinator for Reconstruction and Stabilization (OCRS) in 2004 to allow the United States to respond to "post-conflict" crises in areas of the world hit by war, civil conflict, or natural disaster. In close co-operation with the National Intelligence Council, the OCRS assembles rapid-response teams made up of U.S. aid agencies, big non-governmental organizations, international financial institutions, and private companies that will have "pre-completed" contracts to rebuild the conflicted societies. At the top of the "to do" list is the sell-off of state-owned companies and government programs to private for-profit American corporations.

The Bush administration says the United States is simply bringing democracy, stable government, and a sound market economy to needy regions of the world. Klein argues that the real purpose is not to help societies rebuild themselves, but to use the desperation and fear created by catastrophe to engage in radical social and economic engineering of entire regions, and at the same time, make huge profits. While foreign consultants live high on the hog, local populations have no say in what gets sold or to whom. Wholesale privatizations and land grabs are taking place before traumatized citizens are able to mobilize. From telecommunications systems to water delivery, transnational corporations are raking in money from these projects. "Democracy building" has exploded into a multi-billion-dollar business.

## THE BIG THREE

Between the wars in Afghanistan and Iraq and the huge increase in defence spending, it is little wonder that the U.S. arms industry is making a killing under the Bush administration. The Arms Trade Resource Center is a New School University–based research institute linked to the highly respected World Policy Institute. In a comprehensive October 2004 report called "The Ties That Bind: Arms Industry Influence in the Bush Administration and Beyond," authors William D. Hartung and Michelle Ciarrocca paint a frightening picture of insider dealing. The authors describe a regime in which lucrative government contracts are handed to the arms industry, which in turn bestows historically high contributions on favoured politicians. As well, a revolving door sends industry executives to key White House positions while political insiders serve time inside the industry.

The Pentagon's top ten defence contractors received more than US$80 billion in 2003, almost double what they made just three years earlier. These statistics do not include the money many of the same companies made from the Department of Homeland Security, the Department of Energy, which deals with nuclear weapons and nuclear reactors in the navy, or from recent contracts awarded for the rebuilding of Iraq. The biggest winner in terms of new contracts, the World Policy Institute reports, is Halliburton. In one year, the company went from US$500 million to just under US$4 billion in defence contracts. Again, this figure does not include all the lucrative contracts it received in Iraq. Computer Sciences Corporation, which does missile defence work and also owns Dynacorp, a private military contractor whose work stretches from Colombia to Iraq, saw its military contracts more than triple from

2002 to 2003. Another winner was the Science Applications International Corporation – the same one that tried and failed to overhaul the media in Iraq – which saw its contracts increase from US$2.1 billion in 2002 to US$2.6 billion a year later.

These companies, however, while rocketing up the chart, cannot match the sheer volume of work logged by the "Big Three" – Lockheed Martin, Boeing, and Northrop Grumman. The Big Three's 2003 military contracts represent almost one out of every four dollars the Pentagon doled out that year on items ranging from rockets to rifles.

Lockheed Martin, the world's number-one military contractor, received an astounding US$21.9 billion in Pentagon contracts in 2003, an increase of almost US$5 billion in one year, and US$20.7 billion in 2004. Lockheed Martin made the now obsolete U-2 and SR-71 spy planes. It makes the F-16, F/A-22 fighter jets, the Hellfire and Javelin missiles, the PAC-3 Patriot Missile, the Joint Strike Fighter – a "next generation" combat jet that eventually will replace aircraft used by all branches of the military – and the F-117 stealth attack fighters that were used to "shock and awe" the population of Iraq in the 2003 war. The company also runs Sandia National Laboratories, a nuclear weapons design and engineering facility in Albuquerque, and the Nevada Test Site, where new nuclear weapons are tested, either by underground explosion (currently on hold due to a moratorium on nuclear testing, except for "mini-nukes," under five kilotons) or by computer simulation.

Lockheed is well positioned to cash in on Bush's plans to colonize the moon and militarize space, says William Hartung of the World Policy Institute. Lockheed already has major contracts in space launch, satellite, and missile defence work, plus a partnership to run the United States Space Alliance, the joint venture in charge of launches of the space shuttle. The new presidential commission charged with fleshing out Bush's space vision is being chaired by Edward Aldridge, the Pentagon's former under secretary of Defense for Acquisition, and a current member of Lockheed Martin's board of directors. Meanwhile, Hartung reports, the under secretary in charge of acquiring space assets at the air force is Peter Teets, a former chief operating officer at Lockheed Martin. His position was created in accordance with the recommendations of the Commission to Assess U.S. National Security Space Management and Organization, an advisory panel that published its blueprint for the militarization of space just as George Bush was first taking office. The commission included representatives of eight Pentagon contractors and was presided over by Donald Rumsfeld. "It is possible to project power through and from space in response to events anywhere in the world," the report concluded. "Having this capability would give the U.S. a much stronger deterrent and, in a conflict, an extraordinary military advantage."

Lockheed Martin is more than just a weapons manufacturer, however. It has also built a formidable information-technology empire that sorts mail for the Post Office, totals taxes for the Internal Revenue Service, collects vital information for the U.S. Census Department, monitors air traffic, provides technology for Homeland Security, runs surveillance at sea ports, tracks delinquent parents for the Department of Health and Human Services, provides interrogators for the prisoners at the U.S. detention facility at Guantanamo Bay, Cuba, and sends out millions of cheques on behalf of the Social Security Administration every month. "The melding of military and intelligence programs, information-technology and domestic security spending began in earnest after the September 11 attacks," reports journalist Tim Weiner in the *New York Times* (November 28, 2004). "When the United States government decided to let corporate America handle federal information technology, Lockheed leapt at the opportunity." Its information-technology sales have quadrupled since 1995, and Lockheed Martin is the number-one supplier to the federal government, which outsources almost 85 per cent of its information/ technology work.

"We want to know what's going on anytime, anyplace on the planet," says Lorraine M. Martin, company vice-president. That's made a lot easier by the incestuous relationship between company officials and the Bush administration. The *New York Times* reports that Lockheed lobbyists hold crucial posts, picking weapons and setting policies, at the Pentagon and in the White House. "Former Lockheed executives serve on the Defense Policy Board, the Defense Science Board, and the Homeland Security Advisory Council, which help make military and intelligence policy and pick weapons for future battles." Men who have worked, directly or indirectly, for the company hold the posts of secretary of the Navy, secretary of Transportation, director of the National Nuclear Security Administration's nuclear weapons complex, and director of the National Spy Satellite Agency. The list includes Stephen Hadley, who replaced Condoleezza Rice as National Security Advisor to the president. In turn, when Pentagon and other senior government officials leave public service, many of them head straight for the boardrooms of Lockheed and the other big weapons manufacturers.

Lockheed Martin spends more than any of its competitors in the political sphere. In the crucial 2000 election year, the company spent more than US$9.8 million lobbying Congress and contributed almost US$3 million to presidential candidates, two-thirds of that money going to George W. Bush. It spent US$9.7 million lobbying members of Congress in the mid-term 2002 elections and gave almost US$3 million to re-elect George Bush in 2004.

Boeing, known to the public as the manufacturer of commercial 747s, is second only to Lockheed Martin as a major weapons maker for the Pentagon. Boeing oversees many of the Pentagon's missile defence programs, makes the F-15 fighters and the Apache helicopters, operates the space shuttle, makes the guidance system for the Minutemen and Peacekeeper Missiles, builds precision munitions such as the Standoff Land Attack Missile-Expanded Response (SLAM-ER) and conventional Air-Launched Cruise Missiles, and designed an attack munitions kit that fits over "dumb" missiles, converting them to satellite-guided "smart bombs." Boeing has been at the centre of many scandals. Its "smart bombs" have repeatedly missed their targets in Iraq and Afghanistan, hitting both civilians and U.S. soldiers. As CorpWatch documents on its website on the big weapons manufacturers, the company was caught knowingly selling flawed parts for the Apache that led to thousands of unnecessary landings and at least one fatal crash for which Boeing paid tens of millions of dollars in fines. In December 2004, Boeing CEO Phil M. Condit was forced to resign following revelations that the company negotiated the hiring of top air force procurement official Darlene Druyun while Druyun was setting up a lucrative US$27.6-billion leasing deal involving Boeing's 767 air-refuelling aircraft. Druyun served nine months in a Florida prison for her part in the deal. Nevertheless, Boeing raked in US$17.3 billion in defence contracts in 2004, up US$4 billion from 2002.

Like Lockheed, Boeing gives a great deal of money to friendly politicians. Throughout the nineties, reports the Center for Responsive Politics, Boeing handed out US$7.6 million in political lobbying. In 2000, company election contributions, largely to the Republican Party, totalled US$1.5 million and in 2004, US$1.6 million. Like Lockheed, Boeing executives find a lot of familiar faces at the Pentagon. John Shalikashvili, retired chairman of the Joint Chiefs of Staff, is on the Boeing board. Former deputy secretary of defense Rudy de Leon heads up Boeing's Washington office. And former air force general Ronald Fogelman and former navy admiral David Jeremiah work as consultants to the company. Richard Perle, prominent Pentagon adviser, Project for the New American Century member, and former head of the Defense Policy Board, which advises Defense Secretary Rumsfeld, was a great booster of Boeing. His strong support for the controversial US$18 billion 2003 bid by Boeing to build one hundred 767 aircraft refuelling tankers for the air force almost succeeded until it was revealed that the company had given Perle's venture capital firm Trireme US$20 million the year before.

Northrop Grumman holds the number-three spot through its recent acquisitions of major military shipyards and space and missile defence specialist TRW. Northrop Grumman's contracts dramatically rose from US$5.2 billion in 2001 to US$11.9 billion in 2004.

Northrop Grumman manufactures the infamous B-2 stealth bomber, which costs US$2 billion per plane, the F-14 fighter, the unmanned Global Hawk, and amphibious assault ships. Its Newport News division is the only designer, builder, and refueller of nuclear-powered aircraft carriers in the United States. The company also owns Vinnell Corporation, a private military firm that trained the Saudi Arabian National Guard. Vinnell landed a US$48-million contract with the U.S. occupational authority to train the Iraqi National Army, but botched the job so badly, reports CorpWatch, that the Jordanian army had to be brought in to take over.

Like its rivals, Northrop Grumman has very close ties to the Bush White House. Nelson Gibbs, now assistant secretary of the air force for Installation, Environment, and Logistics, was the corporate comptroller throughout the nineties. Barry Watts, who once ran Northrop Grumman's in-house think-tank, is now the director of the Pentagon's Office of Program Analysis and Evaluation. Other key company connections include World Bank boss and former deputy secretary of defense Paul Wolfowitz, Pentagon comptroller Dov Zakheim, vice-presidential chief of staff I. Lewis Libby, and NASA director Sean O'Keefe, all of whom had consulting contracts or served as paid advisory board members for the company before joining the Bush administration. Northrop Grumman contributed US$1.68 million to the 2004 election, most of it going to the Republican Party.

## THE CULTURE OF CRONYISM

This incestuous and immensely lucrative business is kept in place by a tightly knit group of conservative ideologues who work through a variety of organizations and right-wing think-tanks to shape the Bush security policy. The Project for the New American Century is still going strong and now includes neo-conservative hawks like William Kristol and Robert Kagan (who co-wrote a famous article in 1997 calling for the United States to establish a "benevolent hegemony"). Former Lockheed Martin vice-president Bruce Jackson is PNAC's current director. The influential Center for Security Policy has been a leading voice opposing arms control and promoting "peace through strength" missile defence. Its board is made up of key players in the defence industry and its annual report lists all the major arms manufacturers – who directly benefit from the policy advice the Center gives to the Pentagon – as contributors. The Center's website boasts that no fewer than twenty-two close associates or members of its advisory council now hold influential positions in the Bush administration.

The National Institute for Public Policy, another influential insider think-tank, is a major proponent of the pro-nuclear strategy adopted by the current administration. Its January 2001 report, "Rationale and Requirements for U.S. Nuclear Forces and Arms Control" formed the basis of the Bush nuclear policy, and many of the report's authors, including Stephen Hadley, national security advisor, and Robert Joseph with the National Security Council, are now senior officials with the Bush administration.

World Policy Institute's William Hartung says that more than any administration in history, the Bush administration bases its defence, security, and foreign policies on the expertise of arms-industry officials who benefit directly from the advice they give. "The culture of cronyism that allows arms-industry executives to pull down multimillion dollar compensation packages while wounded veterans are shunted into makeshift medical wards has to end." Republican senator John McCain agrees. He says that there is "compelling evidence" of an "incestuous relationship between the defense industry and defense officials that is not good for America." But don't look for that to change anytime soon. *New York Times* columnist Paul Krugman says that instead of adopting the "leave no child behind" slogan that Bush stole from the Children's Defense Fund, his administration's true motto is "leave no defense contractor behind."

The defence industry makes huge profits through Pentagon support of global conflict. Shockingly, in spite of all the rhetoric of the Bush White House about spreading democracy and freedom around the world, the majority of U.S. arms sales to the developing world go to oppressive, violent, and tyrannical regimes. A May 2005 report by the World Policy Institute found that in 2003, the last year for which complete statistics are available, the United States transferred weaponry to eighteen of the twenty-five countries involved in active conflicts. From Angola to Chad and Ethiopia, to Colombia, Pakistan, and the Philippines, transfers through the two largest U.S. arms-sales programs (Foreign Military Sales and Commercial Sales) to these conflict nations totalled nearly US$2.7 billion. Almost 80 per cent were to countries defined as "undemocratic" by the U.S. State Department's Human Rights Report. The top recipients included Saudi Arabia (US$1.1 billion), Egypt (US$1 billion), Kuwait (US$153 million), the United Arab Emirates (US$110 million), and Uzbekistan (US$33 million). The largest U.S. military aid program, Foreign Military Financing, increased by 68 per cent in the first three years of George Bush's presidency. The largest increases went to countries that were engaged as U.S. allies in the wars in Iraq and Afghanistan, including Pakistan, and Bahrain.

"Billions of U.S. arms sales to Afghanistan in the 1980s ended up empowering Islamic fundamentalist fighters across the globe," the report concluded. "Perhaps no single policy is more at odds with President Bush's pledge to 'end tyranny in our world' than the United States' role as the world's leading arms exporting nation. Arming repressive regimes while simultaneously proclaiming a campaign against tyranny undermines the credibility of the United Sates and makes it harder to hold other nations to high standards of conduct on human rights."

## THE INTEROPERABLE ALLY

This is the foreign policy that the Canadian Council of Chief Executives wants Canadians to become a part of. The CCCE calls for a North American Defence Alliance in order to create "a North American defence community of sovereign nations." This would allow Canada and the United States to defend the continent from missile attacks, share naval protection, and protect infrastructure from terrorist attack. The CCCE states this new commitment would necessitate a reinvestment in Canada's military to ensure the "inter-operability of Canadian and United States armed forces on land, sea and in the air." No mention is made of the fact that Canada is already the sixth highest military spender, dollar for dollar, among NATO's nineteen members. Instead, the business lobby insists that Canada must enhance its "homeland security capabilities within North America" if it is to be a player in this new North American Defence Alliance.

In pushing for "interoperability" the CCCE is reinforcing pressure from the United States on all its NATO allies to spend more on the military, to work toward more integrated planning, and implic-itly to accept increased dependence on U.S. military technology. In Canada, this has sparked calls by a willing military industry to revamp Canadian defence policy and divert spending from peace-keeping and human-security functions to meet the Bush adminis-tration's priorities. If Canada acquiesces, it will be subsumed into a U.S. foreign-policy plan most Canadians would abhor.

One clear objective of the big-business campaign for deeper integration with Bush's America is to force Canada to abandon its historic commitment to multilateralism and align itself with an increasingly unilateralist United States. Under Bush, the United States has either repudiated or opted out of a long list of interna-tional treaties and conventions, including the Kyoto Protocol on global climate change, the Comprehensive Test Ban Treaty on nuclear weapons testing, and the UN agreement to curb the inter-national flow of illicit small arms. President Clinton refused to sign on to the International Criminal Court for war crimes; Bush is steadfastly hostile toward it. The only global institutions Bush's America supports are those like the World Bank and the World

Trade Organization that help the United States impose its style of market capitalism on the rest of the world. In addition, U.S. foreign aid is only 0.1 per cent of their GDP, the lowest in the industrialized world.

The debate over Canada's role in the defence of North America is far from over. Dr. John Clearwater, a specialist in nuclear weapons, says Canada's decision to opt out of missile defence was important to the United States only at a political level. He writes, "The clear and simple fact is that Paul Martin and the Liberals have already given the United States exactly what it sought to begin with – full co-operation by NORAD in missile-defence work. Last August, Ottawa and Washington agreed that NORAD's aerospace warning function would be used 'in support of the designated commands responsible for missile defence of North America.' NORAD was already, by signature of Canadian ambassador Michael Kergin, an integral part of the missile defence structure." Canada is now providing manpower for the NORAD early-warning and battle-command posts at its expense, a "free gift" to the operation of missile defence, adds Kergin (Winnipeg *Free Press*, March 3, 2005). A major U.S. defence contractor, Raytheon, is exploring locations for a radar station in Labrador that would, Defence Minister Bill Graham admits, become part of the North American Aerospace Defense Command's information system, and under the agreement referred to by Kergin, be available to the managers of the missile defence shield.

And the Canadian military is beginning to promote the kind of private-sector engagement and profit-making in areas of conflict more commonly associated with the U.S. military in countries like Iraq. Rick Hillier, the head of the Canadian Forces, called on Canadian business leaders to take a "Team Canada" approach to overseas operations and join his soldiers on missions to troubled nations such as Afghanistan, reported the *Edmonton Journal* (July 23, 2005). Chief of Defence Staff Gen. Rick Hillier said in a speech to a Toronto think-tank that the private sector has a role to play in future military missions. "I think it's a Team Canada approach that we need," he told the Canadian Institute of Strategic Studies. "We need private industry involved . . . you want to come in and make money from us, build our camps, fill our contracts or do our maintenance for us and then ten years later when everything's stabilized and secure you can come and start operating your business. . . . We need you there on Day 1. Take some risks with us on Day 1 as part of a team that we build . . . with you supporting us and us being supported by you," reported the *Journal*.

Essentially, Canada has been asked to surrender some of its sovereignty, says Michael Byers of the Liu Centre for the Study of Global Issues, to a country that would not be prepared to give up any of its own. Proponents of military expansion are now focused on the expansion of NORAD to include the maritime dimension, he says. The prize for the United States is unrestricted access to the Arctic archipelago. Ships from the Canadian navy, the Canadian Coast Guard, and the U.S. Coast Guard are already conducting joint exercises near Esquimalt Harbour and the Strait of Juan de Fuca involving surveillance, interdiction, and simulated explosives disposal. "If space divides us, then maritime should unite us," Colonel Douglas Murray, chair of the social-science division of the U.S. Air Force Academy told the *Globe and Mail* (March 9, 2005). Foreign-policy critic Steven Staples adds his concern that the long-awaited International Policy Statement, released in April 2005, shows that the Martin Liberals are trying to make up for their decision on missile defence by transforming the Canadian military so it is capable of deploying quickly with U.S. forces as well as greatly expanding Canada's secret commando force, Joint Task Force 2 (JTF2), at the expense of peacekeeping.

The decision not to join George Bush's ballistic missile defence plan was popular with the Canadian people. Paul Martin would be wise to remember this as pressure mounts to integrate the military and foreign policies of Canada and the United States at a time of unprecedented arms buildup. A good neighbour needs to be concerned with the protection of shared spaces and few Canadians would reject collaboration with the United States on common defence and meeting the security requirements of the continent. But Canada must retain the ability to form its own foreign and military policy based on an assessment of its best interests and in a way that reflects its long-held values.

# enemy
# creep

*The Rise of the Corporate Security Complex*

On September 26, 2002, thirty-four-year-old Maher Arar was arrested by American authorities at John F. Kennedy airport in New York. He was changing planes on his return to Canada from a vacation and was detained because his name had been placed on the United States' Watch List of terrorist suspects. Arar, who came to Canada from Syria as a teenager and holds dual citizenship, was held for thirteen days and questioned by Homeland Security officials for possible links to another suspected terrorist, a man Arar insists he barely knew. Even though he was not formally charged with anything, Arar was then placed in handcuffs and leg irons and transferred to an executive jet. The plane flew to Washington, stopped in Portland, Maine, and Rome, Italy, and finally landed in Amman, Jordan. Arar told Jane Mayer ("Outsourcing torture: the secret history of America's 'extraordinary rendition' program," *New Yorker*, February 14, 2005) that, during the flight, he heard pilots and crew identify themselves in radio communications as members of the "Special Removal Unit" and learned he was being taken to Syria for interrogation. Having heard about the barbaric police practices in that country, he begged crew members not to send him there as he feared he would be tortured. They did not answer him but invited him to watch a spy thriller they were showing on board.

Ten hours after landing in Jordan, Arar told Mayer, he was driven to Syria where, after just one day of threats, his Syrian guards started to beat him. They whipped his hands repeatedly with two-inch-thick electrical cables and kept him in a windowless underground cell that he likened to a grave. "Not even animals could withstand it," he said. Although he initially asserted his innocence, he eventually confessed to anything his tormentor wanted him to say. "You give up. You become like an animal." A year later, in October 2003, Arar was released without charges and sent back to Canada. The Syrian government said it could find no link between Arar and terrorism.

The Canadian government would have liked to let it go at that. But the public and Arar's family, particularly his wife, Monia Mazigh, had searching questions about the role Canada had played in the affair. The government was forced to call an inquiry in late January 2004, and appointed Justice Dennis O'Connor, assistant chief justice in Ontario, to head it. The United States government refused to co-operate in any way with the inquiry. Until its findings are made public, we can only speculate about how deeply the Canadian government might have been involved. However, testimony from many witnesses at the inquiry has raised some very troubling questions. Bill Graham, who was foreign minister at the time that Arar was detained, testified that he had felt "frustrated" by the lack of information he was receiving from security authorities. Franco Pillarella, then Canada's ambassador to Syria said that, even though he met with Arar while he was incarcerated by the Syrians, he did not take any action as he saw no "proof of torture." Superintendent Michel Cabana, the senior RCMP officer in the 2002 investigation of Arar, testified that he suspected that Arar was being tortured in Syria, but took no action as he felt it "right" to share information and investigative leads with Arar's jailers. "As appalling as it may seem to you, part of our duties in Canada is to protect the Canadian public, which means that from time to time we have to deal with countries that don't necessarily have the same record as we do and don't necessarily treat their prisoners the same way that we do." At this point in Cabana's testimony on June 30, 2005, Maher Arar abruptly left the inquiry and went outside for air.

## HIDDEN AGENDAS

The Bush administration responded to the 9/11 terrorist attacks by implementing a host of draconian domestic laws to fight terrorism, and demanded that other countries follow suit, urging that the U.S. legislation be used as their template. Much of the Bush administration's agenda was backed up by UN Security Council Resolution 1373, under which member states failing to comply risked Security Council sanctions. But the resolution was also backed up by the military, economic, and political might of the United States. Governments around the world have followed suit with a growing web of anti-terrorism laws and measures. The International Campaign Against Mass Surveillance, an organization sponsored by a coalition of civil liberties groups (including the International Civil Liberties Monitoring Group, a network of Canadian civil society organizations), says these measures threaten the human rights and civil liberties of peoples everywhere ("The Emergence of a Global Infrastructure for Mass Registration and Surveillance," April 2005).

The result has been an emerging trend toward the harmonization and integration of security functions on a global scale. In democratic countries, says the report, this has led to a rollback of rights, freedoms, and civil liberties that were won over the course of centuries. Repressive regimes have been strengthened by this trend, and development assistance has been diverted to bolster security apparatuses. Intrusive and discriminatory measures from national ID cards – soon perhaps to become international through biometric technology – to no-fly lists are being introduced in a number of Western countries. Governments are aggressively using information gathered and shared through electronic systems to crack down on dissent, close borders to refugees and activists, and seize and detain people without reasonable grounds. "The object of the infrastructure is not ordinary police work, but mass surveillance of entire populations," says the coalition. "In its technological capacity and global reach, it is an unprecedented project of social control – identity theft on a massive and official scale."

Internationally, the post–Second World War order – which enshrined the universal, inalienable human rights of all individuals – has been seriously eroded, says Gerry Barr, head of the Canadian Council for International Co-operation. Governments tell their citizens they need extraordinary powers to protect their citizens from terrorists. They say citizens should be willing to put up with some "inconvenience" and loss of privacy. "But in this new world where individuals are expected to hide little from governments," the report concludes, "governments are hiding a lot. And, there is a lot to be feared."

An explicit goal of the Canadian Council of Chief Executives is to harmonize Canadian and American security measures so that Canada can take its place in the global surveillance system. In its final report, the Task Force on the Future of North America called for a common security perimeter and a common standard of entry into Canada, the United States, and Mexico. There would be harmonized movement of people and cargo, and a biometric identity Border Card – or "Smart Card" – that people would have to "voluntarily seek, receive, and pay the costs" for. There would be a unified North American Border Action Plan, which would harmonize refugee, visa, and immigration procedures, including "entry, screening and tracking," and joint inspection of foreign nationals at ports. The task force called for trilateral co-operation on counter-terrorism and law enforcement including "tracking, storing and disseminating" intelligence. Training and exercises would be developed to increase co-operation and interoperability "among and between enforcement agencies and militaries."

Canadians reacted with horror to the 9/11 attacks and are good neighbours who want to work with Americans to ensure their safety and ours. But the campaign to harmonize Canadian security measures with those of the Bush administration is dangerous and misguided. If adopted here, measures such as the Homeland Security Project, the Secure Flight Program, the National Security Entry-Exit Registration System, the profiling and registering of residents based on country of origin or religious background (and perhaps eventually on sexual orientation), and many other initiatives would undermine Canadian values and constitutional guarantees as well as national and international rights.

## EVERYONE IS A TERRORIST

Immediately following the September 11 terrorist attacks, Washington established a whole new homeland security regime. On October 26, 2001, the U.S. Congress passed the USA Patriot Act, which, together with the Homeland Security Act and numerous presidential orders, granted sweeping new powers to the executive branch while reducing the powers of the judiciary and Congress and curtailing the rights of American citizens. Under the new laws, domestic terrorism was redefined to include acts that appear to be intended to "influence the policy of a government by intimidation or coercion." Because of this language, those who engage in legitimate dissent might now be considered terrorists. The Patriot Act allows federal authorities to search a home or workplace and seize the property of a suspect without ever informing the person in question. The Act also allows authorities to undertake secret surveillance and searches of library, student, medical, and financial records and to monitor the activities of political and religious groups that are not suspected of criminal activity. It authorizes the FBI to access business records held by American companies and their subsidiaries. It dramatically increases the government's surveillance, search and seizure, and wiretapping authority and allows for the sharing of secret information on American citizens among federal agencies. In the first two years after 9/11, the Bush administration issued at least eighteen thousand anti-terrorism subpoenas and search warrants (*Vanity Fair*, February 2004).

The most contentious measure is perhaps the one that allows the FBI to go to a secret intelligence court to demand access to material from businesses and other institutions as part of an investigation. Some are resisting. The *New York Times* (May 19, 2005) reported that more than 380 governmental bodies, including seven states, have adopted formal resolutions to express their concern about the broad reach of this provision. But others are voluntarily offering the FBI access to their files. Hundreds of colleges and universities, many commercial banks and private corporations, and all major U.S. airlines share personal records with government agencies without the consent of the individuals whose records are involved. As well, the U.S. government is buying personal data on Americans from commercial data companies. One such company, DoubleClick, has information from fifteen hundred firms yielding information on 90 million American households. Outside the United States, reports the American Civil Liberties Union, a company called ChoicePoint has collected information on hundreds of millions of Latin Americans and sold them to the U.S. government.

Several major programs collect and collate private and public information. MATRIX (Multi-State Anti-Terrorism Information Exchange) merges government data from participating American states with a private database that claims to have complete records on millions of Americans. US-VISIT and the Passenger Risk Assessment Center track all travel in and out of the country. TIA (Total Information Awareness) aimed to mine the commercial transactions of Americans until Congress shut it down in 2003. (TIA was run by Iran-Contragate's John Poindexter.) Private corporations are making a fortune from the war on terror. Together with the Department of Homeland Security, they have created what the International Civil Liberties Monitoring Group calls the "Corporate Security Complex" – the modern successor to the Military Industrial Complex that emerged in the Cold War era. Some of these firms are cashing in on the new business of "data mining," that is, analyzing the massive records they have gathered for patterns of behaviour that supposedly indicate propensity for terrorist activity. For information-technology companies like Lockheed Martin, LexisNexis, ChoicePoint, Accenture, Computer Sciences, and Acxiom, the war on terror has been a boon. In 2003, the U.S. government allocated an estimated US$115 billion for research and development related to anti-terror initiatives. Estimated allocations to 2010 are from US$130 billion to US$180 billion a year, according to the *Wall Street Journal* (November 25, 2002).

But the private sector offers something more than technology to government agencies: it offers a way around some of the laws and accountability mechanisms that regulate the public service. For example, says the International Campaign Against Mass Surveillance, by contracting with private corporations, government agencies gain access to databases they would not, under privacy and other laws, be able to maintain themselves. This allows the Bush administration both to evade the privacy issue and to shield government from public scrutiny. There is another ethical issue here as well. These corporations, like the big defence companies, give huge amounts of money to political allies and have easy access to senior White House and Homeland Security officials. They are influencing policy in a very sensitive area in order to maximize their business potential, egging on governments to embrace newer, bigger, and more intrusive systems of social control.

Yet the U.S. Department of Homeland Security wants more. On April 10, 2005, the *New York Times* reported that the Bush administration is developing a plan to give the government access to possibly hundreds of millions of international banking transactions in an effort to trace and deter terrorist financing. To the already voluminous government databases currently tracking financial transactions would be added the logs of international wire transfers into and out of American banks. The Bush administration has authorized the Treasury Department to draft regulations requiring financial institutions to turn over "certain cross-border electronic transmittals of funds" that may be needed to combat money laundering and terrorist financing. As well the Bush administration has broken a promise to cede control of the principal computers that control global Internet traffic – thirteen computers known as "root servers" that inform all Web browsers and e-mail programs how to direct Internet traffic – over to a private international body, reported the *Guardian* (July 2, 2005). Instead, the U.S. government will retain control over this key instrument of global information flow. The FBI used the mandatory review of the Patriot Act, which, in July 2005, made permanent fourteen of the sixteen provisions of the Act, to seek an extension of the Homeland Security tools, such as the right to obtain records without first asking a judge (*New York Times*, May 19, 2005). As well, the United States is considering expanding its screening program for air passengers to include any plane that flies over American territory whether it lands on U.S. soil or not. In April 2005, a KLM flight from Amsterdam bound for Mexico was turned back before it reached U.S. airspace because it had two passengers on the U.S. "No-Fly" list, even though it had not planned to land in the United States.

The U.S. "No-Fly" list has been used to target peace activists, civil rights lawyers, and writers opposed to U.S. foreign policy. In March 2005, Fernando Rodriguez, a prominent Bolivian human-rights activist with no ties to terrorism, was held and questioned by Homeland Security officials at the Miami airport, stripped of his U.S. visa, and forced to board a plane back to La Paz. Rodriguez is a co-founder of the Bolivian chapter of the Inter-American Platform of Human Rights and was on his way to testify at a Washington hearing on abuses by logging, mining, and petroleum companies against indigenous peoples in Bolivia (*Washington Times*, March 30, 2005). Massachusetts senator Ted Kennedy was stopped from getting on a plane from Washington to Boston. He was eventually allowed to fly but was stopped again on the return flight. To get his name off the list, he had to place a personal call to then Homeland Security secretary Tom Ridge. The ACLU says that "hundreds, if not thousands" of innocent people have been singled out because their names are among the over thirty thousand on the list.

Homeland Security Secretary Michael Chertoff is calling for a counterpart to the "No-Fly" list – a global "security envelope" that would allow trusted people like business executives to move freely outside the regular screening process. This echoes a European Community proposal that "trusted economic operators such as business travellers" be allowed to bypass security restrictions between Europe and the United States. Chertoff says that, with proper technology and secure travel documents, certain people and their cargo would be able "to move relatively freely from point to point all across the globe." In their June 2005 Report to the Leaders on the implementation of the North American Security and Prosperity Partnership signed in Waco, ministers from the three North American countries promised to develop a "single integrated global enrolment program for North American trusted travellers." By creating a new super-class of traveller, the governments are legalizing a class-based social system – one they have created with their assault on social programs.

In 2004, the airport screening process was expanded to include most visitors to the United States. People applying for a visa for travel to the United States will now have their fingerprints taken at "virtual borders" outside the country, and citizens of countries from which a visa is not required will be photographed and fingerprinted on entry. The technology used to collect this data is called "biometrics." It records the physical characteristics of a person – such as facial dimensions, fingerprints, iris characteristics, and voice patterns – into a computer database. Eventually, the plan is to create dossiers on all persons entering the United States and store them for one hundred years. As the International Campaign Against Mass Surveillance points out, these records could include information about individuals' medical history, social benefits, passport applications, immigration status, driving record, criminal record, security intelligence file, tax returns, census data, employment history, banking records, credit-card purchases, medical prescriptions, air-travel patterns, e-mails, Internet use, on-line purchases, cellphone calls, and library, bookstore, and video selections. Hardly any vestige of a private life would remain unexamined.

## *AMERICA'S GULAG*

The new laws have led to dangerous abuses. Racial profiling is one. Under the National Security Entry-Exit Registration System, every male over the age of sixteen with origins in a list of designated (mostly Muslim) countries, visiting, studying in, or travelling through the United States was watched and identified. Eighty thousand were registered; hundreds were detained; thousands were deported; and many fled the country in fear. Many told of rough treatment, harassment, and insults by authorities. The Bush administration also authorized the Immigration and Naturalization Service to hold non-citizens for forty-eight hours without charges, and to extend that time indefinitely "in the event of an emergency or other extraordinary circumstances," a clear violation of a U.S. Supreme Court ruling that the government must charge a detainee within forty-eight hours of their arrest. The International Campaign Against Mass Surveillance points out that by holding people on immigration charges while they are in fact being investigated for links to criminal activity (terrorism), the government deliberately denies them their constitutional rights.

Threats to personal privacy, civil liberties, and freedom of movement are bad enough. There's worse. It is becoming clear that the United States and some other countries are engaging in torture, inhumane treatment, and indefinite detention of people suspected of being terrorists or with links to terrorists. The International Civil Liberties Monitoring Group says the United States is operating a "Global Gulag" – a partly secret archipelago of prison camps and detention centres around the world. Some are run directly by the U.S. government, such as Camp Delta at Guantanamo Bay in

Cuba; Bagram in Afghanistan; Camp Justice on the British Indian Ocean island Diego Garcia; a floating detention centre on board a U.S. naval vessel; Camp Cropper, Abu Ghraib, and several others in Iraq; the U.S. airbase in Qatar; and a jail at an undisclosed location referred to by the CIA as "Hotel California" after the popular song by the Eagles, where you can "check out any time you want but you can never leave."

(Not surprisingly, this development has been a boon to the private-prison industry. Companies like Corrections Corporation of America, Correctional Services Corporation, and GEO Group – formerly Wackenhut – operating in many states, were struggling to survive amidst growing criticism about poor conditions, inmate violence, and escapes. However, reported the Associated Press on July 31, 2005, a surge of business from federal agencies seeking to house fast-rising numbers of detained aliens has put these for-profit corporations back in business. Since 2000, the number of federal inmates in private facilities has increased by two-thirds, to more than 24,000. Thousands more detainees not convicted of crimes are confined to for-profit facilities, which now house roughly 14 per cent of all federal prisoners, compared with 6 per cent of state inmates. And business is sure to grow. The Bureau of Prisons estimates that the number of federal inmates is expected to rise from 185,000 to 226,000 by 2010, with private companies likely to be relied on for housing non-citizen immigrants convicted of federal crimes. The number of people detained by U.S. immigration officials is also increasing rapidly, reports the Associated Press, up threefold since 2000 to more than 21,000 at any given time. In December 2004, Congress passed a terrorism prevention bill calling for 40,000 additional beds by 2010 for aliens awaiting deportation.

Lucas Guttentag of the American Civil Liberties Union's Immigrants Rights Project expressed grave concern over the welfare of alien inmates housed in sub-standard, under-regulated, for-profit facilities with an interest in high immigrant incarceration, noting "systemic over-incarceration in the immigration system.")

In the U.S.–run detention centres, prisoners have been beaten, subjected to sleep deprivation, bound in awkward, painful positions, been thrown against walls, forced off bridges, half-drowned in a torture known as water-boarding, covered with their own urine, had lighted cigarettes put in their ears, been chained in the fetal position for over twenty-four hours, humiliated by female personnel, bitten by dogs, banged head-first into doors, forced to sodomize themselves, held naked for long periods of time, and been subjected to mock executions, among other grotesque abuses. In July 2004, the U.S. army admitted that at least thirty-nine prisoners held in U.S. custody had died in violent circumstances and launched an investigation into these deaths. On March 16, 2005, the *New York Times* reported that the investigation was complete and the army admitted that at least twenty-six of these prisoners were victims of criminal homicide. Only one of the deaths took place at the now-infamous Abu Ghraib prison, which shows, said the paper, that the abuses there were not an aberration. The other deaths were classified as "justifiable homicides" and will not be prosecuted.

In spring 2005, Physicians for Human Rights obtained a copy of a new army "detainee operations doctrine" that allows rules of humane treatment to be set aside for "military necessity" in the case of enemy combatants (Boston *Globe*, May 21, 2005). No such exemption exists either in international or U.S. law. Four days after this story appeared, Amnesty International released a scathing report condemning the United States for setting up an international network of detention centres and for evading the Geneva Convention to "redefine" torture.

The army has confirmed that U.S. forces have held more than fifty thousand detainees in Iraq and Afghanistan since 2002. Other detention centres are run by allies of the United States in close co-operation with the CIA, reports the International Campaign Against Mass Surveillance. These are located in Jordan, Syria, Egypt, Morocco, Saudi Arabia, Uzbekistan, and Pakistan – countries well known to employ torture and detain prisoners indefinitely. Among the worst are Far' Falastin interrogation centre in Damascus, Syria (where Maher Arar was held), and the Scorpion jail and Lazoghly Square secret-police headquarters in Cairo. Former CIA agent Bob Baer, who worked undercover in the Middle East, told the *New Statesman*'s Stephen Grey (May 13, 2004), "If you want a serious interrogation, you send a prisoner to Jordan. If you want them to be tortured, you send them to Syria. If you want someone to disappear – never to see them again – you send them to Egypt."

In her *New Yorker* exposé, Jane Mayer chronicled the practice of sending suspects to other countries where they are tortured or "disappeared." It is called "rendition" and it allows the American government to subject suspects to treatment that would be illegal at home. Rendition was carried out in the 1990s on a limited basis, but after 9/11, the program was expanded "beyond recognition" says Mayer. One CIA official told her the scale of rendition operations had become "an abomination." Most of the suspects sent away for torture have not been publicly charged with any crime. Scott Horton, an expert on international law at the New York City Law School, estimates that at least 150 people have been rendered since 2001.

Often, they are taken to their terrible destination by a Gulfstream 5 airplane, nicknamed the "torture jet" by the media. It departs from its base in Fort Bragg, North Carolina (the main U.S. special operations base), makes a short stop at Dulles International Airport in Washington, and then takes off, either with prisoners on board, or to other destinations where it picks up suspects for delivery abroad. The *Sunday Times* (November 14, 2004) reported that it had obtained the logs of some three hundred flights showing "the movements of the Gulfstream 5 leased by agents from the U.S. Defense Department and the CIA." According to this report, the logs show that the plane has flown to at least forty-nine destinations outside America, including Egypt, Iraq, Morocco, Afghanistan, and Uzbekistan, where the "secret police are notorious for their interrogation methods, including the alleged boiling of prisoners."

A 2001 four-part television series in Sweden caused a public outcry when it documented the use of the jet to pick up two

Egyptians living in Sweden. Swedish security police picked up the two men, Ahmed Agiza and Muhammad Al Zery, and handed them over to American agents who shackled, blindfolded, and hooded the men and put them on the jet bound for Egypt. "Disguised agents from an elite American military unit, answering directly to the White House, are allowed to take command on Swedish soil, contrary to Swedish law," said journalist Kalla Fakta, who broke the story. "In a secret and brutal operation, two Egyptians who have been given asylum in Sweden are kidnapped and brought to Egypt to be tortured. They are suspected of terrorism but no evidence is presented." After two and a half horrible years in an Egyptian prison, Al Zery was declared innocent and released. Agiza was given a military trial and sentenced to twenty-five years in prison.

Jane Mayer interviewed a former CIA counterterrorism expert who helped establish the practice of rendition but left when he could no longer stomach the abuses he was witnessing. Michael Scheuer, who wrote the 2003 *New York Times* bestseller *Imperial Hubris: Why the West Is Losing the War on Terror*, told Mayer that Egypt is the favourite destination for rendition because it is a key strategic ally and its secret police, the Mukhabarat, has a reputation for brutality. The partnership between the Egyptian and American intelligence services is extraordinarily close, he said. "The Americans could give the Egyptian interrogators questions they wanted put to the detainees in the morning and get answers by the evening."

Rendition's original purpose was to export to third countries a small number of individuals charged with criminal offences. Now, however, it is regularly used to get rid of a large group of individuals who will likely never have criminal charges brought against them. The names of the vast majority are not known – Human Rights Watch calls them "ghost detainees" – and they will never see justice. The point made by critics of the program is not, of course, whether its victims are terrorists. Some very well may be. But there is a legal process for dealing with terrorist suspects that does not debase and dishonour the entire justice system. When the world's superpower flouts international law in this brutal manner, it sets a terrible example and lowers the human-rights bar everywhere. What the Bush administration has done, says William Schulz, Executive Director of Amnesty International and author of the 2004 book *Tainted Legacy: 9/11 and the Ruin of Human Rights*, is to take the United States back to where it was before human rights were part of the political vocabulary. "The Bush Administration has not only used 9/11 to bypass human rights institutions outside the United States, it has exploited this tragedy to institute an unholy war on its own citizens."

Alberto Gonzales, now the attorney general, authored the infamous "torture memos" to George Bush, giving him almost unfettered latitude in his prosecution of those suspected of being on the wrong side in the war on terror. *Newsweek* (May 25, 2004) broke the story that in a January 25, 2002, memo, Gonzales said the United States was in a "new kind of war" that called for new rules. "As you have said, the war against terrorism is a new kind of war. It is not the traditional clash between nations adhering to the laws of war that formed the backdrop for G.P.W. [The Geneva Convention on Prisoners of War]. The nature of the new war places a high premium on other factors, such as the ability to quickly obtain information from captured terrorists and their sponsors in order to avoid further atrocities or war crimes, such as wantonly killing civilians. In my judgement, this new paradigm renders obsolete Geneva's strict limitations on questioning of enemy prisoners and renders quaint some of its provisions requiring that a captured enemy be afforded such things as commissary privileges."

In this memo and others, Gonzales told George Bush that he did not have to comply with the Geneva Convention in the handling of these detainees. The January 25, 2002, memo called for exempting al-Qaeda and Taliban detainees from the Geneva Convention's provisions on the treatment of prisoners, thus allowing the United States not to assess them on a case-by-case basis. Essentially, the lawyers classified these detainees as neither civilians nor prisoners of war (under which classifications they would be protected by the Geneva Convention), but as "illegal enemy combatants." Eric Lewis, an expert in international law told the *New Yorker*'s Jane Mayer that Gonzales and his team created a "third category of prisoners and cast them outside the law."

Another series of memos opened the door to legalized torture by U.S. officials and their surrogates. An August 2002 Justice Department memo also drafted by Alberto Gonzales and vetted by a large number of very senior White House officials, including Vice President Cheney, voiced the opinion that laws prohibiting torture "do not apply to the President's detention and interrogation of enemy combatants" and that pain caused by an interrogation must include "injury such as death, organ failure, or serious impairment of bodily functions – to constitute torture" (*Newsweek*, June 27, 2004). Another memo of that same month signed by Assistant Attorney General Jay S. Bybee but prepared by Gonzales's team, argued that torture required the intent to inflict suffering "equivalent in intensity to the pain accompanying serious physical injury, such as organ failure, impairment of bodily function or even death." The memo also said that torture only occurs when the intent is to cause pain. "If pain is used to gain information or a confession, it is not torture." (*Guardian*, January 15, 2005.)

Another memorandum declared that the president could override international treaty prohibitions and federal anti-torture law under his authority as commander-in-chief to approve any technique necessary to protect the nation's security (*New York Times*, March 7, 2005). The State Department, shocked by these developments, tried and failed to hinder the process. In a forty-page memo, State Department legal adviser William Taft called the advice to the president "untenable" and warned that Bush could be charged with war crimes. (It was to stop this kind of insubordination that Condoleezza Rice was brought in to replace Colin Powell.)

Richard Swift, a Canadian staff writer for the *New Internationalist*, says that everything in the United States – aid, immigration, economic development, and foreign policy – must now be seen as refracted through the prism of this "mentality of occupation." Not surprisingly, the most vulnerable are immigrants, refugees, the poor, dissenters, and minorities. The politics of this mindset, says Swift, produces "enemy creep." The definition of terrorism is expanded inexorably so that it fits a much wider circle of opposition and dissenters. He points to the Oregon law that defines terrorism as "any act that disrupts the orderly assembly of inhabitants, commerce, transportation, and education, and government institutions" and reports that there are now 5 million people on the U.S. Master Terror Watch list. They cannot all be terrorists. And many domestic civil society groups are targeted as well. Using the Freedom of Information Act for a lawsuit against the Department of Homeland Security, the American Civil Liberties Union discovered the FBI has collected at least 3,500 pages of internal documents on American civil rights and antiwar groups since 2001 - including 1,173 on the ACLU itself and 2,383 on Greenpeace (*New York Times*, July 18, 2005).

Another chilling example of enemy creep is the 2005 report by the National Intelligence Council, "Global Trends 2020: Mapping the Global Future." In this report the council targets the growing indigenous rights movement in Latin America as a "threat to the security and hegemony of the United States," and includes the movement in its list of terrorist threats.

American civil liberties groups are deeply concerned about a new project of the U.S. military. The *New Scientist* (March 2, 2005) reports the military is funding development of a weapon that delivers a bout of excruciating pain from up to two kilometres away. Intended for use against rioters and for crowd control, it is meant to leave victims unharmed. Nevertheless it is coming under scrutiny from pain researchers furious that their work on controlling pain is being used to develop a weapon and who warn that it might leave long-term psychological effects. Others fear it will be used for torture. The research came to light in documents unearthed by the Sunshine Project, an organization based in Texas and in Hamburg, Germany, that exposes biological weapons research. The papers reveal research being done at the University of Florida in Gainesville on Pulsed Energy Projectiles (PEPs), which fire a laser pulse that generates a burst of expanding plasma when it hits something solid like a person. The weapons, designed for use by 2007, will have the power to literally knock protesters off their feet.

Swift argues that this mentality creates political chill, which discourages dissent and debate. A December 2004 poll conducted by Cornell University found that nearly half of Americans support restricting the rights of Muslim-Americans: almost one-third felt they should be required to register where they live (*Detroit Free Press*, December 17, 2004). Swift worries that this tolerance for the suspension of human rights and civil liberties will become a permanent part of American political culture. The notion is not far-fetched given that the White House says that the United States will be on a war footing for years to come.

Meanwhile, wrote Robert Kennedy in *Crimes Against Nature*, the White House has done almost nothing to require better security at the fifteen thousand chemical manufacturing facilities, oil-tank farms, pesticide plants, and other repositories of deadly chemicals that, if attacked, could each put a million or so people at risk of death or injury. Nor has it forced the nuclear industry to beef up security at its 103 nuclear plants. While the Bush administration is asking Americans to give up fundamental rights and freedoms in the name of security, it has let American corporations off the hook. Seven weeks after the 9/11 attacks, Senator Jon Corzine of New Jersey introduced the Chemical Security Act, which would require chemical plants to reduce toxic chemical inventories where practical and switch to less toxic chemicals where economically feasible. The bill passed the Environment and Public Works Committee in a 19-0 vote. Then, says Kennedy, the chemical lobbyists went to work. The American Chemistry Council, which gave many millions of dollars to the Bush campaign and whose chief counsel, James Conrad, served in President Bush's EPA transition team, flooded senators' offices with requests to kill the bill, calling it a radical environmental campaign out to target the industry. Corzine protested that the bill had nothing to do with environmental protection but was meant to protect the public. Senator James Inhofe, who now chairs this Senate committee, backed the Council and by autumn, the Corzine bill was dead. Al Martinez-Fonts, a former executive at JPMorgan then serving as senior aide to Homeland Security head Tom Ridge, defended the move. Even in times of war, he said, the Bush administration is reluctant to interfere with business decisions by the private sector. When reminded by a reporter that the government forced the airline industry to improve security, Martinez-Fonts replied: "Well, the answer is because September 11 happened, and there were airplanes that rammed into buildings. And it was not chemical plants that were blown up."

## SANCTUARY COUNTRY

While nothing in Canada's responses to the terrorist attacks of 9/11 yet approaches the draconian measures implemented in the United States, Canadians have considerable cause for concern. The Bush administration clearly defines "homeland security" as encompassing all of North America, not just the United States. It is not only through its surrogates in the CCCE that it is pressuring Canada to join in the creation of a common security perimeter and to implement the Canadian version of its homeland security package.

The United States has other ways of applying pressure. In April 2005, the Department of Homeland Security announced that all visiting Canadians, including those travelling by car, boat, and train as well as airplane, will need high-security documents, such as a passport or special border-crossing card. It also warned that the United States might end the exemption for Canadians from the controversial US-VISIT screening system, which requires visitors to submit fingerprints and photographs when they cross the U.S. border. When the program was launched in 2004, it applied only to countries whose citizens require visas to enter the United States.

But three months later, twenty-seven "visa-waiver countries" – including key U.S. allies such as Great Britain, Italy, and Australia – were added. The threat to include Canada is a powerful incentive for the Canadian government to comply with American security demands. The United States has also warned Canada that it may soon demand that any Canadian flight passing through U.S. airspace, even if it doesn't land, must submit its passengers' names, citizenship, birthdays, and possibly addresses and credit-card details to U.S. authorities, or the plane will be turned back.

Many Americans believe that the terrorists who attacked the twin towers crossed the border from Canada and that Canada is a safe harbour for terrorists. There was a news report, immediately after the 9/11 attacks, to the effect that most or all of the terrorists came from Canada. (It was completely false.) In early January 2003, the FBI posted an alert on its website stating that five terrorists were heading for the United States from Canada. This, too, was false and the FBI removed the item from its website, but the damage had been done. FOX News regularly whips up hysteria about the "terrorist hordes" training in the "liberal" haven of Canada. On May 10, 2005, FOX reported that a group of freedom fighters in Vermont is resurrecting the "Minutemen Project" and patrolling the Vermont-Canada border, looking for terrorists trying to cross from Canada into the United States. One member of the group, Chris Simcox, said that Canada is a "Sanctuary Country" for terrorists. Carey James, former FBI special agent in Washington, told the news channel that "every terrorist organization in the world" has representation in Canada. But it isn't just the extreme right wing that perpetuates this view. On April 2005, New York senator Hillary Clinton called on the Bush White House to appoint a "border czar" to coordinate security at the Canada–U.S. border because it is a "gateway for people coming into our country."

Part of the problem is that the hawks in the Bush administration are suspicious of Canada's historic values and priorities. An October 2003 U.S. study on countries soft on terrorism actually singled out Canada. The report, "Nations Hospitable to Organized

Crime and Terrorism," written by the U.S. Federal Research Division of the Library of Congress, is critical of Canada's history of human rights and views it as a problem in combating terrorism. "As a modern liberal democracy," says the report, "Canada possesses a number of features that make it hospitable to terrorists and international criminals. The Canadian Constitution guarantees rights such as the right to life, liberty, freedom of movement, freedom of speech, protection against unreasonable search and seizure, and protection against arbitrary detention or imprisonment that make it easier for terrorists and international criminals to operate."

When Michael Kergin, then Canadian ambassador to the United States, responded to the report, instead of praising Canada's continued dedication to human rights, and taking offence that a system based on rights would be regarded as suspect, he instead described the new law-and-order measures Canada adopted after the September 11 attacks. In its October 2004 report, "Canadian Democracy at a Crossroads: The Need for Coherence and Accountability in Counter-Terrorism Policy and Practice," Montreal-based Rights and Democracy said it is concerned that the Bush administration's conception of counterterrorism is taking root in Canada. It cites the response from Kergin as one example.

Indeed, Canada has implemented a host of structures, laws, and practices that come dangerously close to violating the civil rights of its citizens. In its 2001 budget, the Martin government allocated $7.7 billion over a five-year period to fight terrorism at home. It also established a powerful new Ministry of Public Safety and Emergency Preparedness, closely modelled on the U.S. Homeland Security Agency. The ministry, headed by Deputy Prime Minister Anne McLellan, combined agencies under the wing of the Solicitor General, including the RCMP, Canadian Security Intelligence Service, Correctional Service of Canada, and the National Parole Board, with bodies responsible for borders, emergency preparedness, and crime prevention. This included the new Canada Border Services Agency, in charge of all passenger, food, plant and animal inspection, as well as immigration services such as investigations, intelligence, and deportations. This super-agency, like the U.S. Department of Homeland Security, has come under criticism for its size and power and the possible elimination of some of the checks and balances that were inherent when its components were separate agencies. In October 2004, the government established the Integrated Threat Assessment Centre with a $30-million budget to assess terrorist threats and coordinate this information with its American counterpart, the National Counterterrorism Center.

In June 2005, the government announced a huge expansion of the clandestine Communications Security Establishment, a wing of the Defence Department that spies on foreign conversations and messages. Staff levels at the agency will jump from 950 before 9/11 to 1,650 by 2007–2008. Its budget is to be increased by 57 per cent. As well, in June 2005, Public Security Minister Anne McLellan unveiled a sweeping plan to harmonize Canadian entry screens with those of the United States. It envisages common benchmarks on visitor visa screening and processing within the year and committed the three North American countries to "real-time information sharing of high-risk individuals and cargo and greatly expanded use of biometrics to screen visitors to North America."

The government also passed Bill C-36, which amended the Criminal Code, the Official Secrets Act, the Canada Evidence Act, the Proceeds of Crime Act, and several other pieces of existing legislation. C-36 gives security services sweeping new powers to arrest and detain a suspected terrorist without charges for up to seventy-two hours; carry out a preventive arrest without warning; compel a person believed to have information about terrorism to testify before a judge, thereby removing an individual's right to remain silent; prevent the disclosure of sensitive information in judicial proceedings, meaning that an individual could be convicted without knowing the details of his or her alleged crimes; wiretap suspected terrorist groups for up to a year and without notification for three years; lay criminal charges against anyone who knowingly participates in the activities of a terrorist group, raises funds for terrorist activities, or harbours a terrorist; and to seize, freeze, and confiscate property used in, or related to, terrorist activity. C-36 also introduced the definition of terrorism so that it now applies to acts committed "for a political, religious, or ideological purpose, objective, or cause."

Carol Goar of the *Toronto Star* (December 22, 2004) said that C-36, while less sweeping than the USA Patriot Act, mirrors its intent and approach. Many civil and human-rights groups have condemned C-36 for undermining democracy and human rights in Canada. C-36 expands and augments the scope and scale of police and government monitoring and control over its citizens far beyond measures necessary to respond to the potential risks of terrorism, says the International Civil Liberties Monitoring Group. C-36 is part of an "irreversible and incremental process that will alter forever the fundamental values, civil liberties, and constitutional guarantees that Canadians have until now viewed as the pillars of Canadian democracy, particularly with regard to due process, the right to privacy and legitimate political dissent," said the coalition in its April 2005 brief to the House of Commons Standing Committee reviewing the legislation.

There are several other key pieces of legislation in the government's security program. The Public Safety Act (C-7) gives security officials investigative powers and enforcement tools that go far beyond the Emergencies Act of 1988, which it replaces. Unlike its predecessor, the Public Safety Act – which permits the collection and sharing of personal data between law enforcement, intelligence, and security agencies, inside Canada and with its sister agencies in the United States – may get around the Charter of Rights and Freedoms, some fear. The Act grants ministers and bureaucrats a wide range of powers: the issuing of "interim orders," "security measures," and "emergency directives"; the delegation of authority to lower-level officials; and the collection and use of personal information, such as criminal records, passport identification, and travel plans, without adequate Parliamentary approval, scrutiny, or oversight. Privacy Commissioner Jennifer Stoddart told an April 2004 public-safety conference that C-7 is based on the premise that the more information the state has about everyone, regardless of whether they have done anything to incite suspicion, the safer we will be. "I am not clear how reducing the freedom of all individuals in society will prevent further threats to public safety by terrorists on a political mission," she added.

The Privacy Commissioner has concerns about another government initiative as well. On August 18, 2005, Justice Minister Irwin Cotler told a police association meeting in Ottawa that his government will introduce legislation to give police and national security agencies new powers to eavesdrop on cellphone calls and monitor the Internet activities of Canadians. The "lawful access" bill will allow police to demand that Internet service providers hand over a wide range of information on the computer habits of their customers that could include their personal financial and health data.

Bill S-23 created the Airline Passenger Information/Passenger Name Reservation (PNR) data bank, and Bill C-44 authorized the Canadian government to share it with the United States and some other foreign governments if those governments are required by law to collect passenger information. Canada has also entered into an agreement to implement a biometric passport system and a method of making it interoperable with the U.S. Department of Homeland Security. Roch Tasse of the International Civil Liberties Monitoring Group warns, "The Canadian surveillance system will be exactly the same as in the U.S. It will be a North American system with no difference between the two countries." (*Ottawa Citizen*, April 25, 2005).

On August 7, 2005, Transport Canada and CSIS announced they are developing their own "No-Fly" list. A team of officials from Transport, Justice, Public Safety, CSIS, the RCMP, Immigration, and the Border Services Agency are working to sort out problems posed in creating such a list, which violates Canada's privacy laws and the guarantee of free mobility under the Charter of Rights and Freedoms. Under another new law, however, the High Risk Traveller Identification Initiative, the Canada Border Services Agency is already phasing in a program to share information with the U.S. Customs and Border Protection Agency about "high-risk" Canadian air travellers. A secret risk-scoring system is used to determine whether a traveller requires "closer scrutiny" reports Jim Bronskill (Canadian Press, May 20, 2005). Not only is this list secret, a Canadian barred from flying into the United States may not be able to contest the information held by the Americans. Bronskill points out that Canadians, unlike Americans, cannot use the U.S. Privacy Act to obtain personal files from Washington.

Another disturbing new development is the Canada Security of Information Act, an amendment under C-36 to the old Official Secrets Act, which makes it illegal to receive, retain, or communicate safeguarded government information. The Canada Security Information Act was the legislation that the RCMP used to justify its raid on *Ottawa Citizen* reporter Juliet O'Neill's home and to secure warrants against her and her newspaper after she wrote a story about the RCMP investigation of Maher Arar. The Canadian Association of Journalists has called for the repeal of this act, saying that it "appears to make it illegal for journalists to receive or report on confidential documents or information while empowering the government to designate any information secret without an appeal."

The government has also tabled the Restricted Areas and Marine Facilities Restricted Area Access Clearance Program, which will require port workers to provide private personal information to authorities about themselves and their families in order to keep their jobs. They will have to agree to be fingerprinted and to hand over all information on their immigration, school, and employment history, current and past addresses, credit-card use, and international travel. Anyone deemed to have "propensity to aid and abet those likely to be involved in terrorism . . . at risk to be prone or induced to commit an act or assist to commit an act . . . or a propensity to be bribed and blackmailed" can be fired under this proposed new act. The only recourse would be a costly individual application for judicial review. The Canadian Maritime Workers Council says this approach to port security is misguided. Instead of blaming workers for inadequate security, the government should reinstate the Ports Police Program it disbanded in 1997 and replaced with a patchwork of local police services and private security companies. The Canadian government is also developing legislation to modernize laws that define the rules for lawful access to search and seizure of the Internet and cellphones. In its April 2005 report "Securing an Open Society, One Year Later," it says that new legislation will be proposed to compel telephone and Internet companies to make their systems intercept capable and to ensure, when required by law, timely access to basic customer name and address information. As well, the government promises to develop amendments to the Criminal Code and other federal acts to address new technology and permit ratification of the Council of Europe Convention on Cybercrime.

NGOs in Canada are concerned about the new Charities Registration (Security Information) Act, which enables the government to revoke the charitable status of an existing charity or deny a new charitable status application if it is determined that the charity has supported or will support "terrorist activity." It can also lead to the freezing or seizure of the charity's assets and expose its directors to civil liability. In October 2001, reports Rights and Democracy, the RCMP published a report on terrorism stating that "protests against genetically modified food and on-going environmental concerns about water, forest preservation, and animal rights are issues to watch" under the new laws. (Several years earlier, the RCMP put together a threat-assessment list, which included the Council of Canadians, Amnesty International Canada, Rights and Democracy, Greenpeace Canada, and several unions. These groups were safe from such anti-terrorism laws then, but not now.) The RCMP used this provision and amendments to the Foreign Missions Act to establish an "access control area" in downtown Calgary during the June 2002 G-8 summit in Kananaskis. The 2001 annual CSIS report tabled after the adoption of C-36 warned, "Canada is confronted by domestic terrorism issues related to aboriginal rights, white supremacists, sovereignty, animal rights and anti-globalization issues." Rights and Democracy points out that Canadian charities that helped the African National Congress under Nelson Mandela, Chinese student groups at Tiananmen Square, and groups supporting the fight for independence in East Timor could all have been shut down under this law.

Under the terms of the USA Patriot Act, private American companies and their subsidiaries operating abroad must share any business records the FBI deems necessary for homeland security purposes. Section 215 of the Act authorizes the FBI to obtain orders from the secretive Foreign Intelligence Surveillance Court requiring a person, organization, or company to disclose "any tangible thing" that might be of interest to the government. This sweeping language can and often does include entire databases. Within the first two years of the Act, the Court received over fourteen thousand applications for data seizures; not one was denied (Steven Donziger, *The Nation*, September 22, 2003). Further, a company that has been ordered to share information on individuals with the FBI is forbidden under the Patriot Act to tell the individuals in question. There is no way for a person to know if the U.S. authorities have obtained information on him or her and no way to challenge the accuracy of what may have been reported.

There are thousands of American firms operating in Canada; every one of them is subject to the provisions of the USA Patriot Act. British Columbia contracted out the operations of its Medical Services Plan and Pharmacare to Maximus, a U.S.–based corporation. In 2004, David Loukidelis, the B.C. privacy commissioner, investigated whether the U.S. Department of Homeland Security would be able to access the health data of B.C. citizens and found that it is very possible that the U.S. Supreme Court could issue an order to see these files and that B.C. would probably have to comply. A team of federal lawyers agrees with this assessment. Highly sensitive military, personal, and national-security information is accessible by the United States, said Public Works official

Mark Seely in a memo on the findings of the lawyers' report. "The U.S. Patriot Act prohibits the corporations from disclosing that they have given the information to the FBI. As a result, personal information collected by the federal government and disclosed to companies through contracting may be potentially disclosed and collected by the FBI without the knowledge or consent of the Canadian company, the federal government and the affected individuals" (*Globe and Mail*, December 18, 2004).

Federal Privacy Commissioner Jennifer Stoddart is very concerned about the massive outsourcing of Canadians' personal, financial, and medical records to U.S. companies by the federal and provincial governments. A U.S. firm has been given the contract by the federal government to collect the data for Canada's firearms registry, for instance. "Private information on millions of Canadians held by major banks and corporations, including Sears Canada and Canadian Tire, is outsourced to the United States," reported Chris Cobb in a four-part December 2004 investigative report for the *Ottawa Citizen*. "One company – Total Systems of Georgia – handles half of all Canadian VISA business. Credit checks on millions of Canadians are performed by three U.S. companies." In October 2004, CIBC VISA sent out an announcement to its customers that the cardholder agreement had been amended to allow the U.S. government to "obtain disclosure" of all its records.

The Canadian Federation of Students is concerned that private data on hundreds of thousands of Canadians with outstanding student loans is now available on request by U.S. Homeland Security officials, following the sale of a Canadian Imperial Bank of Commerce subsidiary, Edulinx, to a U.S. student-loan company called Nelnet. This former subsidiary of the CIBC had been contracted by the Canadian government to service 1 million outstanding student loans in Canada; the contract is worth over $250 million. Even more alarming is the fact that Lockheed Martin, the world's largest weapons manufacturer, has been given the contract to design the software for the 2006 Canadian Census. Imagine the usefulness of the Canadian Census data to the United States.

(The U.S. Census Bureau provided the Department of Homeland Security with a Zip-code level breakdown of every Arab-American citizen sorted by country of origin for its registration program.) While Statistics Canada has assured those expressing concern that the company will not have access to the data and that none of the information collected from the census will be shared with the U.S. Department of Homeland Security, Canadian civil liberties groups remain worried. Lockheed Martin is an American company that does a great deal of business with the American government. In any dispute, there's no question where its loyalties lie. And it would not be obliged to tell the Canadian government that it had shared this sensitive information back home.

## NOT SO SMART BORDERS

Perhaps most of all, Canadians should be concerned by the potential for abuse of minorities, immigrants, and refugees under these new rules. When the most vulnerable among us become even more vulnerable as a result of deliberate government action, something is very wrong.

The Smart Border Accord started the process of harmonizing Canadian and American immigration, visa, and customs systems. Canada adopted the U.S. list of countries whose citizens require visas. A number of Commonwealth countries whose citizens previously travelled without visas to Canada were affected. It also included a Safe Third Country agreement, which requires Canada to turn back refugee claimants who have arrived at our border via the United States, compelling them to seek asylum in the United States. The agreement is ostensibly based on the principle that refugees must claim refuge in the first country they reach as long as that country is "safe" for them. But it is really based on strong pressure from the Bush White House, which views refugees as a security problem, to create a seamless North American refugee system, with the terms and conditions set in Washington.

The Safe Third Country agreement violates refugee rights established in Canada twenty years ago. The Supreme Court declared that refugee claimants in Canada are entitled to basic rights, including the right to an oral hearing before being denied entry, says Janet Dench, executive director of the Canadian Council for Refugees. How can the country that knowingly sent Maher Arar to be tortured in Syria and that has established the "American Gulag" be considered safe, she asks. Close to twelve thousand refugee claimants a year have passed through the United States to come to Canada in the last few years. Now these asylum seekers have no choice but to stay home or try their luck with the much-less hospitable U.S. system. In fact, in the first six months that the law was in effect, the number of refugee claimants arriving in Canada was about half the average, reported the Canadian Press on August 5, 2005. The Canadian Council for Refugees calls this new practice "a silent killer."

Under the new (and misnamed) Immigration and Refugee Protection Act, Canada now issues Security Certificates on ministerial order to detain people suspected of terrorism for secret reviews that amount to secret trials, explains the International Civil Liberties Monitoring Group. The purpose of the certificates is to detain individuals suspected of having terrorist links. Security Certificates deny the right of due process and a fair and open trial to non-citizens suspected of representing a risk to national security. Under these provisions, a person can be detained indefinitely until a single judge, in camera, determines whether or not the person will be deported, potentially to a country where they will face torture or death. Detainees receive only a summary of some of the evidence against them. The precise allegations and the source of the allegations remain unknown. Evidence may be presented in court in the absence of both the detainee and their lawyer. The Federal Court's decision is final; no appeal is possible. Amnesty International says of this process that it "falls far short of international standards for fair trials and may result in arbitrary detention and violation of the right to liberty." The UN Working

Group on Arbitrary Detention visited Canada for several weeks in June 2005 and said it is gravely concerned about Canada's use of national-security certificates and will report its findings to the UN Commission on Human Rights. Currently five refugee claimants are being held under these certificates in Canada and some of them have been held for five years. Human Rights Watch says that any promises from their home countries of Syria, Egypt, Morocco, and Algeria that they will not be tortured if deported are completely unreliable.

Consider the case of Maher Arar. Lest Canadian citizens think what happened to him could not happen to them, a Department of Foreign Affairs document obtained by the *Ottawa Citizen* (April 3, 2005) through an Access to Information request, says that all Canadian citizens are vulnerable to rendition, not just refugees or individuals with dual citizenship, such as Arar. In this document, officials warned "a person possessing only Canadian citizenship could be involuntarily removed to a third country under U.S. law through rendition."

Distressingly, as the human-rights bar is set lower in Canada, public officials find ways to defend their actions. John Manley, who as deputy prime minister and the lead minister on the security file was responsible for negotiating the Smart Border Accord and many of the other security rules and practices now in place, defends the sharing of intelligence with the United States, even if the American government later uses it to violate human rights. At an appearance before the Arar inquiry, Manley affirmed his support for cross-border information sharing between American and Canadian security agencies of the kind that led to Arar's detention and rendition to Syria. According to the *Globe and Mail* (June 1, 2005), Manley told the inquiry that the sharing of sensitive intelligence information with the United States is justifiable regardless of whether the Americans later use it in ways that violate Canadian notions of human rights.

Supreme Court Justice Ian Binnie appears to agree. He told a March 2005 University of Ottawa symposium on counterterrorism that in a world where the state itself could be destroyed by an act of terror, Canadians may have to reevaluate their traditional belief that "it is better for ten men to walk free than for one innocent man to be punished." That proposition is "tested" when you get to the matter of security and counterterrorism, he said. "The greatest threat to our rule of law is terrorism," Justice Binnie declared. In matters of international security it is "absolutely necessary" for courts to show deference to state agencies because they have more expertise, information, and resources on such matters than do judges, he said (*Ottawa Citizen*, March 21, 2005)

Such dangerous sentiments are uttered more and more frequently by people in authority in Canada. Creating a North American security perimeter of the kind being promoted by the Bush administration, the Canadian Council of Chief Executives, and the Manley Task Force on the Future of North America would shut out dissenting points of view and make Canada a part of the Americans' seemingly permanent war on terror. The International Civil Liberties Monitoring Group warns of the danger of giving in to the pressure to join the security state. "Terrorism must be opposed by reaffirming democratic values and the rule of law, not through the erosion of liberties and increased lawlessness." Or as Benjamin Franklin said, "Those who would give up essential liberty to purchase a little temporary safety deserve neither."

# left
# behind

*The War on the Weak*

It is an article of faith among advocates of an unfettered competitive environment that private ownership is better than public when applied to social services. The discipline of the marketplace, according to true believers, enforces efficiency. Bad choices are quickly remedied by shareholders whose gimlet eye never wavers from the bottom line. True believers, unfortunately, are rarely persuaded to alter their beliefs by mere contrary evidence. So reports showing the inefficiency of private health care in the United States, however devastating, may have no effect.

A "meta-analysis" of all the studies comparing mortality rates between private for-profit and public not-for-profit hospitals in the United States was undertaken by McMaster University in Hamilton, and the results were published in the May 2002 edition of the *Canadian Medical Association Journal*. The massive study found that death rates in for-profit hospitals are significantly higher than in not-for-profit hospitals. This was the case even though patients who use for-profit hospitals are wealthier and can afford a healthier lifestyle than those in the public sphere. The single common factor, the researchers found, was that for-profit hospitals cut corners. They have to, both to achieve a profit margin for investors, and to pay the excessively high salaries of their administrators.

Said Dr. P.J. Devereaux, a cardiologist at McMaster and the lead researcher for the study, "Administrators tend to hire less highly skilled personnel, including doctors, nurses, and pharmacists. The U.S. statistics clearly show that when the need for profits drives hospital decision-making, more patients die."

The message was reinforced by an eminent American physician who testified before the Canadian Senate in 2002. Dr. Arnold Relman, professor emeritus of medicine at the Harvard Medical School told Canadians what life would be like under the U.S. health-care system: "My conclusion from all of this study is that most of the current problems of the U.S. system – and they are numerous – result from the growing encroachment of private for-profit ownership and competitive markets on a sector of our economy that properly belongs in the public domain. No health care system in the industrialized world is as heavily commercialized as ours, and none is as expensive, inefficient, and inequitable – or as unpopular. Indeed, just about the only parts of U.S. society happy with our current market-driven health care system are the owners and investors in the for-profit industries now living off the system."

If the Canadian Council of Chief Executives is aware of these and similar reports, they have chosen to ignore them. After all, privatization may deliver poor health care, but it also delivers huge profits.

## DOING MORE WITH LESS

While Canada's social programs were not directly targeted by the Task Force on the Future of North America in its report, there is no question that deeper integration with the United States would put tremendous pressure on Canada to harmonize its social security system with the American model and open it up to competition from big American service corporations. Nor can there be any question that further privatization of Canada's social security system would be welcomed by the big-business community backing integration. Already in Canada, the same groups pushing for closer ties with the United States are working hard, and with great success, toward the privatization of Canada's health, education, and social services.

Jean Chrétien and Paul Martin, while paying lip service to universal health care, almost killed it with budget cuts. Deficit fighting, support for unregulated free trade, and deep cuts to the country's social security system were the hallmarks of the "new" Liberals when they returned to power in 1993. The 1995 federal budget cut federal cash transfers by a staggering 40 per cent, gutting health care so badly that the resulting waiting lists were found by the Supreme Court in its ruling of June 9, 2005, to violate the Charter of Rights and Freedoms. These cuts, and two-tiered health care, have been continuously supported by almost every major newspaper in Canada for over a decade, including the *Globe and Mail*, the *National Post*, and the rest of the CanWest chain.

The Conservative Party under Stephen Harper's leadership is clearly against universal social programs, notwithstanding its cries of indignation after the Supreme Court ruling. Harper told the House of Commons on October 28, 2002, that privatized health care is a "natural development." This mirrors an interview he gave in 1997 to the National Citizens Coalition newsletter, *The Bulldog*, in which he said, "It's past time the feds scrapped the Canada Health Act." The National Citizens Coalition, with which Harper has long been associated, advocates that corporations and charities take over the social functions now performed by governments (exactly the position of the Bush White House) and believes that the government's role should be limited to national defence, protection of private property, and law enforcement. The corporate-funded, Vancouver-based Fraser Institute considers Canada's social security system both immoral and an inefficient use of taxpayers' money. It advocates a mix of private and public charity for the "deserving poor" and has lobbied for a new definition of poverty that would apply only to those families who lack the "basic necessities for absolute physical survival."

The C.D. Howe Institute, one of the oldest and most influential policy think-tanks in Canada, authored the so-called Green Paper that provided the rationale for the 1995 budget. The Institute, whose board is made up of a corporate who's who in Canada, has called for an end to federal cash payments to the provinces for social services and, in a major 2002 policy paper on health care, said that people who use more public health services should pay higher taxes. Alberta's Friends of Medicare said this would amount to a tax on the sick.

The Canadian Council of Chief Executives has been consistent in its opposition to Canada's public social infrastructure. The CCCE set out its ten-year plan in 1994 when it was still the Business Council on National Issues and the leading proponent of NAFTA in Canada. It called for a freeze on social spending and a return to targeted, not universal, social spending; restrictions on government borrowing for social services; reduced unemployment premiums; lower corporate taxes; the deregulation of energy; a war on the deficit; privatization of public services; and the removal of foreign-investment reviews. Between the Mulroney Conservatives and the Chrétien–Martin Liberals, the corporate lobby group has had tremendous success in moving this agenda forward. Its official position on social programs is "to do more with less, target those in need, and create incentives that encourage individual self-reliance."

In its submission to the Romanow Commission, the CCCE stated that Canada's health care should be taken out of the hands of politicians and bureaucrats and turned over to provincial Crown corporations that would be run by "experienced businesspeople" with performance bonuses and incentives, corporate discipline, and private-sector innovation. The CCCE was delighted with the Supreme Court ruling on the unconstitutionality of Quebec's ban on private health insurance. The Canadian Chamber of Commerce echoed the position of the CCCE before the Romanow Commission, calling for greater use of voluntary, private-sector delivery of health-care services and private-sector investment.

In fact, the same call for smaller government (so dear to the hearts of Bush Republicans) can be heard in the corridors of power – both political and corporate – in Canada. In an April 14, 2005, *Globe and Mail* editorial, former Ontario premier Mike Harris and former leader of the Official Opposition in the House of Commons Preston Manning (both currently senior fellows with the Fraser Institute), provided a précis of a major new report by the Fraser Institute and the Montreal Economic Institute. In "A Canada Strong and Free," Harris and Manning laid out a "dream commensurate with the vision of the Fathers of Confederation and the vastness of our country," namely a "dramatic expansion of freedom of choice and acceptance of personal responsibility in every arena of national life." This would come about as Canada adopts policies to "constrain the size of government," turns huge portions of the federal role over to the provinces, dramatically lowers taxes to individuals and corporations, and turns health care over to the provinces and the private sector – a complete replica of George Bush's domestic-policy agenda.

In the report, Harris and Manning make the clear connection between their social agenda and deeper economic, foreign, and trade ties with the United States. They reiterate the call for a new customs agreement with the United States that would involve the creation and mutual administration of a common tariff and quota system, the elimination of rules of origin, and mutual responsibility for border security. If they are successful, Canada will end up negotiating international trade agreements such as the General Agreement on Trade in Services (GATS) as one bloc with the United States. American education, welfare, health, and daycare service corporations would then have full access to the Canadian market and the right to demand equal access to Canadian government funding that Canadian companies now enjoy. If the big-business community gets its way on its deep integration project with the United

States, it will spell the end of Canada's already deeply troubled universal social programs.

## CUTS AND A COLD SHOWER

Canada's public social programs were born of a people's dream. Living next to the biggest superpower on Earth, Canadians knew that they had to create ribbons of interdependence across the country if they were to survive as a separate nation on the northern half of the North American continent. Canadians rejected the American narrative of "survival of the fittest" and chose instead a vision of "sharing for survival." As a fundamental right of citizenship, they decided that all Canadians, regardless of socio-economic background, ethnicity, or where they lived, had a right to a good education, health care, and assistance for the elderly, the young, the poor, the unemployed, and the disabled. Canada's universal social programs were forged in the twin furnaces of the Great Depression and the Second World War. Veterans observed that the same country that didn't have enough money to feed, house, clothe, or employ its citizens suddenly had all it needed to send them to war. The men and women who returned from that terrible ordeal vowed they would not go back into bread lines and work camps. They set out to build a nation worthy of the fallen comrades they had left behind on the battlefields of Europe. They weren't alone. In 1942, *Saturday Night* magazine said, "Almost everyone agrees that health and unemployment insurance schemes, regulation of business, and a sharp limitation of profits are necessary to provide Canadians with real security."

While Canadians were ready at war's end, it would take almost another twenty years to put the social security system in place. The Medical Care Insurance Act of 1966 established a publicly funded, non-profit comprehensive universal health-care program. It was amended in 1984 as the Canada Health Act to ban user fees and extra billing. The 1966 Canada Assistance Plan consolidated all federal–provincial assistance programs into one comprehensive package, enshrined the right to social assistance for all Canadians in need, and set national standards for social assistance across the country. The Canada Pension Plan guaranteed that seniors and the disabled would receive a government pension adequate to maintain a socially acceptable standard of living. The National Housing Act of 1964 provided funding to the provinces for low-income housing and in 1971, the new Unemployment Insurance Act provided a safety net for the unemployed, making it one of the most comprehensive programs of its kind in the world. In 1973, the Family Allowance Act was instituted. In adopting these far-reaching programs, Canada joined a number of progressive European countries that believed in a collective response to social issues and distinguished itself from the individualistic track that had been chosen by the United States.

Now, one by one, Canada's cherished social programs are being picked off. From the mid-1980s to the early 1990s, the Conservative government of Brain Mulroney savaged Canadian social programs, eliminating universal child benefits, "clawing back" family allowance and old-age pensions, and removing government contributions to unemployment insurance. The 1995 Martin budget killed the Canada Assistance Plan, opening the door to massive provincial cuts to welfare, and rolled funding for health, education, and social assistance into one dramatically underfunded transfer payment. Between them, the Mulroney and Chrétien governments took $36 billion from health-care funding, steadily reducing the federal share of health spending (and influence) from 42 per cent in the mid-1970s to just 10 per cent at the end of Jean Chrétien's tenure. (It is edging slowly up again due to new infusions of money from the Martin government.) A number of provinces, particularly Alberta, British Columbia, Ontario, and more recently Quebec, have slashed funding to health, education, and welfare and endorsed public-private partnerships, turning huge parts of their social security systems over to for-profit companies.

Between these massive cuts and the "cold shower" of deregulation, privatization, and NAFTA, Canada's social security net has been deeply damaged. Not surprisingly, the effects have been felt by the weakest in our society: the young, the old, the poor, new Canadians, the disabled, and First Nations people. In its 2004 report (issued in 2005), Campaign 2000, a coalition comprised of the Canadian Council for Social Development, the Centre for International Statistics, and the National Council of Welfare, says that 15.6 per cent of Canadian children live in poverty – substantially more than in 1989, the year Parliament unanimously voted to wipe out child poverty by 2000. As a result, Canada has slipped to nineteenth place on the OECD child-poverty list. Shockingly, in the last decade, one-third of all Canadian children lived in poverty for at least one year. The child-poverty rate for families with a single female parent stands at over 50 per cent, reports the coalition, and child-poverty rates for Aboriginal children, immigrant children, and children in visible minority groups is more than double the national average. Distressingly, in a country that boasts strong recent job creation numbers, almost half of poor children live in families where the parent or parents work all year. The good jobs of the past have been replaced for many families by precarious low-wage employment.

The National Council of Welfare, a citizens' advisory group to the minister of social development, blames much of this growing poverty on the clawback of federal family benefits and distressingly inadequate provincial welfare services. In its June 2005 annual report, the Council shows many welfare recipients eking out a living on incomes well below the poverty line. A total of 1.7 million Canadians are "suffering" (the council's word) on incomes inconceivable to other Canadians. Moreover, the council reports, when adjusted for inflation, benefits in 2004 were at their lowest levels since the early 1980s. "Miserly" income support means that these Canadians are living thousands of dollars below the poverty line. "Canadian welfare policy over the last fifteen years has been an utter disaster," concludes the report.

The Canadian Labour Congress explains that the economic recovery of the late 1990s was fuelled by a growth in jobs rather than a growth in real wages. In other words, working people have been able to stay afloat only by working longer hours or taking on more than one job. Restructuring of the economy has led to the erosion of labour standards, decreased access to collective bargaining, and the proliferation of low-income jobs with few or no benefits. Non-standard work (part-time, contract, seasonal, or self-employed) now stands at 37 per cent of all jobs in Canada, compared to just 25 per cent in 1980. In the first fifteen years of free trade, Canada created fewer than half as many full-time jobs as during the previous fifteen years. More than one in three workers lack basic benefits with their jobs, says the Canadian Policy Research Network, and their pay has remained virtually unchanged through the so-called boom of the 1990s. Canada is a low-wage country now, second only to the United States among industrialized countries, according to the Canadian Labour Congress's Andrew Jackson.

Public-sector jobs (typically jobs with benefits) have fallen as a percentage of overall employment over the last decade. So have unionized jobs. Those who lose their jobs are out of luck: only 38 per cent of the unemployed in Canada now qualify for unemployment insurance (or Employment Insurance as it is absurdly called now), compared to close to 80 per cent in 1985. And Canadian families are staggering under a mountain of personal debt. The average Canadian household is not only not saving money any more, but holds consumer and mortgage debt equal to 98 per cent of their after-tax income, up dramatically from ten years ago.

In other words, Canada's social structure is looking more and more like the United States'. No wonder; governments have cut social spending to levels not seen since before the 1950s. A recent Organization for Economic Co-operation and Development study confirms that Canada is now spending just 18.9 per cent of its GDP on social programs, 15 per cent less than a decade ago. Statistical comparisons of spending on social security between the United States and Canada show a steadily narrowing gap. Says Jackson,

"There has been a major convergence of Canada towards the small government, high inequality, high insecurity U.S. model."

Deep inequality and the entrenchment of social class have been the hallmarks of this new social revolution in Canada. In its landmark study "Rags and Riches, Wealth Inequality in Canada" (2003), the Canadian Centre for Policy Alternatives found that the gap between rich and poor in Canada, in relative terms, rivals anything in the Third World. Millions of Canadians are living on the brink of financial disaster, while others have accumulated huge slices of the wealth pie. The study found that the wealthiest 10 per cent of family units in Canada now hold 53 per cent of the wealth. The wealthiest 50 per cent of family units control an almost unbelievable 94.4 per cent of the wealth, leaving only 5.6 per cent of the country's wealth to be shared among the bottom 50 per cent of the population. Tax cuts to the wealthy and corporations have helped to achieve this deeply unfair result. In fifteen years, Canada's corporate taxes have been continually lowered and now match U.S. levels. In the same period, Canada's taxation levels have dropped from above-average levels to the bottom third among OECD countries. Corporations are keeping more and more of their profits, thereby removing potential sources of revenue to social programs. And those profits keep going up.

Canadian corporations are on their way to another record year in 2005, Statistics Canada reports (*Ottawa Citizen*, May 28, 2005). Profits in the first quarter surged following a similar increase in 2004. Corporate profit margins continue to reach record highs, up 8 per cent in the past year, compared to average weekly earnings of employees, says Statistics Canada, whose incomes rose only 1.9 per cent – well below the 2.3 per cent increase in the cost of living. "Almost all of the income gains from our supposedly well-performing economy are going to shareholders and to very high income-earners, especially the top 1 per cent," explains Andrew Jackson. A spring 2005 report from the Toronto Dominion Bank says that Canadian corporations are sitting on an unprecedented pile of cash. TD chief economist Don Drummond admits that corporations probably don't need any more tax breaks, adding that low-income workers need a break way more than corporations (*Ottawa Citizen*, April 29, 2005).

The number of millionaires has tripled in just over a decade and corporate compensation has skyrocketed. In its 2004 annual report on CEO earnings, the *Globe and Mail* highlights the growing gulf in Canada between the rich and the poor. That year, Frank Weise, CEO of Cott Corporation, earned almost $22 million; Laurent Beaudoin of Bombardier earned $25 million; Robert Gratton of Power Corp earned over $52 million; Frank Stronach of Magna earned over $53 million; and Robert McEwen of Goldcorp Inc. earned close to a whopping $95 million. Altogether, the top fifty corporate executives took home almost $700 million in 2004.

## BOMBING THE HEALTH-CARE SYSTEM

Next to social assistance, no other social program in Canada has been as targeted by right-wing politicians and the big-business community as public health. Wilfully oblivious to the fact that burgeoning health-insurance costs are nearly bankrupting many American corporations (and were cited by General Motors as one of the reasons for its massive layoffs announced in June 2005), Canada's big-business community continues to push for the full privatization of health care. It has made common cause with the big American health corporations that have saturated their own market and are aggressively seeking new ones. The World Bank estimates that global health expenditures exceed $4 trillion every year and represent a great new investment opportunity. The most promising source of new contracts for the health-services corporations are the lucrative health-care programs, such as Canada's, still being delivered by governments to their citizens on a not-for-profit basis.

In Canada, massive cuts at the federal level have been matched by massive cuts at the provincial level. Most provinces have chopped their own funding to hospitals, laid off registered nurses, and closed beds. The Romanow Commission reported that even with recent investments, provincial government spending on health care as a percentage of the GDP is down one-half of a percentage point from 1990. Like their federal counterpart, most provinces have implemented huge tax cuts, draining provincial revenues. There's not much left to invest.

Deep cuts to Nova Scotia's health system have left many citizens with greatly reduced services; cancer care, liver transplants, and other essential services are either reduced or non-existent. Although the McGuinty government has promised to re-fund the system in Ontario, the province is still reeling from the damage done by the Harris government, which cut 12 per cent of the health-care budget and gouged almost $1 billion from its hospitals. British Columbia premier Gordon Campbell cut government services by 25 per cent in his first term. Thousands of health-care workers were laid off, almost thirteen hundred acute beds were shut down, and the province is now contracting out over one thousand surgeries every month. Alberta's Ralph Klein savaged the health-care system when he first came to power in 1992. He slashed the health-care budget by 22 per cent (and welfare by 40 per cent) and laid off six thousand public-service workers and three thousand nurses. Many hospitals and half of the province's hospital beds were closed.

But Klein did something else. He made Alberta the Petri dish for the privatization of public services in Canada. When their public services were cut to the bone, the people of Alberta were forced to accept private alternatives. In 1997, in what appeared to be an abrupt turnaround, the Klein government began pouring money back into the system and by 2002, spending levels on health care were back where they had been a decade before. This time, however, the funds are supporting what is essentially a two-tier system, and going straight into the pockets of many of the premier's corporate friends. Proponents call it "public-private partnership" and claim that government maintains control of the programs while the more "efficient" private sector runs them. In truth, no matter how efficient a private company may be, it must find ways to turn

a profit for its investors. In the end, as the McMaster study demonstrated, that usually means cutting corners.

Yet many provinces are following Alberta's lead. Ontario
announced in June 2005 a $30-billion public-private partnership
fund for new schools and hospitals. All this money will go to for-
profit corporations. And on August 25, 2005, Provis Infusion
Clinic Inc., a new private cancer clinic in Toronto, opened its doors
to paying customers. In Vancouver, the Cambie Surgery Centre
boasts that it is Canada's "most advanced private surgical centre in
Canada" with "more operating capacity than most B.C. hospitals."
It is proud of its record of servicing "famous athletes and celebri-
ties" and known for the outspoken private-sector advocacy of its
founder, Dr. Brian Day – also known as Dr. Profit. British
Columbia has fourteen private clinics that looked after fifty thousand paying customers in 2004. Montreal was labelled the "private
health-care capital of Canada" by the Montreal *Gazette*, which
conducted an investigation in February 2005. There is a "parallel
system for the wealthy" in that city, said the newspaper, which
reported that ninety doctors in Quebec have opted out of medicare, more than all other provinces combined. (One of them, Dr.
Sheldon Elmer, is Prime Minister Martin's doctor.) There are at
least a dozen medical imaging clinics and a number of knee and
hip replacement clinics. The going rate for hip replacement is
between $14,000 and $18,000. Montreal also has the first private
emergency clinic and was, not surprisingly, the base from which
the Supreme Court challenge was launched.

Normand Laberge of the Canadian Association of Radiologists
called that decision an "atomic time bomb on the health-care
system." The fallout will take time to assess but there is no doubt
that it was a wake-up call for Canadians. Within days of the ruling,
American corporations announced their intention to move into
Canada using the rights they have under international trade rules.
A spokesman for America's Health Insurance Plans told the *Ottawa
Citizen* (June 11, 2005) that the thirteen hundred companies his
agency represents are interested in the new opportunities opened

up by the decision. "Rest assured," said Mohit Ghose, vice-president of public relations for the association, "there will be serious discussion about how we can bring disease management and chronic care management and other tools to those Canadian citizens who might want the option available to them." Moving more of the health-care system to the private sector could create a boom in investment, Jeremy Friesen, senior currency analyst for RBC Dominion Securities told the *Globe and Mail* (June 10, 2005).

Proponents of two-tier health care say they don't want the American system but rather the "kinder, gentler" system of Germany or Sweden. Apparently they imagine that they will have a choice. But while Canada has never entered into a free-trade agreement with either Germany or Sweden, it is a signatory of NAFTA, whose rules are clear. The exemption for health care under NAFTA, which has largely kept the big U.S. for-profit health corporations out of Canada, applies only to a fully publicly funded system delivered on a non-commercial basis. Once privatized, the system must give "national treatment" rights to American private hospital chains and HMOs (health maintenance organizations). Not only would U.S. health corporations have the right to set up shop in Canada, they also would have the same right to public funding as Canadian companies. In no time, the public system would be bankrupt and we would have a corporate health-care system based on the American model. If any level of government tried to resist, the next Canada Health Act legal challenge would likely be held before a secret NAFTA tribunal at World Bank headquarters in Washington.

Even without the Supreme Court ruling, it is possible that these companies have a right under NAFTA to compete in Canada, because the health system is being privatized so fast. Fully one-third of all health-care spending is now private, as services are de-listed and doctors opt out of medicare. There are now at least 240 health-care corporations, many of them American, operating in Canada. There are also 140 private health-insurance companies operating here. The Canadian Life and Health Insurance Association says that at least thirty-seven of them are American. There are also 663 private home-care agencies, and private companies now control at least 10 per cent of the MRI market.

The Americanization of the Canadian system is just fine with Dr. Jacques Chaoulli, the Montreal family doctor who has been waging a campaign to privatize Canada's health care for over a decade. It was Chaoulli who teamed up with Georges Zeliotis, a patient angry at having to wait for a hip replacement, to launch the Supreme Court challenge. Lest anyone thinks that Chaoulli was acting out of compassion for this or any other patient, it is important to note that he has become a darling of the American right and is a highly sought-after speaker for right-wing think-tanks such as the Pacific Research Institute, the Heritage Foundation, and the Cato Institute. The *Globe and Mail* reported on June 22, 2005, that Chaoulli had met with conservatives in Washington shortly after the Supreme Court decision and had offered a helping hand to American health-services corporations who want to set up in Canada. "I would like to make a team with American entrepreneurs and go to Canada and create a private, parallel health-care system," he told the *Globe*. "I'd like to show the Canadian people what it means to provide a good quality health-care system at a good price." Grace-Marie Turner is president of the Galen Institute, a right-wing research group dedicated to free-market health-care reform. After introducing Chaoulli to the select group of influential conservatives, she said, "He's truly a superstar in the health-care movement. I have a tear in my eye. This is truly a fight for fundamental liberty." With friends like him to assist them, it seems clear that American private health-care companies are going to be moving into Canada. Canada may not yet have fully harmonized its health-care system with that of the United States, but we're singing the same song.


## THE COMMERCIALIZED CLASSROOM

The core value behind public education is that every child matters equally, regardless of family income, social status, or race. It doesn't matter whether a child's family has lived in the country for a year or five generations. Public education also honours every student's abilities. It recognizes that not all have equal physical or intellectual abilities. This model, however, is not compatible with the dominant value of economic globalization, namely, head-to-head competition. Nor do public schools serve the economic and class structure so clearly emerging or re-emerging in Canada, the United States, Australia, and Europe.

Canada's demographic make-up is changing. Once egg-shaped, with a small group of wealthy at the top and a small group of poor at the bottom (thanks to the equalizing impact of universal social programs), Canada now resembles a pear, with more wealth concentrated among a small group at the top and many more Canadians trying not to fall out from the bottom. Public schools in Canada and other democracies have been pilloried by the wealthy and the big-business community because they have resisted adapting to this new demographic and have stubbornly clung to their notions of democracy in education. What critics want is a tiered education system much like our emerging tiered health-care system. One tier would cater to the sons and daughters of those in power, providing them with the best education in the world. The other would be a diminished public system to train the rest for the jobs available to their class. Those who are prepared to finance the superior schools for their own children have been very successful in convincing governments to lower taxes (particularly on their class) and have not opposed the massive funding cuts to public education that have taken place in most parts of Canada.

Ontario's Mike Harris and Alberta's Ralph Klein implemented the first of these massive cuts to education, setting the two politicians on a collision course with teachers in their provinces. They closed music, arts, and after-school programs, and libraries. Strapped schools had to start fundraising and charging students for textbooks and programs. Harris brought in a tax credit of $3,500 per child for parents who sent their children to private schools, thus beginning the public subsidization of the private system. Recent reports show a dramatic increase in dropout rates in Ontario high schools that are directly linked to the cuts and to over-reliance on rigorous literacy testing. The cuts mean students with special needs are not getting the attention they require. They mean larger class sizes with the attendant decline in quality. Testing tends to drive failing students out of schools. Children from poorer and immigrant families don't have the same access to assistance to prepare themselves for these tests and just drop out after they fail or even before taking the tests. (Some people think this is the real agenda: many of the jobs created in the globalized economy require little or no education.)

British Columbia has now followed the Harris example. Since the Campbell Liberals came to power, 113 schools have been closed; 2,500 teachers have been fired; and special-ed and ESL teachers have been cut by almost 20 per cent. Class sizes have burgeoned. Teachers report that in some classes, students rush to compete for limited seats and latecomers must stand at the back or sit on the floor. More than one hundred school libraries have been closed. In fact, school libraries across the country have been assailed. The Association of Canadian Publishers released a scathing study on the chronic neglect of school libraries in March 2005. The authors of "Canadian Books in School Libraries: Raising the Profile" report that because of funding cuts, school libraries in every province are in crisis, with serious consequences for students, particularly those from low-income families.

The OECD now ranks Canada nineteenth out of thirty developed countries for elementary and secondary school funding, below most of Europe, Korea, Mexico, and even the United States. At 3.4 per cent of its gross domestic product, Canada not only spends proportionately less than it did ten years ago but also is now below the OECD average of 3.8 per cent. Even with the re-funding taking place in Ontario and some other provinces, Statistics Canada reports that the total represents a smaller slice of the GDP every year (*Globe and Mail*, September 14, 2004). This is a particular tragedy, says Terry Price, president of the Canadian Teachers' Federation, because the decades of adequate funding were beginning to pay off. Where Canada once scored in the middle of the international literacy scale, it now finds itself in the top seven or eight countries. But with the funding cuts, the Teachers' Federation warns, this position may not hold for long.

Funding cuts have parents and teachers scrambling. Erika Shaker of the Canadian Centre for Policy Alternatives reports that parents are spending more and more money on basic school supplies and teachers are spending more than five hundred dollars every year of their own money to subsidize students who cannot afford user fees. Parent advisory councils are becoming full-time fundraising bodies, raising millions of dollars to make up for the cuts. Not surprisingly, the distribution of funds by school is uneven – schools in wealthier areas can raise much more money. In fact, the underfunding of public schools is accelerating the deepening class divisions in Canada. Students from poorer families and communities fall further behind because they cannot access computers, textbooks, special education courses, and educational trips.

The funding cuts are leading to the commercialization of education as schools are forced to turn to the private sector to make up for the shortfall of money. In July 2005, the Canadian Teachers' Federation published a landmark study, "Commercialism in Canadian Schools – A National Survey." Its findings are disturbing. Fifty-four per cent of secondary and almost one-third of elementary schools have ads placed in them. Fifty-six per cent of secondary schools have an exclusive deal with either Coke or Pepsi. Fifteen per cent of elementary schools and 30 per cent of secondary schools participate in a corporate partnership program with such companies as Wal-Mart and McDonald's. Thirty per cent have "Incentive Programs" to encourage parents, teachers, and students to buy a specific company's product or service. The majority of elementary schools report the use of private scholastic materials, including Pizza Hut's "Book It" program and Mr. Christie's "Smart Cookie" program. One-fifth of all secondary schools now sell services such as curriculum or facilities. More than half the schools in Canada now charge user fees, in some cases even for core programs.

Every school in Canada now raises about sixteen thousand dollars a year to keep going. Larry Kuehn of the British Columbia Teachers' Federation warns that by encouraging school districts to become entrepreneurial (his province has set up "school district business companies"), provinces run the risk of undermining equity in education financing, a hallmark of the Canadian system. Wealthy districts can attract tuition-paying foreign students; rural, poor, or Aboriginal districts cannot. Of the $100 million that international student fees brought into B.C. schools in the 2004/2005 year, the vast majority subsidized wealthier areas, enriching the most privileged students. One Ontario school in a wealthy area raised $250,000 through such fundraising activities as a yacht-club gala and a silent auction, which included a weekend getaway on a private island.

The direct assault on education is politically motivated, says education author and critic Heather-jane Robertson. She points out that public opinion has not driven any of the education trends of the last decade: "There has been no massive outcry to make class sizes larger, hallways dirtier, increase the dropout rate, shorten the school week, or drive out good teachers." Rather, right-wing interests have targeted schools because they are so crucial to the formation of culture and are the place where the "spirit of the market" can be taught. "Applying the logic of the market to anything of shared importance merely guarantees that it will not be shared equally," she told a February 2005 B.C. teachers' conference on privatization. "Yet the privatization of other areas of 'the commons' can't proceed unless this truth is disguised, which is why education is such a vital link in the privatization chain."

## THE AMERICAN DREAM DIES

The changes taking place in Canada's social security system and the consequent creation of an entrenched underclass have already occurred in the United States, but in a far more dramatic fashion.

The differences between social classes in the United States are truly breathtaking. In 1960, the wealthiest 20 per cent of the population made thirty times as much as those in the bottom 20 per cent; four decades later, they make seventy-five times as much. The *Wall Street Journal* (May 13, 2005) reports that the top 1 per cent owns more than 40 per cent of the wealth. The top 10 percent owns two-thirds of the wealth, leaving the bottom 90 per cent to share one-third of the nation's assets. According to the UN Human Development Index, the United States, with the second highest GDP in the developed world (after tiny Luxembourg) and the highest per-capita income, ranks dead last in fighting poverty, is at the bottom in terms of functional literacy, has one of the lowest levels of life expectancy, has the greatest income inequality, and has the highest number of citizens without access to health care. With 22 per cent of its children living in poverty, the U.S. child-poverty rate is second only to Mexico says Unicef in its annual 2005 report, "Child Poverty in Rich Countries." The OECD reports that the United States has not only the highest overall poverty rate of all its member countries, but the most persistent. It also scores dead last on the income mobility chart, underscoring recent studies that show the States is now less socially mobile than any other industrialized country. The *Economist* says the United States is calcifying into a "European-style class-based society" of the past.

The number of millionaires in the United States jumped nearly 10 per cent in 2004, says Merrill Lynch in its 2005 "World Wealth Report," trumping the growth rates of high net-worth individuals in other regions of the world for a total of 2.5 million millionaires. In the U.S., corporate CEOs pulled in median compensation of about US$14 million in 2004, up 25 per cent in one year. (Compensation for oil-and-gas executives increased by an astonishing 109 per cent.) United Technologies CEO George David topped the list, taking home almost US$100 million. The average CEO now earns 240 times more than his workers. In 2002, the ratio was 145 to 1. But, says *USA Today* (March 31, 2005), these huge salaries are not necessarily linked to good performance. Merck shares sank 30 per cent after the company's recall of Vioxx (the pain reliever was judged to be unsafe), but the company gave CEO Ray Gilmartin US$55.4 million anyway.

Meanwhile, says the highly respected Washington-based Economic Policy Institute, the situation for working families has not been this bad since the Great Depression. Its report, "The State of Working America, 2004/2005," offers a detailed examination of the situation for working people and their families and concludes that since 2000, unemployment is up, wages and job quality have eroded, and the average household's net worth has fallen. The minimum wage, at US$5.15 an hour, has not been raised since 1997. Family debt is at record levels and less than half (45.5 per cent) the workforce has an employer-funded pension plan. A quarter of all white families and 61 per cent of African-American families have no financial assets whatsoever. Minority families lost income in these years at three times the rate of whites, and median incomes for single-mother families fell to US$26,000, below the poverty line for many. Almost 90 million Americans are "twice-poor," meaning that they live in households with income less than two times their poverty threshold. Welfare benefits dropped an astonishing 13 per cent each year since 2000, leaving these families totally adrift. To add insult to injury, says the Institute, the unbalanced nature of the Bush tax cuts has redistributed after-tax income from the bottom 99 per cent to the top 1 per cent.

Parts of the United States are beginning to resemble apartheid-era South Africa. The *New York Times* (June 7, 2005) reports on the growth of gated communities in North Carolina, Florida, and California, replete with golf courses, spas, country clubs, and multi-million-dollar homes existing side by side with black communities denied sewers, police services, garbage pickup, and even running water. Although the residents of the poor communities are subject to the zoning laws and land-use rules of the affluent hamlets, they are not allowed to vote in their elections. The exclusion of minority neighbourhoods is called municipal under-bounding; it has caught the attention of civil-rights groups, who assert that the denial of basic services such as water is a violation of the Constitution.

In a passionate speech to a June 3, 2004, Washington conference called Take Back America, PBS's Bill Moyers (who was targeted by the Bush administration in its attacks on funding for public broadcasting) decried the new America, where families cocoon themselves in gated communities guarded by private security guards, drink bottled water, depend on private pensions, and send their children off to private schools. He blames the "fanatical drive" to dismantle the political institutions, legal and statutory canons, and intellectual and cultural frameworks that have shaped public responsibility for social harms arising from the excesses of private power. "From public land to water and other natural resources, from media with their broadcast and digital spectrums to scientific discoveries and medical breakthroughs, a broad range of America's public resources is being shifted to the control of elites and the benefit of the privileged."

## SICKNESS MAINTENANCE ORGANIZATIONS

Perhaps in no other sector do Bill Moyers's words ring more true than in health care. Health care has never been seen as a birthright in the United States as it has in Canada, and, unlike Canadians, each American is responsible for his or her own care. Nevertheless, until the early 1990s, most health care was delivered on a not-for-profit basis by private doctors, clinics, and hospitals. It is true that financing was not public and the unemployed were put at a disadvantage because most health insurance comes through employers. But most HMOs only needed to generate enough income to provide an often very good living for doctors, specialists, and others working in them. In the 1990s, however, HMOs came under the control of large insurance corporations and merged with giant drug companies to swallow up hospitals, freestanding clinics, doctors' practices, nursing homes, outpatient clinics, and pharmacies to create huge for-profit health corporations that dominate the Fortune 500. Health care suddenly became a gargantuan business, its corporations listed on the stock exchange and its investors demanding a healthy return on their money. In 1993 alone, at the height of the mergers, the top ten HMOs saw profit increases ranging from 14 per cent at the beginning of the year to 270 per cent at the end. They rose again in 1994 by 732 per cent. Health analyst Colleen Fuller says the takeover of America's non-profit health-care system constituted "the largest transfer of charitable assets in U.S. history."

The annual profit of the health-care market in the United States is over US$1 trillion. It is top heavy, with highly paid administrators making CEO salaries comparable to those in defence, oil, and telecommunications. To afford these soaring salary costs and to make profit for investors, many thousands of front-line health-care workers, particularly nurses, have been laid off and millions of beds eliminated. To deliver cheaper care, administrators cut nurse-to-patient ratios, substituted untrained workers for qualified professionals, and shifted from a full-time to a part-time workforce. Nurses are doubling up on their workload and experiencing high rates of burnout. Because they operate on a for-profit basis, HMOs "cherry-pick" clients, preferring to provide services for those with good health and full-time jobs. Doctors are forced to see many more patients than before, and consequently spend less time with each. Many physicians have seen their incomes decline and report burnout, job dissatisfaction, and poor mental health. And fraud is rampant: the U.S. General Accounting Office reports that almost 10 per cent of all health-care money spent is defrauded through over-billing and other abuses.

Says Dr. Marcia Angell in the *New England Journal of Medicine*, "The private managed-care market has been a miserable failure at delivering health care. It has creamed off even larger percentages of health care premiums in bloated administrative and marketing costs and profits; it has rewarded health plans that cherry-pick the healthy and avoid the sick; and it has resisted at every turn providing adequate services to those unfortunate enough to need them."

The irony is that, according to 2005 OECD statistics, the United States spends about twice as much on health care as Canada when public and private spending is added up, and more than twice the average among the OECD countries.

The result of the wholesale privatization of their health-care system has been devastating for many Americans. More than 45 million do not have any health insurance at all and another 200 million have limited care that would not fully cover catastrophic or long-term care. More than eighteen thousand adults in the United States die every year, according to the Institute of Medicine, because they have no insurance, and at least 10 million American children are currently at risk for the same reason. Nearly half of the 1.6 million bankruptcies declared each year in the United States are the result of an inability to pay medical bills and soaring drug costs. Sick people lose their homes, their savings, and often, their jobs, which means of course, the double loss of health insurance. Alan Freemen reports in the *Globe and Mail* (June 11, 2005) that more than three-quarters of Americans who file for bankruptcy because they cannot pay their medical bills had insurance at the onset of their illness. When a patient leaves hospital, he or she is charged for everything from complicated surgery to medical supplies and consultations. Wrangling over the bill can be long and debilitating for both sides. And health-insurance costs are skyrocketing, with annual double-digit increases leaving more behind every year.

## MANY CHILDREN GET LEFT BEHIND

Public education in the United States is undergoing a similar assault. Years of massive funding cuts to elementary and secondary public schools have left the system open to attack from those with a clear agenda. Ever since Ronald Reagan blamed schools for failing to equip the workforce with the skills necessary to compete in the global economy (*A Nation at Risk*, 1983), right-wing forces have sought ways to take control of the education system and destroy its democratic heart. There are three forces involved in this assault: private corporations making a fortune from testing and the privatization of education; the evangelical Christian right that views the contemporary classroom as the tool of Satan; and social conservatives and foreign-policy hawks who want to purge America's schools of every vestige of liberalism.

Excessive class and wealth differences in the United States have led to a class-based public education system. Because the financing of public schools comes largely from property taxes, wealthy families and communities can afford vastly superior public schools equipped with gymnasiums, swimming pools, language labs, state-of-the-art technology, and arts centres. Children of poor families go to inner-city schools that have rats in the cafeteria, twenty-year-old textbooks, filthy, overcrowded classrooms, and guns. The private sector has benefited from this reality; it provides wealthy schools with the many extras they can afford and it equips poor and middle-class schools, struggling to cope with funding cuts, with technology and textbooks in exchange for free advertising and influence on the curriculum.

The Christian right and social conservatives have exploited their new-found political power with the governing Republicans to make steady inroads on the education system. They want mandatory school prayer and a curriculum that teaches "family values," creationism, moral absolutism, American superiority, and unconditional acceptance of Jesus Christ as the sole guide to eternal salvation. The teaching of tolerance (toward gays and lesbians for instance) found in public schools is particularly abhorrent to them. They believe in rigidly interpreted "revealed truth" and want the school system to deliver it. Their clout in mainstream American society is growing; a majority of Americans (55 per cent) now believe in creationism, the theory that God created humans, dinosaurs, and everything else in the last ten thousand years.

They are heartened by George Bush's support of their views. At an August 2005 White House media briefing, Bush endorsed the teaching of "intelligent design" - that all life is caused by intelligent agents - alongside evolution in America's schools. As *Time* magazine reported in its August 15, 2005, edition, new laws that challenge the teaching of evolution are pending or have been adopted in twenty states, including such traditionally liberal bastions as New York and Michigan.

One of the first acts of Bush's new second-term education secretary, Margaret Spellings, was a highly public, vitriolic attack on PBS for a cartoon named "Postcards from Buster." Buster Bunny, a character popular with children (and created by Canada's Cinar Films), travels around America exploring different regions and religions and celebrating diversity. In one episode, Buster visits Vermont to highlight farming and maple sugaring and chats with a farm couple that happens to be two women. PBS, which gets federal funding from the Ready-to-Learn program, pulled the offending episode after threats that future funds would be cut. Spellings has issued new guidelines for federal education funding to ensure that there will be no depiction of gays and lesbians in future programs.

Christian and social conservatives as well as the big education-service corporations have all benefited from George Bush's 2001 No Child Left Behind (NCLB) legislation. (So did the neo-conservatives. NCLB requires high schools to give military recruiters students' phone numbers and addresses and can cut funding to districts that refuse to comply. *Newsday*, May 26, 2005) The Act requires schools that fail to make sufficient progress toward improving test scores to face escalating sanctions, including allowing students to take their share of federal funding to a for-profit school. If a school fails to meet performance objectives for five consecutive years, it must be turned over to a private management company or converted to a charter school. Charter schools are publicly funded but "chartered" by the state and freed from the rules that apply to public schools. They are run by parents, teachers, or non-profit groups, often churches, and are the tool the right uses to get around the diversity and tolerance required of public schools. The first charter schools were set up in 1991, but the number has risen dramatically since No Child Left Behind was introduced. The Center for Education

Reform proudly reports that there are now over 3,400 charter schools in the United States serving 1 million students and the number is about to explode again thanks to a raft of successful challenges to state rules limiting the number of charter schools.

American education critic Gerald Bracey calls No Child Left Behind the "Perfect Storm." The requirement under the Act that by 2014, 100 per cent of each state's children must achieve at the "proficient" level is totally unrealistic, and the Bush administration knows it, he says. Already, both the California Department of Education and the Minnesota legislative auditor have said that under these rules, from 80 to 90 per cent of their schools would fail. That, of course, is the point, says Bracey, a professor at George Mason University. Failing schools would be turned into charter schools, as would their federal allocation of funds. The Bush team is also promoting the voucher system, which gives money directly to the family for "school choice." The principle beneficiaries of vouchers are religious schools, but parents can also use their voucher to "top up" their own funds, and send their children to for-profit schools. In the end, it is the death knell for the public system. The more charter and voucher schools there are, the poorer the public system, for the NCLB Act takes money directly out of the public system and puts it into the quasi-private charter system. A June 21, 2005, policy brief released by the Education Policy Studies Laboratory at Arizona State University reports that funds flow from the federal government, through the states, and into the hands of private for-profit companies.

No Child Left Behind has provided a great opportunity for the private education companies to move in on the nearly US$500 billion spent annually on elementary and secondary schools. Under the rules, every student in every school must be tested every year. The U.S. General Accounting Office estimates that states will have to spend between US$2 billion and US$5.3 billion to comply with the testing provisions alone. The *Wall Street Journal* (January 2, 2005) reports that business is booming for the big education corporations scrambling to cash in on massive new contracts. The federal law requires struggling schools to provide tutoring and enrichment programs such as those offered by the controversial private school chain, Edison Schools. "We don't have a choice," says an official from the California Office of Student Achievement. "If we don't do this, the federal government will yank our entire federal funding allocation and that's US$27 million." Sylvan Learning Center's revenues grew from US$180 million in 2001 to over US$250 million in 2004 and are due to increase by 250 per cent in 2005–06. Sylvan expects to tutor twenty thousand students in the 2005–06 year at between US$20 and US$40 an hour.

Sales of printed materials related to standardized tests nearly tripled in the last five years, and education corporations from European-based transnationals to start-ups like Ignite, run by Neil Bush, the president's brother, are swarming into the schools offering pre-packaged curriculum, tests, and educational materials armed with the "teach to test" mandate. Teachers are required to teach three hours a day from McGraw-Hill's Open Court materials in Oakland, California. The teachers' union there reports that school-district employees and instructional facilitators inspect the class-rooms to verify that the right posters are on the walls and that everyone in the district is on the same page every day. McGraw-Hill rakes in US$1.4 billion every year, mostly on textbooks and testing materials. People for the American Way reports that the Bush administration has awarded a core group of right-wing edu-cation reformers with lucrative contracts. The Education Leaders Council was formed in 1995 and has consistently attacked public education. It received more that US$77 million in U.S. Depart-ment of Education funds over three years to promote charter and voucher schools. A co-founder of the Council, former Pennsylvania education secretary Eugene W. Hickok, is now the second-ranking official in the federal agency.

Meanwhile, poor, black, disabled, Hispanic, and minority chil-dren are being told they are losers by a rigid system that cannot wait for them. One teacher tells the not uncommon story of a little boy in her class who couldn't stop shaking during a test. Finally, he put his arms over his head, hunched over his desk, and refused to interact with anyone. "He just shut out the world," she says.

## A MATTER OF FAITH

Two major planks of the Bush social revolution are key to his second term: faith-based social services and his "Social Security Reform" to privatize the public pensions of Americans.

To keep a core promise to the religious right, George Bush has championed the notion that faith-based organizations can deal with social problems better than governments. This concept, called "Charitable Choice," was first introduced by then Senator John Ashcroft in President Clinton's regressive 1996 welfare reform package that gutted so much of federal social assistance. The clause allowed religious organizations to infuse religious beliefs into service programs while still receiving government funding, but it was not promoted federally until the Republicans came to power. Nine days after his first inauguration in 2001, Bush created the White House Office of Faith-based and Community Initiatives to remove barriers prohibiting faith-based groups from accessing government funds targeted for welfare, and to allow them to provide an array of social services. He also established faith-based centres in ten federal departments to "promote the Administration's faith-based and community agenda by changing how the federal government operates," according to the White House website.

When Congress refused to pass additional faith-based initiatives in 2002, Bush issued executive orders to increase funding, weaken traditional barriers between government and religious activities, and build a huge network of religious groups to deliver these programs across the country. He also sponsored thirteen regional conferences and additional meetings across the United States to lobby religious groups to apply for US$50 billion in federal funding. This process incidentally produced a politically valuable e-mail list of thirteen thousand faith-based groups. A year later, the Senate passed the Charity, Aid, Recovery and Empower-ment (CARE) Act, to, in George Bush's words, "rally the armies of compassion." While watered down due to fierce opposition, the new act nevertheless constitutes, in the words of Stanley Carlson-Thies, who helped George Bush create the program, "a public policy innovation that's already reshaping how federally funded services are delivered at the state and local levels."

Senator Rick Santorum has been a strong supporter of faith-based social services and works closely with Reverend Herb Lusk, who runs a church-based social-service agency in Philadelphia. Called People for People, the organization receives close to US$10 million a year to run a religious charter school, job-training program, and child-care facility. It is planning to build a mix of housing and retail stores on hundreds of parcels of land it is acquiring. Lusk told the *New York Times Magazine* that he is creating a faith-based empire: "I don't say that to be braggadocious. That's just a fact."

Early reports on these initiatives are disturbing. In a 2003 report, "The Expanding Administrative Presidency: George W. Bush and the Faith-Based Initiative," the Rockefeller Foundation says that the Bush administration has "weakened longstanding walls banning religious groups from mixing spiritual activities with their secular services, thus marking a major shift in the constitutional separation of church and state." The report found that federally funded religious groups are now allowed to consider religion when hiring staff, convert government property to religious purposes, use government funds to build and renovate structures used for church-based social-service delivery, and provide religious training for those seeking church jobs. In its report "Leaving Our Children Behind," the National Gay and Lesbian Task Force said, "Charitable Choice demands no accountability, has no requirement that reli-gious institutions not discriminate, and provides no safeguard against recipients of social services being subjected to proselytizing and other forms of coercive behavior." A 2002 *Washington Post* story caused an uproar when it revealed that top administration officials had tried to solicit support from the Salvation Army by offering a firm commitment that any legislation the White House supported would allow religious organizations to sidestep state and local anti-discrimination measures barring discriminatory hiring practices on the basis of sexual orientation.

Perhaps the most damning reports come from George Bush's home state, which has zealously embraced Charitable Choice. The Texas Freedom Network, a coalition of twenty-three thousand religious and community leaders concerned about the blurring of Church and state, calls the concept "treacherous," and reports that Texas now gives preferential treatment in state contracting to faith-based service providers, often passing over more experienced secular providers. People in need are often given no choice but to seek faith-based treatment and as a condition of treatment, must participate in religious activities. Faith-based providers have been given exemptions from state licensing and health and safety standards, and the "deregulation of faith-based programs" has allowed providers to treat physical diseases like alcoholism and drug addiction as sins. "After five years of aggressively implementing the Bush-led Faith-based Initiative in Texas, positive results have proven impossible to document or measure. Evidence points instead to a system that is unregulated, prone to favouritism, and dangerous to the very people it is supposed to serve."

Yet Charitable Choice is marked for aggressive new support in George Bush's second term, as is his so-called reform of the U.S. Social Security system, which provides retirement, disability, and pension benefits for senior citizens. In 2001, the Presidential Commission on Social Security called for the creation of personal savings accounts that would allow working people to divert a third of their social-security payroll taxes – which currently fund the system – to investment in the stock market, while benefits from the government would be steadily decreased. Bush says that if Americans don't shift to the market for their retirements the fund will go broke. He calls these personal savings accounts part of his "ownership agenda" that will allow people to have more control over their lives. But his warnings of bankruptcy of the system don't add up. Government actuaries, backed by economists from across the political spectrum, say that the Social Security fund will take in more than it pays out for at least thirteen years and that it has built up a reserve of US$1.8 trillion in interest-bearing Treasury bonds for the years after that.

The real reason for Bush's insistent advocacy of this initiative – which is not popular with the American people – is highly political. There are several potential benefits. First, it would undermine the universal nature of the current program, leading to its partial or eventual privatization. Responsibility would shift from society and government to individuals, and make Social Security retirement benefits increasingly dependent upon the vagaries of Wall Street. This is totally consistent with the ideology of the current Republican Party, as the cuts to government pensions would affect working people significantly more than they would affect the rich who can buy private pension plans. It would have the added political benefit of forcing working people to buy into the system of market capitalism because their futures would be dependent on it. This would in turn weaken the voices of opposition to private health care and education, economic globalization, and smaller government. It would also be a body blow to unions, already struggling to survive in Bush's America.

George Bush's Social Security reform would enrich the financial-services industry by transferring trillions of dollars into private plans they would administer. Senator Byron Dorgan of North Dakota calls the Republican plan "one big, wet kiss to Wall Street from the Bush Administration" (*Globe and Mail*, March 5, 2005). It would also pour huge new amounts of money into Wall Street at a time when it is badly needed. Michael Hudson is a Distinguished Professor of Economics at the University of Missouri and writes in the April 2005 edition of *Harper's Magazine* that what Bush is seeking with his social security reform is "a boom – or more accurately, a bubble – bankrolled by the last safe pile of cash in America today." Hudson says that large numbers of American corporations have simply not put away enough money to pay retirees what they are owed. Many are declaring bankruptcy, leaving their employees to seek help from the federal insurer, the Pension Benefit Guarantee Corporation, itself in deep trouble. To save corporate America, the Bush administration wants to transfer the problem to the stock market, and in the bargain, rescue it, along with the fortunes of the Republicans themselves.

For make no mistake; they are in deep financial trouble. With a US$7.7-trillion debt on one side and rapidly rising military costs on the other, they are desperate for money. The U.S. dollar is already dropping and the financial community is watching for signs that foreign banks (which hold 80 per cent of all U.S. dollars) are dumping dollars for currencies that pay better. A deep drop in the U.S. dollar would cause a steep rise in interest rates and a global economic crisis, warns Nova Scotian freelance journalist Ralph Surette. Without raising taxes, which Bush can't do for political reasons, these deficits can't be covered.

U.S. Federal Reserve Board chairman Alan Greenspan agrees. He warns that the mighty U.S. economy is headed for stagnation or even decline unless Washington reins in its swelling deficit (*Globe and Mail*, April 22, 2005). Current budget forecasts predict an additional US$2.6 trillion being added to the national debt in the next decade. Even the International Monetary Fund is issuing warnings about the "truly excessive" U.S. deficit. The Boston *Herald* got a hold of a confidential presentation by Stephen Roach, chief economist at investment banking giant Morgan Stanley, to a senior group of fund managers in late 2004. At that meeting, Roach warned that the United States has no better than a 10 per cent chance of avoiding economic "Armageddon." He said that America's record trade deficit means the dollar will keep falling. To keep foreigners buying T-bills, and prevent a resulting rise in inflation, Alan Greenspan will be forced to raise interest rates, which will be devastating to U.S. consumers already in debt "up to their eyeballs." To finance its current accounts deficit with the rest of the world, he adds, America has to import US$2.6 billion in cash – every day – an amazing 80 per cent of the entire world's net savings. "It's not sustainable," says Roach.

With a current surplus of US$1.8 trillion (expected to grow to US$3.7 trillion by 2018 according to the fund's trustees), the Social Security fund is the "greatest plum of all" says Michael Hudson. The Bush team, as aware of the U.S. government's desperate need for new money as these international financiers, know it. There are trillions more in state public pension funds. Grover Norquist, president of Americans for Tax Reform and architect of Bush's economic policy, has his eye on this money as well.

George Bush has followed to the letter the first two planks of Norquist's three-step formula for transforming government. First, he has radically cut taxes, especially to the rich, thus creating huge deficits. Secondly, he has used these deficits as an excuse to slash non-defence spending. Now is the time for the third step. State by state, Norquist told the *Nation*'s Robert Dreyfuss, and at the federal level, he and Bush will be dismantling and privatizing public pension funds and "liberating" the trillions of dollars now held in trust for retirees. Referring to those who believe in public services such as public pension funds, Norquist stated, "We want to take that power and destroy it."

# deep
# deregulation

*Trusting Business to Do the Right Thing*

In 1998, the giant seed manufacturing company Monsanto, based in Louisville, Kentucky, launched a legal action against Bruno, Saskatchewan, farmer Percy Schmeiser. Monsanto claimed that Schmeiser was growing its patented, herbicide-resistant canola without having paid for the seed. It was seeking some four hundred thousand dollars in damages.

Schmeiser is a respected member of the community. He has been both mayor of Bruno and a member of the provincial legislature. And he has farmed the land for more than forty years. In that time, like many farmers, he had saved the seed from one year's crop to plant the next one. And he had experimented with his own seed varieties to produce a strain of canola singularly well suited to his corner of the province. He had neither purchased nor planted any of Monsanto's Roundup Ready canola seed and he responded to the lawsuit by declaring his intention to fight it.

Monsanto withdrew its original claim that Schmeiser had knowingly planted its canola. Schmeiser contended that it had either been blown onto his land by the wind – Saskatchewan is a windy province – or had landed there by some means of cross-pollination. But Monsanto argued that it didn't matter how the seed had found its way onto Schmeiser's land. It was his responsibility to root it out, even if it landed there accidentally. The case was fought in federal court, appealed, and finally taken to the Supreme Court of Canada. Percy Schmeiser was not required to pay costs or damages but, on the chief point, Monsanto won its case. The right of a company to protect a patented life-form – in this case, a crop seed – was entrenched in law. Schmeiser and his wife, Louise, have spent over two hundred thousand dollars to fight Monsanto and may lose their farm. They have become role models all over the world to farmers fighting to protect their seed heritage. In the eyes of millions of family farmers, Monsanto was the loser in this case.

Increasingly, in recent years, the Canadian government has abandoned support for the rights of individual farmers to take up the cause of agribusiness. In an earlier age, the Canadian ministry of agriculture actively invested in crop research that was freely shared with farmers striving to improve yields in a sometimes inhospitable climate. But now the department's research subsidies are invested in companies that use their discoveries to augment shareholder profits. It's just one more way in which Canadian regulatory practice is falling in line with the American way of doing business.

## THREE-PART HARMONY

Deeper integration between Canada and the United States is not a theory or a fear. It is a reality. For several years, a plethora of task forces, working groups, commissions, coordinating committees, and cross-border consultations have been operating to harmonize Canada–U.S. programs and procedures. Some of this work is simply the way two neighbours act together for mutual protection in the face of a shared threat; no one would wish this kind of co-operation to stop. But much of it goes far beyond common-sense coordination of security and trade. What is taking place now, totally off the radar screen of most Canadians, is the incremental and systematic harmonization of Canadian and American regulations and standards governing health, food safety, and all aspects of the environment. Because this harmonization is taking place during the tenure of George Bush, it is leading inexorably to massive deregulation in these areas, putting Canadians, their health, and their environment in terrible danger.

This harmonization process has been central to the demands of the big-business community in Canada. This is because, thanks to the trade regime the business community created, the economy of Canada is now bound almost exclusively to that of the United States. In the first decade of free trade, exports to the United States increased by 250 per cent, and the United States is now the destination for almost 90 per cent of Canadian exports. As Canada has become more dependent on U.S. markets, trade within Canada and with the rest of the world has declined, in spite of Jean Chrétien's "Team Canada" trade missions to other countries. This dependence has made Canada more vulnerable to U.S. trade disputes such as the contentious softwood lumber issue. And it has left the business community terrified of tighter border controls in the wake of 9/11.

The only way to secure that border in a way that gives big business continued access to the U.S. market, contends the Canadian Council of Chief Executives, is to merge trade and border policies, including all regulatory, environmental, and inspection systems. That this would have the added bonus of doing away with many pesky regulations and standards is not mentioned in most briefs, but it is clear that deregulation would serve the bottom line of these companies very nicely.

In its North American Security and Prosperity Initiative, the Canadian Council of Chief Executives argues that, because the economies of the two countries are now so integrated, our domestic laws are essentially redundant. The CCCE would remove three areas of "significant sensitivity": the use of trade remedies within a "de facto integrated market"; regulatory restrictions on access and ownership in major industries; and impediments to the mobility of skilled labour. The C.D. Howe Institute would create a full Customs Union, establishing a "common external tariff toward the rest of the world, allowing for the free circulation of goods and services within the common area"; and a Common Market, which would totally free up internal trade in goods and services (including health care and education) and "harmonize existing standards, regulations, and policies to a common norm." These dramatic recommendations, if combined with joint Canada–U.S. inspection and security procedures, would essentially wipe out the Canada–U.S. border.

The Task Force on the Future of North America calls regulatory differences between Canada, Mexico, and the United States "the tyranny of small differences" and recommends the adoption of a North American approach to regulation and the creation of a "seamless North American market." To "improve competitiveness," the members call for "regulatory convergence . . . mutual recognition . . . and interoperability" in the "collaborative development of new standards." They agree to "unilateral adoption of another country's rules" (but don't say which country) and propose a "tested once" policy for biotechnology and pharmaceuticals, meaning that if a permit, licence, or patent has been given to a product in its country of origin (which would be the United States in the vast majority of cases), it must be accepted in the other countries of the bloc. Task-force members, including senior Liberal John Manley and the CCCE's Thomas d'Aquino, also want regulatory co-operation on human and veterinary drugs, medical devices, pest control, and chemicals. Citing the deep integration that already exists in the North American food system, the group calls for "integration of rules on food, health, and the environment." Further, all new rules in any of these areas should not be designed by the individual nation states, but rather done by a "new mechanism" to create North American rules and standards.

The process of North American regulatory harmonization is well underway. In a leaked 2003 memorandum, "Securing Growth: Beyond the Border Accord," the Department of Foreign Affairs and International Trade (DFAIT) made it clear the Canadian government is already putting many of these pieces in place. The memo calls for operationalizing a common North American approach to standards, testing, qualifications, regulations, labelling, procurement, and environmental protection in order to "free up resources that could be devoted to our shared security interests." DFAIT officials give the green light to the "tested once" policy for pharmaceuticals and other consumer goods, doing away with rules of origin requirements. In a truly stunning departure for the department supposedly responsible for protecting Canadian interests in international trade negotiations, the memo also endorses a common North American trade position at the WTO.

The Policy Research Initiative, a research arm of the Privy Council, has undertaken a major review of regulations under its "North American Linkages" project. It is concentrating on three areas. It has set up the "International Regulatory Co-operation" project "to identify the differences in regulatory frameworks between Canada and the U.S. that may be having a detrimental impact on trade and investment" and to propose options for "enhanced regulatory cooperation with the U.S." This group is studying a possible customs union between Canada and the United States, which would harmonize external tariffs and eliminate the rules of origin of products. On its website, the Policy Research Initiative admits that a customs union would mean a common trade policy between the two countries and a subsequent loss of sovereignty for Canada. Finally, the group is studying the emergence of cross-border regions and the impact of regulatory harmonization on "sub-national governments."

## GETTING SMART

At their Ottawa meeting in December 2004, and then again in Waco, Texas, in March 2005, Prime Minister Paul Martin and President George W. Bush signed agreements pledging to pursue joint approaches to partnerships, standards, and regulations in order to increase cross-border trade and improve the "efficiency and competitiveness" of North American business.

They established an ongoing series of cross-border working groups (overseen by designated cabinet ministers in Canada) that produced its first "regulatory convergence" action plan at the end of June 2005. In the plan, the three governments laid out ambitious targets toward deeper regulatory integration of their economies. The topics covered included invasive species, water quality, and food safety. They also announced their intent to relax "rules of origin" requirements for intercontinental trade that would allow billions of dollars of additional goods coming from offshore to move freely across North American borders. Canada will now have to abandon any health, safety, or environmental standards on imports that are more stringent than American standards. Canada, the United States, and Mexico also set 2007 as the date by which they will put in place a "regulatory co-operation framework" to cut red tape that hinders trade between the three countries.

To enable Canada to fulfill its commitment to this process, the Canadian government launched its "Smart Regulation" initiative, right after the Waco summit. Treasury Board president Reg Alcock ordered a massive government-wide review of all current regulatory practices as well as an assessment of the criteria for new ones in order to begin this process of regulatory harmonization. "Smart" stands for Specific, Measurable, Attainable, Realistic, and Timely, but Hugh Benevides of the Canadian Environmental Law Association says the term is just a clever but empty vessel into which to pour the real agenda, "fewer regulatory barriers" and "less regulatory duplication" – code words for downward harmonization.

Smart Regulation is a process to bring regulatory regimes in line with international trade and investment policies. The OECD defines Smart Regulation as "market-oriented, trade-and-investment-friendly regulation." Member countries, including Canada, have agreed to ensure "mutual coherence and complementarity between regulatory and trade policy." In other words, what Canada has promoted internationally, Canada must provide at home. Under the WTO, member countries, including Canada, have been steadily ceding corporate patent rights to large drug companies and "intellectual property rights" to companies privatizing seeds and genes. As well, under the GATS, the services negotiations of the WTO, all countries have agreed to lower "barriers to trade" in all services until every barrier in every service is gone. To ensure compliance with these commitments domestically, the Canadian government has been putting all policy and regulations under the microscope of experts from DFAIT and Industry Canada. All this work is further scrutinized by the big-business community. All regulation in Canada must now conform to a dual (and almost always conflicting) mandate: to protect the health and safety of Canadians while promoting Canadian competitiveness in a global economy that is increasingly deregulated.

This transformation of Canada's regulatory system was far advanced before 9/11. What the "crisis" at the border has given big business is a powerful new tool to speed it up. Canada will not be deregulating in isolation. All regulatory reviews will be harmonized between Canada and the United States. The fact that Canada's food, health, and environmental rules will be allied to those of the increasingly deregulated United States of George W. Bush is a big-business bonus. Deregulation will, of course, be effectively permanent and irreversible because it will be part of a contractual obligation with the United States. And the process will be difficult to follow because it will be implemented by bilateral or trilateral committees. Fewer and fewer decisions will be made in Canada. The Smart Regulation initiative is a major undertaking that could result in the abandonment of regulatory sovereignty by the Canadian government.

Alcock's mandate is largely based on the recommendations of the External Advisory Committee on Smart Regulation, established in 2003, which will continue to meet and advise government departments as they prepare their reports. Representatives from industries with a stake in deregulation, including energy, mining, biotech, agribusiness, pharmaceuticals, and forestry dominate the

Advisory Committee. It held no public hearings during the two years it took to write the report for the government. Instead, it relied heavily upon the complaints it heard from industry about the taxing burden of existing Canadian regulations. In its report, the Advisory Committee recommends support for "important new industries like biotechnology" and underscores the desirability of "not inhibiting competitiveness, productivity, investment and the growth of key sectors." It proposes adding additional "tests" to the current rules that already concern many health and environmental groups. As it is now, the benefits of a regulation or standard must outweigh the costs – not always easy to prove when industry is forcefully arguing against regulations – and no "unnecessary regulatory" burden should be imposed upon industries. The Advisory Committee would add further limitations to the government's ability to establish regulations. It calls for a reduction in the number of made-in-Canada regulations. It argues that Canada should develop its own regulatory requirement only when "necessary" in order to meet national goals or values. In the absence of international consensus on a standard or regulation, it proposes that Canadian governments adopt the standard of "key trading partners," which would of course mean the American standard.

The Advisory Committee says that the government should focus on those areas "necessary for the health and safety of Canadians." It recommends "the removal of regulatory impediments to an integrated North American market" and echoes the warning of the Task Force on the need to "eliminate the tyranny of small differences" between the regulatory frameworks of the two countries. (When he launched the Smart Regulation initiative at a Press Gallery breakfast, Alcock made light of regulatory differences between Canada and the United States and gave an amusing speech featuring the picayune differences between Canadian cheese doodles and American cheese doodles.) The Committee calls for a prescriptive "mix of instruments" to replace current statutory regulations, including "education programs," voluntary industry codes, and "voluntary compliance."

The Committee clearly comes down on the pro-business side of the conflicting dual mandate of regulatory agencies: "The regulatory system must enhance market performance, and support innovation, competitiveness, entrepreneurship, and investment in the Canadian economy." The clear mandate of the Smart Regulation initiative is to enhance Canadian corporate competitiveness, increase cross-border trade by harmonizing the regulatory regimes of Canada and the United States, and make Canada a more desirable place for private investment. In fact, the Advisory Committee says there is a need for a "major change" in the culture of government if this new approach is to succeed and advises training programs for government regulators and senior bureaucrats. Canadian Environmental Law Association's Hugh Benevides says that this process is the next logical step after free trade, which was the preliminary step toward full continental integration. Regulatory policies lie at the heart of a nation's rule of law and must be abandoned if "deep integration" is to take place.

Large numbers of government committees and working groups are now toiling away to implement the political commitment to deep border integration. Fifteen different government ministers and departments have set up committees to overhaul their regulatory frameworks. In the next three to five years, Alcock's Treasury Board office plans a sweeping review of all the rules governing how foods are grown and labelled, how drugs are approved, how industrial projects are assessed, and how livestock are treated, to name just a few of the areas to be examined. The House of Commons Standing Committee on Industry, Natural Resources, Science and Technology has launched a study of Canada's industrial strategy and regulatory and foreign-investment frameworks, including a review of "progress in implementing its Smart Regulation initiative" in order to respond to the recommendations of the Advisory Committee. The mandate of the newly launched Automotive Partnership Council of North America is to fully integrate the North American auto industry. One of the top goals of the automakers is to harmonize manufacturing regulation. They already have their sights on Canada's higher safety standard for vehicle steering columns.

## HEALTH AND DRUG SAFETY AT RISK

One of these teams is hard at work lowering the standards for food and drug safety in Canada. In February 2004, Mark B. McClellan, then commissioner of the United States Food and Drug Administration; Diane Gorman, assistant deputy minister of the Health Products and Food Branch of Health Canada; and Ernesto Enriquez Rubio, commissioner of the Federal Commission for the Protection from Sanitary Risks of Mexico, signed a "Trilateral Cooperation Charter." Its mission is to "enhance communication . . . develop partnerships . . . and harmonize positions" among the countries in the areas of drugs, biologics, medical devices, food safety, and nutrition. The Charter, says Health Canada on its website, is an important initiative for the "development of regulatory cooperation" between the three agencies and includes the participation of Canada's Competition Bureau and the Canadian Food Inspection Agency. One of the working groups is the "Canada–U.S.–Mexico Compliance Information Group." This has been set up "to increase the exchange of information and explore areas of mutual interest on regulatory compliance decision-making approaches." The fact that the Competition Bureau is a participating member of this cross-border harmonization team is evidence that its mandate goes far beyond protecting the health and safety of Canadians and probably will be giving equal time to the health and well-being of Canadian corporations.

On June 29, 2005, Health Minister Ujjal Dosanjh announced a memorandum of understanding between Health Canada and the U.S. Consumer Product Safety Commission to "establish mechanisms" to collaborate on the setting of standards on consumer goods, including risk assessment and management, enforcement and compliance activities, laboratory testing, recalls, regulatory development, emergency management, and public health and safety information.

It can be no coincidence that Health Canada has undertaken these major new reviews of its health and consumer protection legislation and is preparing to replace the Canada Food and Drugs Act, the legislation under which the federal government has a statutory duty to protect Canadians from hazardous food, water, air, prescription drugs, and medical devices. The eventual goal is to write a whole new Health Protection Act. The government claims it simply wants to modernize the current legislation. Mike McBane of the Canadian Health Coalition says the real motivation behind the review, called "Health and Safety First! A Proposal to Renew Federal Health Protection," is to give a boost to Canadian industry by lowering safety standards. Smart Regulation means that instead of government regulation intervening in the market, the market will now intervene in government legislation. He says that profits are to be put before safety.

The OECD has singled out the Canada Food and Drugs Act as a barrier to Canada's trade commitments. In a 2002 study, "Enhancing Market Openness Through Regulatory Reform: A Review of Regulatory Reform in Canada," the organization says: "Major pieces of legislation, such as the Canada Food and Drugs Act, often constrain regulators to adhere to the command-and-control, prescriptive style of regulation and perpetuate an old-style approach ill-suited to the dynamics of good regulatory practice in general and trade and investment-friendliness in particular." The OECD adds that where the Canadian government has tried to move to a more "flexible" system, the power of "special interest groups" in Canada was enough to dissuade it from "trusting business to do the right thing."

In its own internal documents, Health Canada concurs, saying the current Act focuses too narrowly on safety and "does not allow" other considerations, such as the "need to improve the economy and to promote competitiveness." The drive within the department to include a business component in its mandate goes back a decade but Smart Regulation has given it new life. Health Canada now is quite explicit in stating that it will work to "contribute to innovation and economic growth, and reduce the administrative burden on business."

The Canadian Health Coalition believes that Health Canada wants to replace the current standards which require proof of safety, with a weaker industry standard requiring evidence of harm. The presumption going forward will be that technology and products are safe unless proven otherwise. The Precautionary Principle, which places the primary burden of proving a product's safety on the manufacturer, would be replaced by a "risk-cost-benefit" regime. Under this regime, the burden of proof that a product may be harmful is shifted to the public. This new system would actually have officials weigh the economic benefits of a proposed new drug, genetically engineered food, or new medical device against the number of injuries or deaths they might cause. The coalition calls this position indefensible. The Precautionary Principle was developed as an approach appropriate to situations where scientific knowledge is limited or incomplete, McBane explains. It allows governments to be cautious when they simply don't know if a product is safe or not. The risk-cost-benefit approach is an industry-friendly standard that permits risk if there are offsetting benefits to consumers or the industry. This standard was applied first to environmental and health regulations under Ronald Reagan. It has been used in the United States to justify "acceptable" levels of pesticides, hormones, antibiotics, genetically modified organisms, and compounds that cause adverse side effects in pharmaceuticals.

The risk-cost-benefit approach also depends heavily on the "evidence" produced by industry itself. The lion's share of biotechnology testing in Canada and the United States, for instance, is done by the biotech industry. Its assurances that a product is safe are much more likely to be accepted under a risk-cost-benefit regime than one in which safety is paramount. The Canadian Health Coalition is very concerned that the proposed new legislation would speed up drug approvals at Health Canada, a process already heavily dominated by the industry. The department is facing billions of dollars in liability suits for failing to meet its legal "duty of care." Less stringent safety criteria could mean that Canadians would lose recourse to the courts for claims of regulatory negligence.

Similarly, under a harmonized regime, Health Canada could very well approve direct-to-consumer advertising of prescription drugs. This is currently against the law in Canada, but allowed in the United States, where the big pharmaceutical companies spend billions of dollars in marketing their drugs. The *New England Journal of Medicine* (February 2000) reported that drug advertising is having a significant, negative impact on the practice of medicine in the United States. It reported that 80 per cent of patients who asked their doctor for a drug had seen it advertised on television. Doctors, according to the report, are finding themselves under pressure to prescribe medicines they would not independently have chosen for these patients. Drugs are not advertised in the mass media to inform the public, but to sell a product, and for this reason no other country in the world allows direct-to-consumer advertising except the United States and New Zealand. New Zealand is reviewing the policy because of public criticism.

Another health issue that could be affected by Canada–U.S. harmonization is the price of prescription drugs. Although drug costs are the single most significant factor accounting for the rise in health costs in Canada over the last decade (a direct result of trade rules giving the big drug companies twenty-year patents), drugs are still substantially cheaper in Canada because Canada maintains price controls. But deeper integration with the United States could change all that, warns Robert Chernomas, a health economist at the University of Manitoba. In order to protect the big American drug companies that gave him record high contributions in both presidential elections, Bush wants to drive the price of drugs around the world up to U.S. levels. On January 1, 2005, the United States and Australia signed a free-trade agreement that gives American pharmaceutical companies the right to challenge the Australian public insurance plan if it approves generic drugs that would undercut their prices. This was the first international trade agreement to allow the United States to tell a foreign industrialized country how to operate its national health plan and provide drugs to its own citizens. In late July, Congress signed a regional free-trade agreement with the small countries of Central America (CAFTA) with similar provisions. These poor countries are now prohibited from providing cheaper generic drugs for people suffering from HIV and AIDS.

Chernomas says that this is the first skirmish in a war. The United States has put a "marker" down that it will now use with other countries. Over time, the Bush administration is seeking a "world price" for prescription drugs, a price that will be set in the United States. There is no way that Canada, locked into a common trade bloc with its neighbour to the south, could maintain lower prices for its citizens. Interestingly, the man who spearheaded this initiative for George Bush and the big American drug companies is Mark McClellan, former Food and Drug Act Administration commissioner now in charge of Medicare and Medicaid, and the same man who signed the Trilateral Cooperation Charter with Health Canada.

## FOOD SAFETY AT RISK

A similar story is unfolding over at Agriculture and Agri-Food Canada. (Several years ago, the department changed its name from Agriculture Canada to Agriculture and Agri-Food Canada to reflect its new mandate to promote competitiveness in the agri-food sector. At the time, it adopted a "business-risk management" approach to regulation to build a "stronger, more profitable agriculture sector for the 21st century.") A trilateral body has been set up to oversee the integration of North American agriculture policy and the harmonization of its regulatory framework. Called the North American Agrifood Market Integration Consortium, the group is made up of representatives of industry, government, and academics from the three NAFTA countries. It meets regularly. The coordination body is the U.S.–based Farm Foundation, whose mandate is "to improve the productivity and competitiveness of U.S. agriculture."

One issue being targeted for regulatory harmonization is the border inspection of food. Agriculture and Agri-Food Canada's Canadian Food Inspection Agency (CFIA) is responsible for protecting Canada's food safety supply. However, the Agency has a conflicting mandate, which is to facilitate trade in food, animals, plants, and related products. The way it has handled this dual responsibility is to depend heavily on industry self-regulation and by adopting a risk-cost-benefit system in assessing safety. Public health advocacy and farmers' groups have warned the government that it is impossible for one agency to promote agribusiness trade on one hand while trying to establish a credible regulatory regime on the other.

They were right. CFIA is the agency in charge of preventing BSE (bovine spongiform encephalopathy, otherwise known as mad cow disease) in Canada. It refused to heed the warnings of senior Health Canada scientists such as doctors Shiv Chopra, Margaret Haydon, and Gerard Lambert, who were fired after going public with their criticisms. The result of the BSE crisis was the loss of thousands of family farms, billions of dollars, and Canada's international reputation. The auditor general has been highly critical of the CFIA, calling it one of the most secretive agencies in government. In her reports, Sheila Fraser has also criticized the agency for the exceptionally heavy presence of industry on its advisory committees.

However, instead of forcing the CFIA to enhance protections for Canadians, the Martin government has introduced C-27, the Canadian Food Inspection Agency Enforcement Act, to ensure the agency complies with the Smart Regulation initiative. C-27 will mean the end of any independent policy on food production, inspection, and enforcement in Canada, says Beyond Factory Farming, a coalition of organizations that promote sustainable farming. C-27 will give the CFIA the power to make bilateral agreements that force Canada to adopt the regulatory practices of the United States. It will authorize it to privatize Canadian food-inspection services; force it to share information about Canadians with the U.S. government; and enshrine the risk-cost-benefit approach to the enforcement of all food and agriculture legislation. Essentially, C-27 links Canada's border food-inspection practices with the U.S. Homeland Security Act and the U.S. war on terror. The sweeping powers accorded to the CFIA under C-27 mean that the agency will enter into information sharing and investigative arrangements with the United States. The act also ties Canada into the U.S. regulatory system by providing for U.S. inspection, testing, and regulatory standards to apply in Canada.

Cathy Holtslander of the Beyond Factory Farming Coalition notes in her brief to the House Standing Committee on Agriculture and Food, that C-27 is designed to make Canada's food-inspection process conform to the recommendations of the External Advisory Committee on Smart Regulation, which include: adopting international approaches to regulation wherever possible; minimizing the impact of regulatory differences between Canada and the United States on trade and investment; moving to a single North American review and approval system; putting in place an integrated North American regulatory process for food; accepting product approvals by the United States; adopting a risk-management approach to regulation; and collaborating with "appropriate partners" from outside the public service, meaning the private sector. "Our central concern with C-27 is that it creates a framework to permit an unelected bureaucracy, the CFIA, to re-structure the regulations that govern Canada's food and agriculture in a way that will put trade ahead of public safety, and will put integration with the U.S. regulatory system ahead of legitimate Canadian democratic control over the rules that govern the food we eat," says Holtslander.

Allowing the United States to set Canadian food safety standards is a dangerous move, Dr. Lester Friedlander, a former USDA

(United States Department of Agriculture) veterinarian, said in an April 12, 2005, address before the Canadian House Standing Committee on Agriculture. "Rules and regulations are broken every day in the United States because the government is not enforcing them, allowing, for instance, animal protein to be fed back to cattle. The public must insist that the food safety regulatory function be separated from the governmental agency promoting corporate agribusiness." (Feeding ground-up animal parts to cattle, a practice that once seemed to be a cheap and efficient means of adding protein to their diet, is now widely assumed to be a cause of BSE.) The Associated Press reports (June 22, 2005) that eighteen months after promising major reforms in the cattle-feed industry to prevent an outbreak of BSE in the United States, American cattle are still eating chicken litter, cattle blood, and restaurant leftovers. "Once the cameras were turned off and media coverage dissipated, it's been business as usual," says John Stauber, author of *Mad Cow U.S.A.: Could the Nightmare Happen Here?* "No real reform, just more feeding of slaughter house waste. The entire U.S. policy is designed to protect the livestock industry's access to slaughterhouse waste as cheap feed." Stauber was not surprised when the first American case of BSE was found in June 2005 and believes there are likely more cases. While it is true that BSE was allowed to find its way into the Canadian system due to the CFIA's negligence, a made-in-Canada regulatory system can still be fixed. However, if C-27 becomes law, Canada will be adopting the standards George Bush refuses to improve. And that means adopting the American regulatory system, which favours industrial livestock production over the family farm – a system that is destroying rural communities.

Two other Smart Regulation initiatives threaten the Canadian food supply. The government is putting final touches on C-28, an amendment to the Food and Drugs Act that will give the health minister "interim marketing authorization," the right to temporarily approve drugs and food that might ordinarily be considered "adulterated." Under Article 4 of the current Act, the minister's duty is to prohibit the sale of food or drugs that are adulterated.

However, this amendment would allow the government to "temporarily" permit the sale of cancer-causing chemicals, pesticides, food additives, and veterinary drugs such as antibiotics and growth hormones. Roger Thibault, parliamentary secretary to the minister of health, told the House of Commons that C-27 is "in line with the ongoing intent of the Government of Canada's Smart Regulation initiative" and will "support the ongoing work under the North American Free Trade Agreement Technical Working Group on Pesticides." Mike McBane of the Canadian Health Coalition says that food and drugs are either adulterated or they are not. The minister will have the power, he says, to expose Canadians to dangerous chemicals, additives, and pesticides if it is in the industry's interest to do so.

Similarly, the proposed "tested once" policy, a key recommendation of Smart Regulation, would mean that any hormone, chemical additive, antibiotic, or genetically engineered food approved in the United States would have to be accepted in Canada. In the 1990s, Canadians were successful in denying Monsanto a patent for bovine growth hormone – a controversial hormone that increases milk production in cows but has negative side effects for both cows and humans. But American health and consumer groups were not able to get their government to ban it, and it is now used in most milk production in the United States. Under a "tested once" policy, Canada would have little choice but to allow bovine growth hormone into the Canadian dairy industry.

## THE SEED CORPORATIONS CASH IN

Equally alarming to many Canadian farmers are proposed CFIA amendments to the Plant Breeders' Rights Act, which would give powerful new rights to the big seed companies like Monsanto, mirroring their position in the United States. A quarter of a century ago, Canada had a fully public seed system, writes agriculture researcher Devlin Kuyek in his 2004 study, *Stolen Seeds:*

*The Privatization of Canada's Agricultural Biodiversity.* Farmers saved, shared, and traded seeds, successfully creating a wonderfully diverse food system in an often-harsh climate. The open exchange of seeds prevented seed companies from developing a monopoly and kept the prices too low to attract the interest of major corporations. Biotechnology, with its potential for corporate control over seed and gene production, changed all that. Suddenly, huge biotech and agribusiness companies were seeking access to seed through trade agreements and governments friendly to the private sector. In the 1970s and 1980s, the Canadian government started pumping subsidies into private Canadian seed companies, which were bought up by big American corporations as soon as they started to make money.

In the next decade, the Canadian government started to put in place monopoly rights for corporations. The practice of seed saving by farmers became criminalized in the process, as Percy Schmeiser discovered when he lost his battle with Monsanto in 2004. Successive Canadian governments have slashed funds for agricultural research in the public sphere and replaced them with public-private partnerships or outright subsidies to the corporations. A handful of corporations now control seed production in Canada and around the world. The seed industry's ultimate goal, according to Kuyek, is full-scale protection for its patents. It is going after regulatory reform and wants the Canadian government to protect it from charges of genetic contamination – when, for example, seeds from its plants are accidentally blown or dropped onto other farmers' lands – as it introduces under-tested genetically modified seeds and genes into the system.

This is where the proposed amendments to the Plant Breeders' Rights Act will be helpful to the corporations, says the National Farmers Union. These amendments would encourage or compel farmers to buy certified (corporate) seed; give up the right to sell common seed; streamline regulatory approval of genetically modified crops; collect royalties on farm-saved seed; and extend royalty payment periods on seeds, giving seed corporations a powerful new enforcement and collection tool, including the right to seize farmers' crops. All the "rights" are extended to the companies: farmers are left with "privileges." If a "rights-holder" like Monsanto says that its seed is growing on a farmer's property, the onus will be on the farmer to prove that it's not. This is a corporate practice started in the United States and promoted under the Bush administration. The Plant Breeders' Rights Act, combined with C-27, the legislation to make Agriculture and Agri-Food Canada's policies conform to the Smart Regulation initiative, will further harmonize the North American seed system under corporate control and leave Canadian farmers without the sovereign power to fight it.

If anyone has any illusions that the Canadian government is not 100 per cent behind deregulation, they have only to examine the shameful position Canada has taken on the most controversial corporate seed technology of all, Genetic Use Restriction Technology, or "Terminator" seeds as they have come to be known. Terminator seeds have been genetically modified to produce crops that are sterile so farmers cannot save them. As a result, farmers are forced to buy new seeds each year from the seed corporations. Terminator was developed by the U.S. government and Monsanto who now jointly own the patent. (Several other seed companies are developing clones.) The National Farmers Union calls Terminator the most problematic application of genetic engineering to date because it gives the seed companies total control of the food supply and spreads sterility to local crops and wild relatives, posing a huge threat to biodiversity. So strong has public reaction around the world been that, since 1998, there has been an international ban on Terminator seeds.

Monsanto and the U.S. government have not given up the fight to sell this technology abroad. They stacked a February 2005 UN meeting on biological diversity in Bangkok with corporate representatives from the biotech industry where they launched an attempt to lift the ban. But because the United States has not signed the Biodiversity Convention, its many government representatives had to observe the meeting from the sidelines. This meant that the

United States and Monsanto had to find a friendly government to introduce their motion. Canada stepped up.

On the first day of the meeting, the Canadian proposal was leaked to the ETC Group (The Action Group on Erosion, Technology and Concentration, an international civil society coalition headquartered in Canada), who made it public. Ottawa's instructions to the Canadian delegation (comprised of officials from the Canadian Food Inspection Agency, the Department of Foreign Affairs and International Trade, Agriculture and Agri-Food Canada, and the Biosafety Convention division of Environment Canada – the very team tasked with upholding the ban) called for an all-out push for field-testing and commercialization of sterile-seed technologies, a move that would have ended the ban. Worse, the Canadian delegation was instructed to "block consensus" by governments if it didn't get its way, and wrote to all its embassies in the week leading up to the meeting instructing them to seek support for this move from the governments to which they were assigned.

Following these revelations, the Canadian government was inundated by thousands of e-mails critical of its position from all over the world, as well as some negative media. It backed off, saving the ban for now. But as Pat Mooney from ETC Group warns, these companies and the U.S. and Canadian governments are not going to drop their quest. Terminator is on the agenda for future conferences and meetings. Mooney reminds governments that there are 1.4 million farmers in the world whose very lives and livelihoods depend on saved seed and who could never afford to buy seeds from companies like Monsanto. "Terminator continues to represent the greatest threat to crop diversity and food security the world has ever known," he says. "Without greater support from governments and civil society, it is only a matter of time before some ambush somewhere is successful."

(Perhaps it was just a coincidence, but three distinguished visitors highly critical of Canada's position on biotechnology were denied entry to Canada to speak at the May 2005 meeting of the UN Convention on Biological Diversity. Professor Kavulakunpla

Ramanna Chowdry, a farmer, retired professor of agriculture economics, and adviser to the Andhra Pradesh state government in India and Kaka Ramakrishna, an Indian farmer who suffered huge losses when genetically engineered cotton was introduced to his region, were denied visas. Dr. Tewolde Berhan Gebre Egziabher, the Ethiopian government's chief scientist and its representative to the Convention, was denied his visa until the very last day of the meeting and was let into Canada only after protest from many groups.)

## FARMERS FIGHT FOR SURVIVAL

Canadian farmers, while not as vulnerable as Third World farmers, are nevertheless experiencing great hardship as a result of these corporate depredations, and the fallout from years of what Fred Tait of the National Farmers Union calls the "dysfunctional free trade market." This system, which Canada has fully adopted, is characterized by traits that are hostile to individual farmers. Large operations push out smaller ones. Rural employment continues to decline as technologically dependent production systems take over. There is a consequent erosion of farmer control, and increased reliance on herbicides, pesticides, commercial fertilizers, and genetically modified crops. High-yield crops that pose higher environmental risks have become prevalent, further enhancing environmental unsustainability and economic insecurity among farmers. Although agriculture exports have doubled since Canada signed the Canada–U.S. Free Trade Agreement in 1989, net income for family farmers has dropped by 24 per cent. Sixteen per cent of Canadian farmers have been forced off the land in this period, and farm debt has doubled. Consolidation has created huge livestock operations that are fouling land, air, and water.

The dysfunctional free-trade market demands ever more deregulation of the agriculture industry, says Tait, a process that will be speeded up as Agriculture and Agri-Food Canada prepares its response to the Smart Regulation initiative. Corporations that supply agriculture services and inputs – that provide transportation, or that process food or market production – receive the benefits of deregulation. The cost of deregulation is borne by the farmer. The next deregulation targets are statutory rail freight rates, "single desk" selling of hogs, Supply Management, and the Wheat Board, all of which benefit farmers and give them more control. (The United States has launched ten complaints through various trade tribunals over the last fifteen years against the Wheat Board. Smart Regulation, with its mandate to harmonize the food system of the two countries, will give the United States a powerful new weapon in its assault.)

Fred Tait says that the removal of regulations designed to protect agricultural producers is being accompanied by a corresponding increase in the concentration of corporate power. Two packers – Cargill and Tyson – kill and pack 75 per cent of Canada's beef. Three transnationals make most of our cereal. There are three manufacturers of farm tractors, a reduction of 50 per cent in fifteen years. Five corporations market most of our food.

"Government regulation of agriculture is being replaced with regulations imposed by American transnational corporations," Tait told the October 28, 2004, Citizens' Inquiry on Canada–U.S. Relations. "The only legitimate purpose of government regulation is to serve the public good. The only purpose of regulations imposed by transnational corporations is the enhancement of corporate control and profitability. Free trade transnational-regulated agriculture is destroying the social and economic base of rural Canada. Transnational-regulated agriculture contends that it is determined to feed a starving world. The irony is that transnational-regulated agriculture is not only destroying the sustainability of the agricultural communities that produce food for export, but at the same time is destroying the sustainability of agricultural communities in the food importing countries. Left to its own principles and values, transnational-regulated agriculture will create a starving world."

## ENVIRONMENT CANADA EMBRACES DEREGULATION

Not to be left behind, Environment Canada has embarked on its own process in order to comply with the Smart Regulation initiative. It is called the Environment Competitiveness and Environmental Sustainability Framework and sets the stage for a public-private partnership on environmental regulation between Environment Canada and industry. Environment Canada's deputy minister Sammy Watson says the federal government is changing its approach to environmental protection and calls the Framework a "mechanism for industry-government collaboration." Environment Minister Stéphane Dion has launched what he calls a new "Industrial Revolution," which will lead to the integration of the objectives of health, the environment, and economic competitiveness. In an October 24, 2004, speech to the Canadian Chemical Producers' Association, Dion promised to convert his department's mandate to enable "Canada and Canadian business to become global leaders in terms of environmental innovation, competitiveness and excellence." He also announced the creation of a new cabinet committee – the Ad Hoc Committee on Environment and Sustainable Economy, chaired not by himself, but by the minister of industry.

(When Environment Canada was established, its mandate was the protection of Canadians and their environment. The departments of Industry and Trade looked after Canada's competitive position in the world. It was assumed that there would be tension between these departments; a department totally devoted to the protection of the environment was seen as a healthy check on industry. However, the department's mandate and commitment to the Precautionary Principle has been changing under the terms of international trade agreements that set out detailed rules to constrain the extent to which governments can regulate trade or the behaviour of corporations.)

In an inter-government memo, Deputy Minister Watson outlines his department's plan to set up "Value-Chain Sector Sustainability Tables" to "strengthen the well being of Canadians, the health of our planet and our long-term competitiveness." In other words, the department will be subject to the same conflicting and contradictory instructions as those that govern food and health safety. These "tables" will be permanent committees established around business sectors and each will approach sustainability issues based on "how corporations make decisions." Watson says they will be charged with identifying desired "national outcomes" and the proposals they come up with will be "tailored to reflect business realities." Each sector table will be co-chaired by a corporate leader and a senior government official from departments other than Environment Canada, and initially will cover the energy, automobile, forestry, mining, and chemical industries. The government and industry co-chairs named so far are: Larry Murray, deputy minister at the Department of Foreign Affairs and Gerry Protti of Encana Corp. for the energy table; Alan Nymark, deputy minister at Treasury Board and Richard Ross of Inmet Mining Corp. for the mining table; Suzanne Hurtubise, deputy minister at Industry Canada and Steve Griffiths of Imperial Oil Ltd. for the chemicals table; and Mark Carney, senior associate deputy minister at Finance and Russ Horner of Norske Canada for the forestry table.

The implication to be read from early government documents is that the new government policy will allow large corporations to police themselves on their compliance to regulatory standards that they themselves are going to set. The tables will form a "community of purpose" to set "long-term standards and objectives" for the department. The chairs of the tables will constitute a committee that will meet regularly to "address crosscutting national environmental issues" and "help develop coherent government views." They will set targets for "corporate level agreements" and negotiate "environmental performance agreements" firm by firm. There will be "incentives to reward leadership and compliance." In true business doublespeak Environment Canada says, "Facilities and corporations complying with their environmental performance agreements will meet regulatory requirements. Small and medium-sized businesses will continue to be governed by regulations." It appears that large corporations will no longer be subject to Environment Canada regulations but will be negotiating a whole new set of agreements as equal partners with the department. Watson does add lamely in a briefing note on the Framework that for "those who fail to act," there will be "some kind" of regulatory system.

Jim Abraham, Environment Canada's acting regional director general, added his understanding of the Framework in a keynote address he gave to a Toronto meeting of the Canada–U.S. Great Lakes Binational Toxics Strategy group on May 17, 2005. The title of his address captures its content: "A Competitiveness and Environmental Sustainability Framework – Transforming the Way We Do Business." "Environmental sustainability is emerging as a new basis for competitiveness," he said. He restated the terms of the new, conflicting Smart Regulation goals of Environment Canada: "To advance the health and well-being of Canadians, preserve our natural environment, and advance our long-term competitiveness." He compared Canada's environmental performance to OECD "competitors" – what some people still call "countries" – and says that the "real long-term outcome" of the Framework is "collaborative mechanism" with industry to deliver on national environmental goals. Although he mentioned that the new approach will be "backstopped" by regulations, all emphasis is on education, incentives, and "performance promotion." Abraham said that the Framework will "brand Canada" as an international model of environmental performance.

David Coon, policy director of the Conservation Council of New Brunswick, is not so sure. "Environmental regulation is one of the few remaining constraints on the economic activity of corporations in Canada. Regulations concerning investment and trade have all but been abandoned in the past twenty years. Yet here we have a proposal, which has been circulating at the highest levels of the federal government, based on the assumption that corporations and governments have a common purpose, and therefore government can abandon its authority to decide what corporations must do to protect and restore the environment." Coon observes that the influence of corporations has been growing for the past twenty years. "This proposal institutionalizes that influence, by making corporations 'partners' in environmental protection."

This attempt to launch a bold initiative at Environment Canada is partly a response to those who say the department has become irrelevant. Environment Canada took a particularly serious hit in (then Finance Minister) Paul Martin's 1995 federal budget. Almost one-third of its budget was cut and fourteen hundred employees were laid off. Other departments that impact on the environment were also disproportionately hit. The Department of Natural Resources was "downsized" by fifteen hundred employees and suffered budget cuts of 69 per cent. The Canadian Forest Service was gutted. At Parks Canada, two thousand employees were laid off and one-third of the budget was cut. At the Department of Fisheries and Oceans, cuts of 70 per cent crippled the world-famous Freshwater Institute. The Sierra Club of Canada follows Canada's Rio commitments closely and says the cuts forced Environment Canada to wholly abrogate the promises it made at that famous 1991 summit. Just two years after the cuts, the *Ottawa Citizen* said that Environment Canada "has little influence on anything you eat, drink, or breathe."

The Martin budget was just the beginning of the department's troubles. In 1998, the federal government negotiated a new arrangement with the provinces to allow them, through the Canadian Council of Ministers for the Environment (CCME), to assume much of the federal responsibility for environmental regulation. Because this group operates from consensus and includes ministers from provinces that are cutting or have cut environmental regulations (Alberta, British Columbia, Alberta, Quebec), it has adopted a "lowest common denominator" approach to environmental issues such as climate change. And just as ending the Canada Assistance Plan (in the same budget) created a patchwork of standards for social welfare across the country, so did ceding federal authority over environmental regulation in this accord. The new deal actually allows provinces to opt out of regulatory regimes and implement a voluntary code for many items.

With the blessing of the CCME, for instance, the fossil-fuel industry negotiated a voluntary compliance code to fulfill its "partnership" commitment to lower greenhouse-gas emissions under the Kyoto Protocol. Under this code – the Voluntary Challenge and Registry – greenhouse-gas emissions have risen at between 2 and 3 per cent a year over the last decade. Further, as Peter Calamai of the *Toronto Star* (February 12, 2005) explains, the government told major polluters in the oil- and gas-, thermal electricity, mining, and heavy manufacturing industries that they would have to cut no more than 55 million tons of gas emissions each a year. The result, of course, has been a huge increase in gas emissions (due to voluntary compliance). Because there is a cap on what industry must cut, the burden of meeting international environmental targets is shifting to such strategies as energy conservation, fuel-efficient vehicles, renewable energy, natural carbon sinks, and emissions trading. It is highly unlikely that the targets can be achieved by these means alone.

So it is no surprise that environmental groups were unhappy when the government released its long-awaited Kyoto plan in April 2005. "The primary problem is that big business, responsible for 50 per cent of the greenhouse gas pollution in Canada, is being let off the hook," said Greenpeace. "Because big business is not doing its share of greenhouse gas reductions, very high targets have been assigned to several large government programs at enormous cost to taxpayers." The Suzuki Foundation agrees: "Canada's climate change plan lets big polluters off the hook and doesn't send a strong message to industry that our economy must become cleaner. . . . By bending over backwards to make targets for large polluting industries so low, the federal government puts a disproportionately large burden on Canadians. Even though individual Canadians are only responsible for about 28 per cent of Canada's emission, they may end up being responsible for at least 74 per cent of emission reductions. That's not fair."

Smart Regulation is making a bad situation worse. Like all the other departments, Environment Canada has essentially been instructed to make its regulatory regime conform to that of the United States. Under this regime, the onus is on the regulator to prove the need for regulation to the industry, and voluntary codes and performance targets are substituted for enforceable standards. The Bush administration, of course, has refused to ratify the Kyoto Protocol and continues to insist that concerns over global warming are exaggerated. British prime minister Tony Blair has taken a different position, and says that greenhouse gases from human activity may cause catastrophic floods, heat waves, and storms and drive many species to extinction. The science academies of all G-8 countries as well as of China, India, and Brazil have stated unequivocally that the burning of fossil fuels in power plants, cars, and factories is the leading cause for warming. Yet Bush continues to rely on advice from industry-funded scientists like Dr. Fred Singer, who cut his teeth defending the tobacco industry, and who claims, "Surface warming is nothing to be worried about."

Canada has already harmonized pesticide residue standards, as agreed to in the Canada–U.S. Free Trade Agreement. The United States had higher allowable residue levels than Canada in the 1980s. Canada often turned back U.S. fruits and vegetables at the border, saying that the high pesticide residues contaminated them. The United States called this an unfair trade practice and threatened a trade challenge. To avoid a trade dispute, the Canadian government entered into a process of negotiation with the United States that ended in capitulation. Canadians now get to eat more pesticides on their imported fruit and vegetables. Similarly, when the Chrétien government was challenged with a trade dispute under NAFTA to its 1997 ban on cross-border trade in MMT, a toxic gasoline additive, it backed down. Ethyl, the American company that manufactures

MMT, used the controversial Chapter 11 provision of the trade agreement, which allows corporations of another NAFTA country to sue governments. Even though he had called MMT a "dangerous neurotoxin" in the House of Commons, Chrétien reversed the ban, allowed MMT back into Canadian gasoline, and paid $20 million in compensation to the company for the year of lost Canadian sales.

Now the stage is being set for yet another retreat. At the heart of the softwood lumber dispute between Canada and the United States, says Bruce Campbell of the Canadian Centre for Policy Alternatives, is the fundamentally different way in which the two countries harvest wood. In Canada, 90 per cent of timber is cut from public or Crown land, while in the United States 95 per cent is cut from privately owned land. In the United States, private market auctions determine the price for cutting timber. In Canada, the price charged by government to companies is based on a number of factors: production costs, market calculations, and company obligations regarding conservation, employment, and local processing. While Canadian forestry practices are destroying old-growth stands at an alarming rate and the Canadian government is leasing huge tracts of land to U.S. corporations, there is still a theoretical ability within the existing structure to implement a sustainable forestry system in Canada.

However, the United States is intensifying pressure on Canadian governments to harmonize their forest management practices with those of the United States. The U.S. government has lost repeated trade panels on this issue, the most recent on August 10, 2005 (a ruling that the White House dismissed as irrelevant). Not only does the U.S. government refuse to abide by them, it refuses to return the $5 billion in tariff revenues it has collected illegally from Canadian exporters. The price of getting a resolution and the return of this money, says the U.S. Department of Commerce, is to give in on a number of issues. The Americans are pressing Canada to remove the requirement to maintain a processing facility in the community where the timber is cut; remove conditions for mill closures; remove minimum cut regulations that reduce production cutbacks and layoffs during downturns; adopt market-based pricing; increase the sale of timber at private auctions; and privatize Crown lands. All this, and the United States wants to cap Canadian market share at 30 per cent. Campbell says making these concessions would "foreclose decades of public policy linking company harvesting rights with obligations to maintain production, employment, and stability in scores of communities, and weaken their capacity to undertake sustainable forestry conservation practices."

Yet it seems that Canada is prepared to do exactly that. In a March 8, 2005, memo, Canadian negotiators, led by former deputy chief free trade negotiator Gordon Ritchie, tabled a proposal that would allow provinces to be excluded from payments of export taxes in exchange for adopting the kind of policies outlined by the U.S. Department of Commerce. Provinces would notify the Canadian government of these changes, and the Canadian government would then seek agreement from the United States that they are sufficient. Only after obtaining agreement from the U.S. government would Canada be allowed to reduce or eliminate the export tax, even though every single trade panel has ruled it should never have been set in the first place. Fred Wilson of the Communications, Energy, and Paperworkers Union says that this proposal is unprecedented in that it would force Canadian provinces to seek approval from the U.S. Department of Commerce in setting policy. "This is the Americanization of Canadian forest policy," he warns. In essence, the United States is using the dispute settlement mechanism of NAFTA to force Canada to harmonize and deregulate in exchange for limited market access. Gordon Ritchie admitted in his autobiography that this was a possibility: "The FTA," he wrote, "reaches into the very core of government regulation of our society. Mishandled, it can do great damage to our interests."

And what system would Canada be adopting? The Bush administration has gutted its forestry protection regime. In late 2004, the U.S. Forest Service rewrote the National Forest Management Act, which thirty years ago set standards for managing the nation's 190 million acres of forest. The Natural Resources Defense

Council says the changes will open up protected lands to industry to log, drill, mine, and build roads and will destroy old-growth habitat and wildlife. The new rules eliminate the environmental review process for forest-management plans and lock the public out of decision-making about these protected areas. In addition, the revised regulations eviscerate some of the nation's most effective wildlife protections, which required the Forest Service to ensure "viable populations" of endangered fish and animals. They also require "independent peer audits" conducted by timber companies.

## BUSH GUTS REGULATIONS

Forest regulations are not the only ones being gutted by the Bush administration. This process of environmental, health, and safety deregulation – now in full forward motion in Canada – has been a key feature of George W. Bush's government from the first day of his presidency. In fact, it started when he was governor of Texas and brought in the 1995 Texas Audit Privilege and Immunity Law and the 1999 Voluntary Emissions Reduction and Immunity Law. These laws allow companies to monitor their own pollution, report their violations to the government, and promise to clean up. There are no fines, no public disclosure, and no government follow-up.

The process at the federal level is located inside the Office of Information and Regulatory Affairs (OIRA), a branch of the White House Office of Management and Budget (OMB). Its mandate is to review every regulation proposed by any department of the federal government that might have an economic or trade impact, and report its findings to the White House. While the process of developing these rules and regulations may take years and has gone through a long and public process, once they reach the OMB, they often either disappear entirely or re-emerge radically watered down. This is because they have gone through a risk-cost-benefit analysis conducted by the man who almost single-handedly developed the concept.

One of George Bush's first acts in his first term was to put an old friend, John Graham, in charge of the Office of Information and Regulatory Affairs. John Graham was the founder and director of an industry-funded think-tank called the Harvard Center for Risk Analysis, where he developed the "science" of weighing the costs of a proposed new law against its benefits to society and devised complicated mathematical formulas for assessment. Here, he trained many students who are now called on regularly to prove a hazardous product is, in fact, safe and published a bimonthly journal, *Risk in Perspective*, featuring, for example, articles discounting the risks of children's exposure to pesticides or power-plant emissions. Since the costs of most new health, safety, food, and environmental regulations usually are charged to industry, big corporations flocked to John Graham's Harvard Center, and jumped to fund his new science. Corporate backers of the Center include Monsanto, Dow Chemical, DuPont, General Electric, Union Carbide, Boise Cascade, the American Petroleum Institute, and the American Chemistry Council. Graham is famous for a 1996 study that examined ninety environmental regulations and claimed that sixty thousand lives could be saved if the government abandoned them.

OMB Watch, an independent organization devoted to more transparent government, points out that Graham now sits in judgment on virtually every new rule affecting workplace and consumer safety, public health, food, medicine, education, and the environment. His input has contributed to the rejection or weakening of hundreds of public health and environmental regulations in his term. He also set up a corporate advisory committee to help him create a hit list of existing rules for "reform." His targets have included the EPA's plan to reduce arsenic in drinking water, the preservation of roadless wilderness, laws prohibiting snowmobiles in national parks, a ban on dumping radioactive waste in landfills, and rules controlling coal-burning power plants. And as Riverkeeper founder Robert F. Kennedy reports in his book *Crimes Against Nature*, after meeting with the National Pork Producers Council, the National Turkey Federation, Farmland Industries, and

the National Cattlemen's Beef Association, Graham instructed the
EPA to modify the provisions of the Clean Water Act so that the
toxic waste oozing from giant lagoons on factory farms is no longer
subject to the Act.

In March 2005, the OMB released a report that lists seventy-six
federal rules and regulations it wants revised to "reduce the
burden" on the manufacturing sector. Some of the new targets
include the definition of solid waste, inventories on toxic releases,
cleanup standards on polychlorinated biphenyls (PCBs), pre-
treatment for water dischargers, and methods for monitoring leaks
of volatile air pollutants at industrial plants. This action is in compliance with a new directive from the Department of Commerce
to boost domestic manufacturing by calling for departmental
studies on how environment, health, and food safety rules impede
industry. The White House issued its own hit list of 189 regulations.
They include rules that limit the number of hours a truck driver
can be behind the wheel without a rest, and regulations on the meat
industry introduced by President Clinton to fight outbreaks of the
deadly pathogen Listeria. This bacterium is particularly dangerous
to pregnant women, often resulting in miscarriages or babies with
developmental disabilities. But Clinton's new rules angered the big
food companies, who gave millions to the Bush–Cheney election
campaign. Their reward is yet another regulatory rollback.

The number of voluntary regulatory programs has doubled
under this president, according to the Natural Resources Defense
Council. The White House has also directed all federal agencies to
weigh the cost of regulation to industry before even submitting
them to the OMB, a move critics say will create an incentive to
develop industry-approved regulatory policies. In late 2004, the
EPA introduced new voluntary guidelines that will rely on industry to secure drinking water and waste-water treatment plants
against terrorist attack. The agency even funded industry to write
the guidelines.

And for the first time ever, science used by federal agencies to
support regulations must pass muster with nongovernmental "peer"

reviewers, says the White House. Specifically, the rules require "independent" review of government scientific findings if that research supports a policy of regulation that would cost the industry or state or local governments US$500 million or more to implement. Critics are concerned that the White House could easily use the peer reviews to slow or block the release of scientific information, thus holding up or weakening new federal regulations for safety, public health, and environmental protection.

As Robert Kennedy outlines in his book, for the peer reviews, George W. Bush is using a group of pseudo-scientists funded by corporate-backed think-tanks and front groups such as the Advancement of Sound Science Coalition, the American Enterprise Institute, the Heritage Institute (which has vowed "to strangle the environment movement"), and the American Council on Science and Health (which employs the so-called tobacco scientists who defend a range of dangerous industry practices). Among its media releases are "Evidence Lacking That PCB Levels Harm Health," "The Fuzzy Science Behind Clean Air Rules," and "At Christmas Dinner, Let Us Be Thankful for Pesticides and Safe Food."

John Graham is deeply involved with all of these groups and is a guru of the Wise Use movement, an anti-environmentalist group heavily influenced by Christian evangelicals such as Pat Robertson, who says environmentalists are the new communists, and Tom DeLay, who considers DDT "safe as aspirin." DeLay also says the Endangered Species Act is the greatest threat after illegal aliens. Wise Use founder Ron Arnold, who wrote the bible of the anti-environmentalist movement, *Undue Influence: Tracking the Environmental Movement's Money, Power, and Harm*, sums up the movement's objective: "Our goal is to destroy, to eradicate the environmental movement. We want you to be able to exploit the environment for private gain, absolutely."

What a friend he found in George W. Bush. In his 2006 budget, President Bush is cutting environmental programs another 10 per cent – by US$3.3 billion. Major targets include clean-water programs, the Superfund toxic-site remediation program, national parks, watershed rehabilitation, and forest conservation, all of which were hit to some extent in Bush's first term. He also announced a ten-year sunset clause on all environmental regulations: Congress would have to re-authorize them. Kennedy says that George W. Bush has launched over three hundred major rollbacks of U.S. environmental laws, and will go down as the worst president in the nation's history. The Bush team is convinced that the government and its laws are illegitimate, he says, and that illegitimacy makes it perfectly permissible to violate all the rules.

# too late
# to panic

*Energy and Water Are on the Table*

The Athabasca tar sands in Alberta constitute an immense reserve of oil, one of the last great deposits on the planet, but in a form that is devilishly hard to extract. The sands are made up of sand and bitumen, a tarlike mix of petroleum hydrocarbons that require intensive processing before they become finished petroleum products. Essentially, the extraction of oil from tar sands is more of a mining operation than conventional oil production. While conventional crude oil is either pumped from the ground or flows naturally, tar sands must be recovered in situ by open-pit mining. About two tons of tar sands must be dug up, moved, and processed to produce one barrel of oil. Currently, 2 million tons of tar sands are hauled away every day from the Athabasca tar sands. This output is set to double in the next five years and triple in a decade. There are at least three major environmental concerns with tar-sands mining: the enormous quantity of greenhouse-gas emissions produced by the operation; the destruction of vast quantities of water; and the destruction of forests, rivers, animal species, and habitat to make the whole production worthwhile financially.

It takes from five to ten times more energy, land, and water to mine, process, and upgrade tar-sands oil than it does to process conventional oil. In fact, it takes almost as much energy to produce tar-sands oil as the extracted oil generates. Not surprisingly, therefore, tar-sands mining produces two and a half times as many greenhouse gases as conventional oil production. The National Energy Board estimates that approximately 125 kilograms of carbon-dioxide equivalents are released for every barrel of synthetic crude oil that is produced from tar sands. The Sierra Club of Canada reports that, with production plans now underway, the Athabasca tar sands project will make the single largest contribution to Canada's greenhouse-gas emissions by 2010, producing seventy megatons – 12 per cent of Canada's Kyoto target – for that year. Development of the tar sands could very well make it impossible for Canada to fulfill its Kyoto commitments.

Even more troubling is the destruction of freshwater sources for the mining of tar sands. Alberta's oil industry is currently licensed to use 26 per cent of the province's groundwater. Every year about 45 billion gallons of ancient aquifer water is injected into conventional wells where it remains after it has forced the oil out. Unlike the water used for irrigation, livestock, or other agricultural purposes, this water is lost from the hydrologic cycle. Another 60 billion gallons is allocated for oil-sands recovery. It takes three barrels of water (35 gallons) to produce one barrel of oil from the tar sands, and of those three barrels of water, one is lost forever. It takes another forty-four barrels of water to further refine the oil into other by-products. Many scientists believe that the strain on the province's water is already too great. The University of Alberta's Dr. David Schindler warns that the Athabasca River is already in danger because of the demands being made on it. But the projected mammoth growth in the tar sands is going to dramatically increase the demand. And so far, every drop of this water is free to the industry.

Third, there is the exponential destruction of wilderness, lakes and rivers, forest wildlife, and habitat. It is hard to describe the size of the tar-sands project in a way that conveys its overwhelming scale. The environmental impact of the exploitation of the tar sands is unprecedented, Myles Kitigawa of the Toxics Watch Society told writer Don Gillmor ("Shifting Sands," *The Walrus*, April 2005). While some individual elements are monitored, no one is assessing the overall cumulative effect of the operation. "It adds up to more than we've ever seen in one place."

Perhaps no other project reflects more graphically the cost to Canada of the failure of successive governments to protect energy and water resources. There will be no let-up in the pressure to exploit these resources in the years to come.

## AMERICA'S GAS TANK

The United States is running out of energy.

Its growing oil shortfall has been widely reported and its gas reserves are diminishing quickly. Natural-gas supplies in the lower forty-eight states are virtually gone and the United States hasn't built a single new oil refinery since 1976. The Bush administration is eager to reduce its dependence on Middle East energy supplies and secure its needs with less troubled and more reliable "economies." Recently, Canada replaced Saudi Arabia as the major energy supplier to the United States and the Bush administration wants to cement favoured and easy access to these supplies. The United States has long considered them to be "North American," not Canadian, and 9/11 hardened this view.

As Sierra Club of Canada's Elizabeth May says, "The U.S. Administration has an energy plan. Canada has none. The U.S. Administration's energy plan is all about boosting the supply of cheap energy. Canada is, de facto, part of the expansionist energy planning of Bush and Cheney. In a real sense, Canada is becoming 'America's gas tank.'"

In its North American Security and Prosperity Initiative, the Canadian Council of Chief Executives calls for a "Comprehensive Resource Security Pact," highlighting energy, based on the core principles of open markets and the compatibility of regulatory frameworks. The Task Force on the Future of North America echoes this recommendation, calling for a North American Energy Strategy within a larger North American Resource Strategy. So do George Bush, Paul Martin, and Vicente Fox in their North American Security and Prosperity Partnership signed at the summit in Waco, Texas. There, they promised to "strengthen and update energy regulation" and "strengthen the North American energy market." In their June 2005 "Report to the Leaders," on the regulatory convergence action plan, senior ministers from the three countries reported that they are "taking action to create a policy environment that will promote the sustainable supply of energy in North America," and added that the plan will include "joint cooperation in the areas of regulation, oil sands production, and nuclear energy."

A month after the terrorist attacks, then U.S. ambassador to Canada Paul Cellucci said that an integrated North American energy market is vital to U.S. security interests. "There is a much more focused approach to energy than before September 11," he told an industry meeting in Toronto. He also pointed to the need for Canada and the United States to streamline their approvals process to get the energy where it is needed quickly. "Our two federal governments have to do a better job of permitting these projects – pipelines and other transmission projects. We have to have a sense of priority about this" (*Globe and Mail*, October 31, 2001). At that time, the Bush administration set up a special task force on energy security headed by Vice President Dick Cheney. Testifying before Congress in 2002, Cheney declared that the "continued development" of the Athabasca tar sands in northern Alberta could be a "pillar of sustained North American energy and economic security."

## DESPERATELY SEEKING OIL SOURCES

The United States has just 5 per cent of the world's population, but it uses 25 per cent of the world's energy. Americans burn 20 million barrels of oil every day (two-thirds of it in their ever-bigger vehicles) but Vice President Dick Cheney told the London Institute of Petroleum back in 1999 that by 2010, the United States will need an additional 50 million barrels a day, largely to fuel its escalating military operations. Oklahoma senator Don Nickles said, "We look at ways to improve our national security since September 11. We cannot have national security without energy security. The two go hand in hand." Along with the rest of the world, the United States is facing a coming energy crisis. Its huge and growing appetite for oil faces two deeply troubling realities: many of the nation's traditional suppliers are politically unstable or no longer dependable, and the world is running out of oil just as global demand is skyrocketing.

Since 1965, demand for oil has increased 150 per cent worldwide. While estimates vary, there is growing consensus in the scientific community that the oil supply has either recently peaked or will peak within the next ten years. Even the most optimistic predictions by the industry are measured in decades. As predicted by senior Shell scientist Dr. M. King Hubbert in the 1950s, oil production reached its highest level in the 1970s and has been declining ever since. The respected British Oil Depletion Analysis Centre, a non-profit think-tank run by scientists, says that there will be an "unbridgeable supply/demand gap" opening up after 2007. Petroleum geologist Colin Campbell, a senior analyst at the Association for the Study of Peak Oil and Gas, another British research institute, supports this prediction. Mark Anielski, economist and adjunct professor of Corporate Social Responsibility and Social Entrepreneurship at the University of Alberta, reports that the United Kingdom and Norway experienced peak oil in 1999 and 2001 respectively, and Saudi Arabia, once thought to have endless supplies, will peak in 2008, followed by Kuwait in 2015 and Iraq in 2017. Because conventional land supplies are drying up, more than a quarter of the world's drilling rigs are now located under lakes, in the oceans, or in tar-sands deposits. This crisis helps explain why the price of crude has risen from US$10 a barrel just seven years ago to breaking the US$70 mark in 2005. Many industry analysts say the price could double again in the next few years.

At the same time, China and India have both entered the international market as competitive buyers. China's oil consumption has nearly quadrupled since 1980. It is now at 5.7 billion barrels a day and is expected to double again by 2025, reports the *Globe and Mail* in its May 2005 series on oil. Until recently a net exporter, China is now the world's second-biggest petroleum consumer and a net importer of oil. Within fifteen years China is predicted to have as many as 140 million private cars on its roads, up from 24 million today. As well, natural-gas supplies are also depleting. Matt Simmons, a Houston-based investment banker and adviser to the Bush administration on energy policy, notes that 65 per cent of the world's gas supply is in decline and experts are not even sure of the rate at which the decline is accelerating.

## FULL ACCESS, GUARANTEED

To deal with these impending crises, the United States is looking more and more to Canada for secured energy supplies. The United States has long considered Canada's energy to be its own and a key component of American economic and military security. In 1985, a joint congressional report called Canada's then regulatory control over natural gas a "direct restriction of American rights to Canadian gas" and called for the government to make guaranteed access to Canadian supplies a point of national security. Guaranteed access to Canada's energy was a central objective for the United States in both the Canada–U.S. Free Trade Agreement and NAFTA. Ann Hughes, the ranking U.S. Department of Commerce trade negotiator, was forthright about her country's wasteful energy habits, and admitted that Canada's energy, secured by the free-trade deal, would allow the United States to forestall conservation practices. Edward Ney, then U.S. ambassador to Canada, said that Canada's energy reserves were the prime motivation on the American side for the first free-trade agreement. The Reagan administration had a friend in Prime Minister Mulroney, who told an American business audience in 1984 that the practice of maintaining emergency energy provisions for Canada was "odious," and declared that Canada had not been built by expropriating "other people's property." He promised the audience full access to Canada's energy supplies.

Good to his word, Mulroney deregulated oil-and-gas exports and dismantled most restrictions on American foreign investment in the energy industry, opening the way for an ever smaller and more powerful group of transnational corporations to take over the energy patch. The trade agreements exempted Canadian government subsidies for oil-and-gas exploration from trade challenge, ensuring that Canadian public funds would continue to pay for uncontrolled and environmentally destructive fossil-fuel exploration. Such exploration has already destroyed habitats in the North and threatened sensitive spawning grounds in Cape Breton and Newfoundland. The National Energy Board was stripped of its powers, and the "vital-supply safeguard," which had required the government to maintain a twenty-five-year surplus of natural gas, was dismantled. The only power left to the National Energy Board to protect the public interest is that natural gas or oil exports are not to be approved unless the oil or gas involved is surplus to "reasonably foreseeable requirements for use in Canada." However, the big American energy companies get around even this provision by having their access renewed automatically by the NEB – they skip the process of applying for a new licence. The Energy Board has been going along with this.

Following the signing of the free-trade agreements and the changes to Canadian law that the Mulroney government passed in order to comply with them, export applicants, either Canadian or American, were no longer required to file an export-impact assessment and the all-Canadian gas distribution system was abandoned. This set off a frantic round of North-South pipeline construction. Export taxes on energy supplies were banned. And, most important, Canada agreed to a "proportional sharing" provision according to which Canadian energy supplies to the United States are guaranteed in perpetuity. In an astonishing surrender of sovereignty, the government of Canada agreed that it no longer has the right "to refuse to issue a licence or revoke or change a licence for the exportation to the United States of energy goods," even for environmental or conservation considerations. This led to a spectacular increase in the sale of oil and natural gas to the United States, because with its large market, the distribution companies were able to negotiate long-term contracts at much lower prices than their Canadian counterparts. This left Canadian consumers to compete for their own rapidly diminishing supplies against an economy ten times bigger.

As a result of proportional sharing, 65 per cent of Canada's oil and 61 per cent of its natural gas is now exported to the United States – up from 33 per cent and 25 per cent respectively in 1985. But Canada is not producing enough oil to maintain these levels of exports to the United States. Canada's conventional oil production peaked in 1973, and its gas production peaked in 2001. In order to fulfill its NAFTA commitments to the United States, Canada is now importing almost half the oil it uses, even though its production has grown by 64 per cent since the FTA was signed. It is at the break-even stage on gas, just able to maintain its own needs after fulfilling its export quotas to the United States. But as demand for natural gas rises in the United States, Canada may well end up having to import gas as well. In other words, the States now has first call on Canada's energy, even if Canada is running short.

These massive exports have set back Canada's economic strategy by decades. "As of 2004," economist Jim Stanford wrote in the *Globe and Mail* (December 6, 2004), "Canada is once again officially a hewer of wood and drawer of water for the global marketplace. Well over half of our total merchandise exports this year consist of natural resources, especially oil and gas, and bulk commodities like nickel and aluminium. Less than half consist of higher-value products." U.S. ownership in the oil patch is creeping up again. The *Toronto Star* (January 22, 2005) quotes an Investment Canada official who says the agency has not turned down one single foreign investment in the energy sector since 1985. By 2003, over half of Canada's oil-and-gas production was controlled by foreign companies, mostly American, and some analysts predict that foreign ownership in the Athabasca tar sands will reach 60 per cent by 2010.

But somehow this is not enough. The United States is seeking more access and Canada's big-business community is calling for a new North American Energy Strategy. One is left to wonder what the real agenda is when Canada has abandoned its control over its energy supplies, conceding that they are now North American and subject to no control but the market. In essence, Canada's energy policy is set in Houston and Washington. What more do the Bush administration and the big-business community want?

## SANDS STORMS

There are two possible explanations. The first is China and its desire to get its hands on the Athabasca tar sands, the largest hydrocarbon deposit in the world. The Athabasca tar sands is seventy-seven thousand square kilometres – roughly the size of New Brunswick – and holds 2.5 trillion barrels of oil, enough to pave a four-lane superhighway the entire four hundred thousand kilometres to the moon, complete with off-ramps. About 311 billion of this is "recoverable" with today's technology, but money is being poured into research to advance technological capacity. Already, China has signed a $2.5-billion deal with Enbridge and bought a one-sixth share in Calgary-based MEG Energy Corp. It has also bought a 40 per cent stake in Synenco Energy Inc.'s planned bitumen-mining operation for $105 million, but that will lead to a $2-billion outlay once construction begins on its project. This is just the beginning, say analysts. The state-owned Chinese National Offshore Oil Corp. (CNOOC) relentlessly pursued a counter-bid for Unocal against Chevron until it was forced to withdraw its bid in early August 2005 under intense opposition from Washington.

Another Chinese oil company, Sinopec, is considering a bid on Husky Oil, which is controlled by Hong Kong billionaire Li Ka-shing, who in turn owns oil-sands leases.

Mark Anielski told Don Gillmor ("Shifting Sands," *The Walrus*, April 2005), "China will eclipse the U.S. consumption in twenty years or less. And there's not enough oil to feed two superpowers." In its June 6, 2005, edition, *Time* magazine says that American competitors fear that China will warp the market. Because most Chinese oil companies are state-owned, they will accept a lower rate of return. But *Time* points out that there is more to this situation than money. "Power and geopolitical influence are oil's handmaidens." Securing sources at whatever cost may be the overarching motivation for this emerging and suddenly fierce scramble for energy. Gillmor, in his article in *The Walrus*, writes that China's presence in Alberta has created a growing uneasiness in the United States. He quotes a December 2004 *New York Times* story entitled "China is emerging as a rival to U.S. for oil in Canada," which said that China's thirst for oil has brought it to "America's doorstep." He notes that Paul Cellucci said it was the first time in more than four years that the word Canada had appeared above the fold in the *New York Times*. Keng Chung of the Alberta Energy Research Institute told Gillmor, "The biggest concern for the Chinese in the oil sands is the Americans. And the biggest concern for the Americans is the Chinese."

This is where things get tricky for the Canadian government. Prime Minister Martin told the *Toronto Star* during his January 2005 Beijing trade promotion trip that the ownership of an energy company investing in Canada is a "valid consideration" for the Canadian government. Industry Minister David Emerson backed this up, saying, with breathtaking naïveté in light of NAFTA, that the government thinks it should be concerned about who owns Canadian resources. "We have to be thinking about the overall position of our natural resources and the degree to which we want to lose control of our natural resource base." Alberta reacted at once, citing past energy wars with Ottawa. Alberta would welcome a bidding war between the two superpowers and analysts warn that the Klein government would go "ballistic" if Ottawa interfered in any way.

However, Washington analysts are already warning that the Bush administration might not look kindly on a Canada that allows too much involvement by China in the tar sands. The failed CNOOC bid is a good example that Washington is prepared to play hardball. In early July 2005, the U.S. House of Representatives voted over-whelmingly – 398 to 15 – to oppose the proposed takeover of Unocal on the basis that a successful takeover would "threaten to impair the national security of the United States." Several promi-nent politicians warned a House of Representatives Armed Services Committee hearing into the CNOOC bid that China is waging a stealth campaign to lock up the tar sands. "They are hunting around the world for reserves of oil, gas, tar sands and other energy-related assets to acquire," said Richard D'Amato, chairman of the U.S.– China Economic and Security Review Commission. "Their goal is to acquire and keep energy reserves around the world and secure delivery to China above and beyond any market considerations." (*Globe and Mail*, July 14, 2005) The Senate has also expressed con-cerns. On July 13, 2005, Finance Committee chairman Charles Grassley – a Republican – and Senator Max Baucus – a Democrat – wrote President Bush saying that the CNOOC bid raised a key question as to whether it was appropriate for state-owned enter-prises to subsidize investment transactions to acquire scarce natural resources needed in the United States. That same week, a *Wall Street Journal*/NBC poll found that 73 per cent of Americans disliked the potential deal, which forced the Bush administration to take sterner measures to block this and other energy grabs by China. CNOOC cited "implacable opposition" and "hostile reaction" from the American Congress as its reason for dropping its bid for Unocal and said in its news release, "The unprecedented political opposition that followed the announcement of our proposed transactions was regrettable and unjustified."

Duncan Hunter, the Armed Services Committee chair, called on the Bush administration to pressure Canada to review Chinese investments in the tar sands: "China is building a military that at some point will be formidable," he said (*Wall Street Journal*, July 14, 2005). James Woolsey, former CIA director, added, "I would hope that some American diplomat or other part of the U.S. government is expressing these sorts of concerns to Canada." Republican congressman Richard Pombo, chairman of the House Committee on Resources, called for the U.S. Department of Energy to launch a separate investigation. Referring to a bid by another Chinese company to take over the appliance manufacturing company Maytag, which does not concern him, Pombo said, "We don't go to war over washing machines. But energy is another matter." (*Time* magazine, July 4, 2005).

One suggestion is for the United States to guarantee a fixed price for the tar-sands oil in return for unrestricted and guaranteed access. In what appeared to many observers as less than a coincidence, the Canadian government tabled C-59, in late June 2005, legislation that would give it the authority to review and block foreign investment on grounds of national security. The move stirred up a "maelstrom of controversy" said the *Globe and Mail* (July 15, 2005), because it is seen by many as a potential tool to ward off Chinese investments in the tar sands in order to protect U.S. national security interests, a charge Industry Minister David Emerson denied. But observers from different sides of this issue will be watching closely to see how the bill is used. Meanwhile the big-business community is working hard to secure the tar sands for the Americans. It will be particularly interesting to watch Thomas d'Aquino and his pro–free-trade, pro–free-markets, pro-competition big-business lobby group explain its support of what will be essentially an American monopoly in the tar sands if its energy pact with the United States comes to pass.

## BARRIER-FREE ACCESS

The second explanation for the emphasis on a North American energy pact or strategy is the desire for further deregulation. While regulations affecting the export of natural gas and conventional oil to the United States have by and large been eliminated, there are still environmental rules in place for the development of new sources. These rules could have a bearing on the development of new mining sites in the tar sands and for building the proposed Mackenzie Valley pipeline. The pipeline would bring natural gas twelve hundred kilometres from the far Northwest through fragile watersheds to provide the energy for the mining operations. Environmental assessments are required to proceed before the pipeline is built, for instance, and fourteen different federal, provincial, territorial, and First Nations governments jointly share the responsibility. While many environmentalists feel that the process is badly flawed and that the energy and construction companies are essentially running the show, there are nevertheless rules and procedures in place to slow down production. The Mackenzie Valley pipeline has been stalled for several years by wrangling over land-claims settlements and under fierce opposition from environmental and some community groups.

Canada has also signed the Kyoto Protocol to reduce greenhouse-gas emissions and the United States has not. American politicians and energy companies do not want to be subject to Canada's commitment to curb greenhouse-gas emissions, especially as they move to take control of what may become the single largest source of greenhouse-gas pollution in North America.

The government of Canada is already hard at work on energy regulatory harmonization. In a 2003 internal memo leaked to the *Toronto Star*, Department of Foreign Affairs and International Trade officials wrote that 9/11 created a "unique opportunity" to expand NAFTA, and listed among the department's priorities the need to "examine and address the regulatory environment for trade in oil, gas, and electricity to eliminate all impediments to North American energy security" and "expedite a review of energy infrastructure, including pipeline capacity." A North American Energy Working Group was established in 2001 to examine, among other items, "regulatory barriers" to North American energy production. But the Task Force on the Future of North America lamented that it has seen only "modest progress," so in June 2005, the governments established a "Regulator's Expert Group" to speed up regulatory harmonization. In its report, the Task Force itself zeroed in on the "vast oil sands" – avoiding the messy image conjured by the word "tar" – and targeted "regulatory approval processes that can slow down both resource and infrastructure development significantly."

The Energy Council of Canada, a government-industry group that proposes policy around energy issues, has unveiled an "Energy Framework for Canada" to provide input into the Council of Energy Ministers in their upcoming meetings. Speaking at the May 30, 2005, Executive Energy Forum in Kananaskis, Alberta, Energy Minister Greg Melchin said that governments and industry in Canada and the United States must work together to quickly develop improved coordination of regulation and a reduction in overlap between different jurisdictions relating to the Mackenzie Valley pipeline and the Alaska-Canada pipeline based on the Smart Regulation initiative. And there is, of course, the new "Framework" being put into place at Environment Canada, whereby the government is preparing to negotiate separate voluntary environmental and regulatory codes with companies and industry sectors, including energy companies.

## TAKE OIL YOU WANT

Intensive deregulation of environmental rules has been a cornerstone policy of the Bush administration since the beginning of his first presidency. George W. Bush brought the same group of big energy company backers who put him in power in Texas with him to the White House. Thirty-one of his transition team's forty-eight members came from the energy industry, and his cabinet and White House staff is an impressive list of former industry officials. No industry has made more money from the deregulation agenda of this administration than the big energy companies. Just days after his inauguration, George Bush launched the National Energy Policy Development Group, chaired by Dick Cheney, to analyze America's energy needs and prepare legislation that eventually became the controversial Energy Bill. This bill was still winding its way through the House and Senate in the summer of 2005.

Robert Kennedy, Jr., in *Crimes Against Nature*, tells the sordid story of how Cheney and Energy Secretary Spencer Abraham packed the Group with cronies from the industry and met in secret for three months to prepare their May 17, 2001, report to the president. Kennedy calls the report "an orgy of industry plunder, transferring billions of dollars of public wealth to the oil, coal, and nuclear industries, already swimming in record revenues." Using the looming national-energy crisis as the backdrop, the report focused almost exclusively on three areas: deregulation, giant subsidies, and corporate tax breaks. To lobby for congressional passage of the plan, more than four hundred industry groups enlisted in the Alliance for Energy and Economic Growth, a coalition created by oil, mining, and nuclear companies. The prerequisite for joining, said the official fundraising letter, was that the company had to agree with and support the Bush–Cheney energy program in its entirety and not lobby for changes. All through the winter and spring of 2001, reports Kennedy, executives from the American Gas Association, the American Petroleum Institute, the National Mining Association, and the Nuclear Energy Institute tramped in and out of the cabinet rooms and Cheney's office. The group got total buy-in from the president for the plan and didn't want to wait for a full-fledged energy bill. So the carnage began right away.

The American Petroleum Institute wanted the United States to pull out of the Kyoto negotiations and got their wish. It also wanted an executive order to weaken environmental regulations, so in May 2001, Bush issued an executive order requiring reviews in all relevant agencies to ensure that regulations were not inhibiting energy supply and distribution. The oil companies petitioned for expanded oil-and-gas exploration and production on federal lands. They got that too. For the hydro-electricity industry, Bush brought in new rules to allow power plants to avoid limits on carbon dioxide and exempted fifteen hundred old plants from the Clean Air Act. The Nuclear Energy Institute wanted a loosening of environmental controls, reduced public access to decision-making, and billions of additional dollars in subsidies. It got them. The Bush administration refused to renew tax deductions to encourage fuel-efficient cars, but created a US$100,000 tax break for Hummers and the thirty-eight other biggest gas-guzzlers. On August 27, 2002, the administration announced that it would redefine air pollution so that carbon dioxide, the primary cause of global warming, would no longer be subject to the Clean Air Act.

In August 2003, the government introduced a proposal to limit the authority of states to object to offshore drilling and ordered federal land managers across the West to ease environmental restrictions for oil-and-gas drilling in national forests. And it gutted the Superfund program, which cleans up massive toxic sites, by cancelling the tax on forty-three hazardous chemicals and another on crude oil that funded it. By the end of George W. Bush's first term in office, says Kennedy, the body of environmental law that had been carefully constructed over the last three decades had become a virtual piñata for energy moguls, delivering new gifts at every blow. One Congressman – Republican Christopher Shays of Connecticut – told Kennedy that it was as if the Bush administration actually wanted to alienate people who care about the environment in order to send a message to core Republican supporters – anti-government, anti-tax conservatives, and evangelical End-Timers.

The full Energy Bill, finally passed on August 8, 2005, gives further huge tax breaks and subsidies to energy companies. It facilitates the building of oil refineries on old military bases, removing a number of restrictions and environmental regulations that previously regulated the practice. The new bill eliminates many of the rules and restrictions on nuclear-energy facilities. It exempts many federal energy projects from the National Environmental Policy Act. This means that many oil-and-gas projects will no longer be analyzed for their environmental impact, they will be closed to public comment, and there will be no environmental studies of water discharged from wells used in methane-gas production. The Energy Bill also paved the way for drilling in Alaska's Arctic National Wildlife Refuge. The Bush administration hopes to earn over US$5 billion in royalties from drilling in this pristine wilderness, one of the few left in the United States. On March 16, 2005, the day the Senate agreed to allow drilling in the Refuge to be added to the Energy Bill, John Bennett of the Sierra Club of Canada said it was "a sad day for the planet."

## TURNING GOLD INTO LEAD

Between Smart Regulation, the potential evisceration of Environment Canada's regulatory oversight, and regulatory harmonization with the United States, the business practices introduced with the Bush–Cheney Energy Bill are very likely to become the norm in the Athabasca tar sands unless Canadians say no. After all, most of the major players in the American Petroleum Institute who so successfully promoted energy deregulation in the United States are operating in the tar sands now. These include ExxonMobil, ConocoPhillips, Shell, and ChevronTexaco, who, along with BP, make up the five most powerful energy companies operating in the United States, according to Public Citizen. The stakes are incredibly high for these companies. Between them, they earned more than US$60 billion in after-tax profits in 2004. Over the last three decades, US$34 billion has been spent to get the tar sands operating. More than eighty massive new projects worth US$87 billion over the next decade are in the works, making the tar sands a capital spending spree unprecedented in modern Canada (*Globe and Mail*, April 4, 2005). The tens of billions being spent there would pay for the Terminal 1 expansion at Toronto's Pearson International Airport twenty-four times over, according to the *Globe and Mail*, making Fort McMurray "home to one of the greatest concentrations of investment on the planet."

The damage to the environment that will result from the exploitation of the tar sands is staggering. In "America's Gas Tank: The High Cost of Canada's Oil and Gas Export Strategy," the Sierra Club of Canada and the United States–based Natural Resources Defense Council sum up the cost already exacted: "Oil and gas exploitation has had a disastrous effect on Canadian wilderness areas. In their search for oil and gas deposits, companies cut paths through the forest along which they plant dynamite charges. These paths are called 'seismic' lines, and thousands of kilometres of them are cut each year, typically with bulldozers. The sound waves from the exploded dynamite charges are measured to find out whether oil or gas is present underground. After exploration comes construction of roads and well sites, followed by pipelines, all causing further environmental harm. All told, oil and gas exploration destroys and degrades habitat for such rare and endangered species as grizzly bears and woodland caribou and brings further industrialization by human settlement and loggers." One study found that where the lines crossed streams, just half the crossings were constructed properly. Northern Alberta is pockmarked with thousands and thousands of wells, some in production, many abandoned. The result of all this activity is that less than 9 per cent of Canada's boreal forest can still be called wilderness.

Of equal concern is the $7-billion plan by a consortium of energy companies, including Imperial Oil, Shell Canada, Conoco-Phillips, and ExxonMobil, to take massive amounts of natural gas from the ecologically pristine Mackenzie Delta of the Northwest Territories and ship it twelve hundred kilometres, much of it through permafrost, to provide the energy for the Athabasca tar-sands operation. The Mackenzie Valley Pipeline Group plans to develop three major gas fields in the western Arctic and then build a series of pipelines to carry the gas to the TransCanada Pipeline, which will carry it to northern Alberta. Critics warn that a pipeline would encourage the kind of exploration in the Northwest Territories that has taken place in northern Alberta, spurring aggressive energy development that will endanger the environment of Canada's last wild frontier. The Canadian Arctic Resources Committee predicts that several hundred new wells will be drilled in the area if the pipeline is built.

The Mackenzie Valley is an important calving ground for beluga whales and the nesting habitat for thousands of birds. The pipeline project would destroy forests and wetlands, damage permafrost, and prejudice the creation of protected areas, asserts the Mackenzie Wild Declaration – a project of Sierra Club of Canada to protect the area. Forests would be clear-cut and heavy machinery deployed to build the infrastructure. The new underground pipelines would tunnel under or cross 580 rivers and streams along the way. And while some First Nations groups have agreed to the project in exchange for economic benefits, others are resisting, citing studies that show that the only benefits will come in the construction phase of the project. Very little of the $50-billion-plus of natural gas that is expected to flow from the Mackenzie Delta will stay in the North.

A final concern is both environmental and political. Canada is running out of natural gas. At current production volumes and with remaining gas reserves, Canada has less than ten years of natural-gas production remaining. Yet recent analyses show that at the rate the tar sands are being developed it will probably need to claim all of the gas from the Delta. So Canada would concede one of the few remaining major untapped gas sources to supply oil to a super-power that refuses to implement conservation measures while allowing Canadians to go without.

Alberta environmental writer Andrew Nikiforuk argues that using the Mackenzie gas fields to make oil from the tar sands is akin to turning gold into lead (*Business Week*, January 17–30, 2005). The highest-value uses for natural gas are home heating, fertilizer production, and petrochemical manufacturing. Given Canada's rapidly depleting gas reserves, politicians will have to decide whether the reserves will be used to keep Canadians warm, exported for electrical generation to keep Americans cool, or burned to cook up bitumen. "Yet no federal or provincial government ever stopped to question the logic of rapidly disposing of a declining non-renewable resource at mostly rock-bottom prices," writes Nikiforuk. In his book *High Noon for Natural Gas*, British environmentalist Julian Darley says the situation is so grave "it is too late to panic. It is time to plan." If Canadian politicians were sensible, he told Nikiforuk, they would recognize that Canada is a cold country. They would cut production and exports and work out depletion rates.

Instead, Canada is planning to plunder the Mackenzie Delta and use its supplies to fulfill its NAFTA obligation to provide oil to the United States, even though doing this will leave Canadians short. To add insult to injury, the Canadian taxpayer is footing a large part of the bill to make this happen. Public subsidies to the tar sands include low royalty rates, publicly funded research and development, tax breaks through the use of Income Energy Trusts, non-taxing of fuel used in vehicles for exploration, income-tax depletion allowance, generous water licences for use without metering, the building of massive infrastructure, including roads, power corridors, and railways, and direct grants. The Canadian government provided $60 million in research and development funding for the tar sands between 1996 and 2002. The Pembina Institute reports that Canadian oil companies receive about $1.4 billion in government subsidies a year.

The Sierra Club of Canada adds that these subsidies, grants, and tax breaks often favour the worst kind of projects. In the tar sands, royalties are reduced from 25 per cent to 1 per cent until the company recovers its capital costs. As a result, while tar sands production increased by 74 per cent between 1997 and 2002, royalties to the citizens of Alberta, who technically own the tar sands, decreased by 30 per cent. Companies pay no federal income tax until the tar-sands project has written off its capital costs. The energy companies get around repaying these royalties and taxes by simply expanding their operations, thus making them available for the breaks all over again.

This is energy policy on the fly. Canadians will soon be competing for energy on world markets, having lost total control of depleting domestic supplies, while destroying the environment in the bargain. And make no mistake, that is the plan behind the North American energy strategy of George Bush, the big energy companies, and the Canadian Council of Chief Executives. Already-deregulated tar sands, increasingly controlled by American energy companies, will lock in Texas-style self-regulation, all to serve American military domination of the world. And that's just fine with former Reform Party leader Preston Manning. In a November 26, 2004, editorial in the *Calgary Herald*, he writes that since the U.S. military commitment to the Middle East is now "astronomical," Canada must accelerate exploitation of Northern gas and the tar sands in order to provide even lower cost continental energy to the Americans. Vancouver youth activist and writer Macdonald Stainsby sees it differently. He writes that the never conquered land of the Inuit and Dene Nations is about to be sacrificed for the worst possible reason: "The rush to destroy the land of these nations should be seen as a Canadian front in what Dick Cheney told us is war 'that will last beyond our lifetimes.'" (*Znet*, November 3, 2004)

## AMERICA IS GETTING THIRSTY

Energy is not the only Canadian resource the Bush administration has its eye on. Canadians know about the energy shortages in the United States. Less well known is that parts of the United States are also running out of water. Americans now depend on ground-water for more than 50 per cent of their water supplies and are mining it far faster than nature can replenish it. California's aquifers are drying up. The Colorado River is strained to the limit, no longer reaching the sea. The water table under the San Joaquin Valley has dropped nearly ten metres in some places in the last fifty years. Overuse of underground water supplies in the Central Valley has also resulted in a loss of more than 40 per cent of the combined storage capacity of all human-made surface reservoirs in the state.

California's Department of Water Resources predicts that, if more supplies are not found, by 2020 the state will face a shortfall of fresh water nearly as great as the amount that all of its towns and cities combined are consuming today.

Another huge concern is the Ogallala Aquifer, the largest single water-bearing unit in North America, which is being mined far beyond its capacity. Made of ancient fossil water and stretching from the Texas Panhandle to South Dakota, it is believed to contain 20 per cent more water than Lake Huron. But there are more than two hundred thousand bore wells draining the Ogallala every day, all day, to provide water to irrigate one-fifth of all the irrigated lands in the United States, much of it water-intensive, large-scale High Plains farming on arid soil. At a withdrawal rate of 50 million litres a minute, water is being depleted fourteen times faster than it can be replenished by nature. Some estimate that it is more than half depleted now, and the current drought in the American Mid- and Southwest (which many scientists say is not a drought at all but a permanent water shortage) is putting more demand on the aquifer. Human and industrial growth in the desert areas of the Southwest are exploding. Municipal development in Phoenix, Arizona, for instance, is occurring at a rate of an acre every hour. Arizona has run out of water and is now importing it from other states. New Mexico has only a ten-year supply left.

The U.S. government is ill-prepared to confront increasingly severe water shortages across the country, warned a June 2004 study by the National Academies of Science and the U.S. Geological Survey. The parched Interior West is probably the driest it has been in five hundred years, said the scientists, and the water level of the Colorado River had the lowest flow on record. Committee chair Henry Vaux, a resource expert with the University of California at Berkeley, warned, "water crises are not confined to western states." He cited as an example the recent conflict between Maryland and Virginia over Potomac River rights that had to be settled by the Supreme Court.

In Florida, the EPA reports, reservoirs below and above-ground are badly depleted and becoming briny with saltwater seepage. In 2003, during one of the worst droughts in Florida's history, the state government finally admitted it needs a plan to deal with a burgeoning population, high demand, and declining water resources. More than half of Kentucky's 120 counties ran short of water or were near shortages in 2004. Washington, Oregon, and Idaho are also experiencing a warming trend that could cause a major shortage in their water supply. Many of their communities depend on the storage of snow packs for their water, but snow packs are among the victims of global warming. Southern Illinois University published a major new report on May 30, 2005, warning that the Chicago area's thirst for water will escalate a whopping 30 per cent over the next twenty years, exerting pressure for big increases in withdrawals from Lake Michigan. Ben Dziegielewski, lead author of the report, says that by 2025, thermoelectric power plants will suck up as much as 85 per cent of the state's water, forcing the population to turn to the Great Lakes for daily water use. An earlier report by a regional planning commission stunned people in the Chicago area when it said that parts of six counties were facing serious water shortages in twenty years.

Consecutive U.S. governments have done nothing to address this problem. The National Academies of Science reports that overall federal funding for water research has been stagnant in real terms for the past thirty years, and the portion dedicated to research on water use and water quality has declined. Many American waterways are already deeply polluted, adding to the problem of scarcity. Massive amounts of chemical fertilizers, nitrates, and toxins find their way into lakes, rivers, wetlands, and groundwater sources. The U.S.–Mexico border, thick with industrial and human waste, has been called a "3,400 kilometre Love Canal." The runoff from industrial farming in the American Midwest is so great that it has created an eighteen-thousand-square-kilometre "dead zone" in the Gulf of Mexico, where no life can survive. The Sierra Club says,

"We have crashing ecosystems in every river basin in the West." And, true to form, the Bush administration has undone many of the previously established protections of America's drinking water supplies. The Energy Bill contains provisions to weaken the Clean Water Act by exempting a toxic cocktail of chemicals used in oil-and-gas drilling, and a liability waiver for the manufacturers of MTBE, a methanol-based gasoline additive that can contaminate a mid-sized aquifer with just a few drops.

## NO ONE IS MINDING THE STORE

There are several possible explanations for the apparently wilful ignorance on the part of Washington politicians toward their country's looming water crisis. Like many industrial countries, the United States has assumed that whatever gets broken can be fixed by technology. And, in fairness, water shortages have been perceived as cyclical droughts and only recently have scientists sounded the alarm. For the Bush team, there is the additional antipathy to anything "environmental" felt by small-government conservatives and the evangelical right, many of whom consider fouled air and water to be a welcome sign that Armageddon is near. There is also a pervasive notion that Canada has untold reserves and that, when the time comes, the United States will, in the words of writer Robert Kaplan (*Atlantic Monthly*, July 1998), simply look to the "wet, green sponge to the North."

Speaking to a group of journalists only six months into his first term, George Bush acknowledged that he is deeply concerned about meeting the water needs of his home state, where "water is more valuable than oil," and that he "looked forward" to discussing the issue with then prime minister Jean Chrétien. He added, "A lot of people don't need it, but when you head south and west, we need it . . . some have suggested abandoned pipelines that used to carry energy. That's a possibility. I would be open to any discussions."

Why ever wouldn't the United States think it could help itself to Canada's water? There is no body of law in place to protect it. No one is minding the store. If one goes to the official Environment Canada website and punches in "Federal Water Policy" (as of July 2005), one will find the "latest" proposal for a national water policy of the federal government, complete with Tory-blue background, a photo of Environment Minister Tom McMillan (Mulroney's environment minister until McMillan was defeated in 1988), and a "note" that reads: "What follows is the text of the 1987 Federal Water Policy. Despite the date of publication, many of the issues and strategies outlined in the 1987 Policy remain valid today. Since no more recent published policy can be offered at this time, the text of the 1987 Policy is offered for information purposes only."

In 2003, leading Environment Canada scientists with the National Water Research Institute published a comprehensive study on the status of Canada's water, "Threats to Water Availability in Canada." The report outlined a whole variety of threats, including industrial farming, global warming, melting glaciers, wetland and forest destruction, energy and mining extraction, and high urban demand. The Institute reports "substantial shortcomings" in government protection of Canada's freshwater resources and points out the need for "urgent and sustainable action" in order to "ensure future access to adequate water supplies." Fresh water is "inadequately resourced" and its care is "poorly coordinated" said the scientists, who called for a reliable inventory of Canada's lakes, rivers, glaciers, reservoirs, and aquifers and the multiple threats to them. "At the most fundamental level, this report reinforces the need for strong leadership and an enhanced spirit of team work over the long term at the highest levels of government," the study concluded.

An earlier report from the Institute, "Threats to Sources of Drinking Water and Aquatic Ecosystem Health in Canada," published in 2001, examined a multitude of pathogens, toxins, agricultural pollutants, and medicines finding their way into Canada's water systems and came to the same conclusion about the urgent need for government research and action.

An internal Environment Canada assessment of the state of Canada's water policy prepared for Environment Minister Stéphane Dion, "Clean, Safe, and Secure Water – The Need for Federal Leadership," was obtained by researcher Ken Rubin in May 2005. It is a scathing indictment of the federal Liberals. A national water crisis looms, say the officials, and no one is in charge. Current approaches are fragmented, short-term, and inadequately informed. Canada has become a nation where provinces and industries squabble over urgent water issues such as pollution, shortages, and sovereignty in an atmosphere of distrust, and with no national leadership. The blunt note warns that this lack of leadership could hurt Canada internationally and cost lives at home. Water shortages on the Prairies caused $5 billion in damages in just one year. Lowered water levels in the St. Lawrence and the Great Lakes are placing limits on shipping. Diseases from contaminated water cost our health system $300 million a year. Between 20 and 40 per cent of rural wells are contaminated. Canada needs infrastructure investment badly, say the officials, as 22 per cent of our waste water is not treated.

The Canadian government doesn't even know how much groundwater there is in Canada. In "Buried Treasure," a 2005 study on groundwater in Canada funded by the Walter & Duncan Gordon Foundation, Alfonzo Rivera of Natural Resources Canada admits, "It is impossible to know how many aquifers exist in all of Canada as there has never been a comprehensive national inventory done. . . . The amount of groundwater stored in Canadian aquifers and their sustainable yield and role in ecosystem functioning are virtually unknown." Rivera's summary, which he calls "The Consequences of Limited Knowledge," says there is simply not enough information on government-wide water programs to support policy development and this "lack of understanding" could lead to "bad management practices." Tony Clarke in his 2005 study on bottled water in North America reports that groundwater takings in Canada are regulated – or not – by a hodgepodge of provincial practices, in some cases all but giving the resource away. He calls the bottled-water business the "most unregulated industry in Canada." He reports that the Canadian Food Inspection Agency is so lax in its reviews, Canadian bottled water plants are inspected on average only once every two or three years.

Not only is the Canadian government not protecting Canada's freshwater supply, however, it also has put it directly at risk in free-trade agreements. Despite intense opposition, "ordinary natural water of all kinds (other than sea water)" was included as a "good" in the Canada–U.S. Free Trade Agreement, and a "good," a "service," and an "investment" in NAFTA. Since under the deal, "no party may adopt or maintain any prohibition or restriction on the exportation or sale for export of any good destined for the territory of another party," once Canada starts exporting fresh water to the United States for commercial purposes, the tap can't be turned off. Canada could soon find itself under export obligations on water of the kind that now exists for energy. Furthermore, the Canadian government would not be allowed to restrict these sales to Canadian businesses. Under the "National Treatment" provision of the deal, American water companies would have equal access to sell Canada's water, just as American energy companies have in the oil patch. If any government tried to limit access to these exports to Canadian companies, American companies could invoke "Chapter 11" and sue the Canadian government for financial compensation.

Canadian agrologist Wendy Holm explains that American companies already have established water rights in Canada, for instance, in the use of water for tar-sands production. Because water is protected as a private "good" in NAFTA, any time water is used in a commercial context by an American company or investor, NAFTA rights apply. Water that is being used by American energy companies in Canada is now theirs to use in perpetuity. These rights include continuity of use, proportional sharing, no price dis-crimination, and the right of American companies to set new envi-ronmental conditions on its use, or even limit the amount available to industry. Under NAFTA, Canadian companies do not have these rights and would have to abide by new regulations. (Holm rightly says that the sooner water is exempted from NAFTA, the better.)

Canada has had a couple of scares with respect to private water exports. In 1998, a flurry of opposition from Canadian activist groups and U.S. Great Lakes states forced the Ontario government to revoke a licence it had given to the Nova Group of Sault Ste. Marie for a five-year permit to draw up to 10 million litres of water a day from Lake Superior for export to Asia. The same year, the McCurdy Group in Gander applied to export about 52 billion litres a year from Gisborne Lake in southern Newfoundland to ship to the Middle East. Fierce opposition forced the Newfoundland government to back down the next year and again several years later when the issue resurfaced. While these sales were not destined for the United States, under the "Most Favoured Nation" obligations of the WTO, once a "good" is being traded or sold to one WTO member country, it must be traded and sold to all. Commercial exports to Asia would open up exports to the United States, where U.S. investors would have additional NAFTA rights.

## NO SURPLUS

The public outcry arising from the two cases of attempted water export forced the Canadian government to deal with the issue. In 1999, the House of Commons adopted a motion introduced by NDP MP Bill Blaikie to ban bulk-water exports. However, knowing that an outright ban (which had been promised in the 1993 Liberal Red Book) would violate its NAFTA commitments, the Canadian government introduced a "Voluntary Provincial Accord," which, while helpful in getting some provinces to agree not to sell their water, can never have the same weight as a federal ban. If any one province – like British Columbia under the Gordon Campbell government – decides to export bulk water for commercial purposes, bans in other provinces would become null and void. For its part, the federal government also chose what it called an "environmental" approach, and passed C-36, an amendment to the Boundary

Waters Treaty of 1909, under which the Canadian and U.S. governments jointly administer shared boundary waters.

C-36 prohibits the removal of water from "Water Basins" instead of imposing an outright ban on exports. However, as international trade expert Steven Shrybman notes, its effectiveness is limited to only some boundary waters, like the Great Lakes, for which it was primarily devised, and would not prevent export of coastal waters or lakes and rivers not touching the border. As well, C-36 is domestic legislation. Technically, it is not an amendment to the Boundary Waters Treaty because the United States did not pass similar legislation, and both parties must agree to a treaty amendment. In any case, under Vienna Convention rules, NAFTA supersedes the Treaty. Finally, and most dangerously, C-36, in attempting to remove the right of provinces to issue out-of-country export licences, instead allows the minister of foreign affairs and international trade to issue licences for the "use, obstruction, or diversion of boundary waters," thus for the first time formalizing water withdrawals and exports. Shrybman says Canada was better off without any legislation than one so flawed.

The third action Canada undertook along with the United States was to ask the International Joint Commission (IJC), the body that oversees the Treaty, to undertake an examination of the issue of water diversions from the Great Lakes. The Great Lakes and St. Lawrence River are the world's single largest source of fresh water: they supply drinking water to 45 million people. But they are becoming increasingly polluted again after years of improvement (Lake Erie's "dead zone" – a wide swath of water devoid of oxygen and therefore lethal to aquatic life – is back and growing), and water levels are dropping from increased demand. In 2004, 28 billion litres of lake water disappeared forever, tapped for irrigation, reports *Time* magazine (December 6, 2004). In its 2000 "Final Report on Protection of the Waters of the Great Lakes," the IJC declared emphatically that there is no surplus water in the Great Lakes and explicitly warned against any new diversions. However, on the American side of the Lakes, pressure has been steadily mounting from thirsty communities and industry off the Basin to gain access to these waters.

So the Council of Great Lakes Governors – a partnership of the governors of the eight Great Lakes states and the provinces of Ontario and Quebec, established in 1983 – set out to examine the demands for new water takings on its own. In 2001, the Council published a draft Annex to its 1985 Charter, which had created a notification and consultation process for water diversions. The Annex, which would allow major new diversions, caused an uproar on both sides of the border. After heated public hearings, the Council released its re-drafted version on June 30, 2005. While there were minor improvements, the proposed Annex is still cause for great concern for all Canadians.

The most egregious aspect of the plan is that it gives unilateral approval for Great Lakes diversions to the Great Lakes governors. The Annex is composed of two elements: a non-binding Agreement addressing the chronic neglect of water stewardship of the Lakes that includes the two Canadian provinces but which has no authority; and a binding and legally enforceable Compact setting out terms and conditions of new diversions among only the eight states. The Compact provides legal authority for U.S. states to license the diversion of unlimited quantities of water to communities that are partially or entirely outside the Basin. Neither Canada nor the provinces would be able to veto these diversions regardless of their duration, scale, or impact on the waters of this shared ecosystem. Nor does the plan require diversions to be approved by the IJC, even if Canada objects. The Compact would establish the same legal right to Great Lakes waters for consumers and companies outside the Basin as is now claimed by those within it, if governors dependent on those voters for re-election approve them. And as Leigh Thomson, an Ontario activist who opposes the Annex, points out, all the big water-service corporations, including Suez, Vivendi, and RWE Thames, are moving into many American communities to privatize public-water services, where they could potentially transfer Great Lakes waters to subsidiaries in communities off the Lakes out of view of public scrutiny.

Ontario Natural Resources Minister David Ramsey admits that pressure from thirsty American states forced his government to abandon its previous opposition to the plan, saying he could not ignore the growing demand on the American side. Waukesha, Wisconsin, is located west of the subcontinental divide that forms the edge of the Basin. It has a daily need of 20 million gallons of fresh water and has applied to be the first "test case" of the plan. Wisconsin's governor is lobbying the other governors hard for access. Thus begins a negotiating process among the Great Lakes governors for access to the Basin that completely ignores Canada, even though Canada has joint ownership of the Lakes. Bear in mind also that the Chicago diversion, which allows Illinois to divert 2.1 billion gallons of water from the Great Lakes each and every day, is grandfathered in the plan. Given the recent Southern Illinois University report of Chicago's burgeoning need for water over the next twenty years, this exemption poses a serious problem.

Both cash-starved municipalities and covetous entrepreneurs are eyeing the Great Lakes and its groundwater as sources of easy money. Several years ago, the mayor of Webster, New York, placed ads in the *Wall Street Journal* and *New York Times* offering to sell "crystal clear" well water. He was forced to back off when the Great Lakes governors pointed out that his water feeds the Great Lakes and is considered part of them. John Febbraro, the Sault Ste. Marie businessman whose original plan to export Lake Superior water set off this chain of actions, says he hasn't given up. Sooner or later, he told *Time* magazine (December 6, 2004), Great Lakes water "will be a commodity." Nova Corp. will be waiting in line. Eugene Corrigan, president of Flow Inc., of Charleston, South Carolina, has identified forty nations interested in buying North American water. He told *Time* that he has opened "serious discussions" with Saudi Arabia and other Persian Gulf countries.

Even if these businessmen do not obtain licences from the Great Lakes governors to take water directly from the Great Lakes in the foreseeable future, the more water is allowed to leave the Basin, the more access industry of all kinds will have to it. Meanwhile, all the world's largest bottled-water companies, including Nestlé (which owns seventy-eight brands of bottled water), Coca-Cola, and Pepsi are already taking massive quantities of groundwater and water from springs that feed the Great Lakes, with almost no oversight in terms of sustainability and no approvals process from either U.S. states or Canadian provinces. Under the terms of NAFTA, the water rights these companies have established just by being there are permanent. Canada could face a trade challenge if it tried to assert a claim to half of the Great Lakes waters. And the proposed Annex explicitly allows the bottled-water industry to withdraw Great Lakes water and bottle it for sale within the Basin. But as Karl Flecker of the Polaris Institute pointed out at a public hearing on the Annex in Kingston on July 7, 2005, can anyone expect a company such as Nestlé, with a $70-billion annual profit, to abide by such a rule? The huge water volumes it currently extracts in Michigan and Wisconsin are exported anywhere the company chooses. Who would monitor these takings to ensure the water stays in the region when oversight is already so poor? Flecker also reminded the hearing that Halliburton planned to export 3 million bottles a day of Great Lakes water to Iraq in November 2004 until a public outcry forced it to drop the plan.

And what is the Canadian government's response to the Annex? Nothing.

There is no response to this potential water grab from these shared waters. The Martin Liberals have abandoned Canada's freshwater heritage. It is no wonder, then, that the federal government was caught totally off-guard when the government of North Dakota decided to drain Devils Lake into the Sheyenne River, a tributary of the Red River, which flows northward into Canada, in order to keep it from flooding. Michael Byers of the Liu Institute for Global Issues calls Devils Lake "an ecological time bomb" (*Globe and Mail*, January 31, 2005). It is a shallow, stagnant pothole, he writes, just south of Manitoba, fed by industrial runoff, a "noxious brew of salt, arsenic, boron, mercury, nitrogen, phosphorous, and sulphate," so polluted, it is unsuitable for irrigating crops. The people of Manitoba rightly fear that it will destroy an already damaged Lake Winnipeg. Yet the Canadian government waited until almost the last minute to seek a solution with the Bush administration and the government of North Dakota. In mid-August 2005, just days before the Devils Lake diversion began, the Martin government announced a "breakthrough." On close examination, the agreement – which everyone agrees is "non-binding" – is pathetic: some government (which one is not specified) will build a "$50,000 rock and gravel filter that, at best, might keep out large invasive species. However, it will do nothing to stop invasive microscopic species or the myriad chemical contaminants contained in the Lake from flowing into the Red River system."

Contrary to public perception, Canada does not have an unlimited supply of fresh water. While it contains many lakes and rivers, it holds just 7 per cent of the available freshwater supplies – water that can be used without damaging the ecosystem or decreasing the overall water stock. Looming permanent droughts face Western Canada if water abuse doesn't stop, scientists such as David Schindler warn. There is no spare water in the Great Lakes and most of the mighty rivers so coveted by thirsty U.S. politicians, flow north. Using them to supply water to the United States would require monumental engineering feats. Ecological devastation would result from reversing the flow of entire water systems. There are people who say it will never be economically feasible to divert water from Canada to the United States. Not very long ago, people said the same thing about developing the tar sands.

The demand for Canada's water – and hydro-electricity – may come sooner than many think. Lake Powell on the Arizona-Utah border and its sister Colorado River reservoir, Lake Mead, may end up short of the water needed to power the turbines at the Glen Canyon and Hoover dams in the next few years, Agence France Press journalist Maxim Kniazkov reports (January 3, 2005). Ever since severe drought hit the U.S. Southwest in 2000, the lake has been the unofficial barometer of crisis. If the water level drops below 1,063 metres, the minimum power pool, there won't be enough of it to rotate the eight turbines installed in the generating room. Ken Rice, manager of the Glen Canyon Dam, says that if the drought continues, minimum power could come as early as between 2007 and 2009. Under a worst-case scenario, says Kniazkov, Glen Canyon could grind to a halt as early as 2006. The Hoover Dam, which powers Las Vegas, would last a little longer, because it would draw on Lake Powell water, but that lake is at record lows as well. The possibility of the Hoover Dam shutting down is sending shock waves all the way to Washington.

None of the big-business groups openly supporting an energy pact have dared to publicly promote a pact in fresh water. The Canadian Council of Chief Executives even has a disclaimer in its report, saying that water is not on the table. However, in the leaked minutes of the Toronto meeting of the Task Force on the Future of North America (co-sponsored by the CCCE), water was clearly part of the discussion. "Serious obstacles remain to deeper regional integration and Task Force members favoured articulating a bold vision for regional integration even if elements of that vision could not immediately be put into practice. Participants divided their suggestions for more intensive cooperation into those that are politically feasible today, and those that, while desirable, must be considered long-term goals. One implication of this approach is that no item – not Canadian water, not American anti-dumping, not Mexican oil – is 'off the table'; rather, contentious or intractable issues will simply require more time to ripen politically."

The leaked minutes show agreement on the crafting of a "North American Resource Pact" of the kind that both the CCCE and the Canadian government publicly favour, with one major difference: the list from the minutes the public wasn't supposed to see includes fresh water. Members note that the issue of water is "invested with great emotion in Canada. . . . Consequently, policy recommendations on these issues are best considered longer-term goals."

Unless Canadians become involved in this debate soon, the process for deeper integration between Canada and the United States will ensure that Canada's freshwater resources become North American freshwater resources, with water policy set in Washington.

# a rogues'
# gallery

*This Revolution Has Been Brought to You By . . .*

During their first term in office, George W. Bush and his team lied about the existence of weapons of mass destruction and Iraqi connections to al-Qaeda, launched a brutal and unsuccessful war in Iraq, lined the pockets of powerful and corrupt corporations, and bankrupted their country to pay for this insanity. As well, they implemented a far-reaching deregulation program that dismantled decades of environmental safeguards and health and food safety standards, putting millions of Americans at risk. And they cut aid projects internationally while escalating an aggressive policy of pro-market "reforms" and pro-American agribusiness food policies in Third World countries, policies that have actually deepened poverty and hunger for the world's poor. Yet, in their second term, all who took part in this scandal are back with secure positions or promotions. Anyone who voiced dissent is gone. As Tim Harper wrote in the *Toronto Star* (April 17, 2005), "It appears the easiest route to success in the Bush White House was to be at the centre of a war that was waged under false pretences, then mismanaged from the day Saddam's statue was toppled." Allan Lichtman, political analyst at Washington's American University, adds that the promotions are not for messing up the war, but for staying with the program. "You certainly don't get rewarded in this administration for being a voice of dissent," he told Harper. Here is a snapshot of the leading players.

## KARL ROVE, WHITE HOUSE DEPUTY CHIEF OF STAFF AND SENIOR ADVISER

The Bush Revolution could not have taken place without a group of political masterminds working behind the scenes. Karl Rove has had a thirty-year plan to remake the political landscape in America. His mandate was not just to deliver two elections to George W. Bush, which he did, but also to marshal the energy and resources of the religious and conservative right in America to forge a whole new culture. Karl Rove has set out to transform every institution, including the courts and state and federal government, in order to entrench conservatism at every level of American life. He has been remarkably successful. The Republicans now control the presidency, the Senate, and the House of Representatives. The new target is the third source of power in Washington – the Supreme Court.

Karl Rove was a committed and already-driven Republican in high school and gave up a post-secondary education to work for Republican candidates. He went to Washington during the Watergate scandal (he was one of a group of young Republicans who approved of the Watergate break-in as a necessary tactic to win the election), where he wrested control of the College Republicans, a radical group in the Nixon era. Controversy inspired by his aggressive tactics caught the eye of the incoming Republican National Committee chairman, George H. Bush, who hired Rove and introduced him to his son George W. Years later, Rove recalled how impressed he was by the younger Bush: "Huge amounts of charisma, swagger, cowboy boots, flight jacket, wonderful smile, just charisma – you know, wow!" In 1977, Bush, Sr., sent Rove to Texas, ostensibly to run a political action committee, but really, according to insiders, to babysit George W., who was drinking and partying hard at the time.

In those years in Texas the power of the once-dominant Democrats was crumbling. It was here that Rove discovered the secret to his – and the Republicans' – success: thoroughly researched, targeted, direct-mail campaigns mixed with aggressive attacks on the opponent's character – so-called Smashmail politics. He likes to point out that mail is largely immune from press coverage – invisible media that "allows you to say anything about anybody and not get caught." Election by election, with Karl Rove behind the scenes, the Republicans began to take over every level of state government. As they did, they removed Democrats from every level of office. It was also in Texas that Rove instilled in his candidate the advice for political conduct to which George W. Bush still faithfully adheres: Don't confuse yourself with the issues. Find three points you want to make to the voters and stay with them at all times. As one grudgingly admiring detractor puts it, "Karl Rove's strategy is one part in-your-face, eye-gouging politics, and another part translating complex policy into simple-to-understand concepts."

Rove, while not a fundamentalist himself – he calls the religious right the "new labour unions" – knew that, if he could find and marshal the millions of conservative Christian voters, he could assure back-to-back Republican victories. He secured lists of church members all across America and scoured the mailing lists of credit-card companies such as VISA, right-wing media such as FOX News, hunting magazines such as *Field and Stream*, and openly right-wing companies such as Coors Beer. Using these sources, he compiled a list of millions of social conservatives and set out to contact them. These lists formed the backbone of both electoral strategies.

Rove also perfected the attack campaign. He is widely believed to get surrogate groups to smear rival candidates, while keeping his own candidate out of it. In 1994, when Rove was running George W.'s campaign for governor against incumbent Democrat Anne Richards, Texan voters received calls from phoney "pollsters" who asked such questions as: "Would you be more or less likely to vote

for Governor Richards if you knew her staff is dominated by lesbians?" Rove allowed a surrogate group called Veterans for Truth,
run by a group of Republican Texans, to smear John McCain's
impeccable war record (and insinuate that he was gay) in the 2000
Republican nomination race. The same group used the same
smear tactic on Senator John Kerry, a decorated war hero, in the
2004 election.

Rove came under considerable pressure because of his alleged
role in the Wilson–Plame scandal, which was partly the result of
his bare-knuckle approach to political warfare, but he remains an
indispensable adviser to President Bush.

## RICHARD CHENEY, VICE PRESIDENT

A bona-fide neo-conservative as well as social conservative, Dick
Cheney was the chief of staff to President Ford, secretary of defense
under President George H. Bush, and is a two-time vice president
to the current administration. A Yale dropout, he managed to obtain
five draft deferments, thus avoiding the Vietnam War. (He and other
pro-war neo-conservatives who did the same are referred to as
"chicken hawks" in Washington.) As a congressman (he was elected
to congress in 1978 to represent Wyoming), he embraced every far-
right cause around. He opposed the ban on selling armour-piercing
bullets; sanctions against apartheid in South Africa; a resolution
calling for the release of Nelson Mandela from prison; school
busing; Head Start (an early child development program for poor
children); the Equal Rights Amendment; extending the Clean
Water Act; support for the United Nations; and a ban on guns that
can escape detection through metal detectors. A charter member of
the Project for the New American Century, Cheney is a Middle
East hardliner and one of the principal architects of the consolidation of foreign policy in the Pentagon.

Cheney was a key hawk in the first Gulf War and was determined to find reasons to invade Iraq. He told the Saudis that he

had photos "proving" a massive Iraqi troop buildup on their border and used this report to convince King Fahd to allow American troops into his country. As reported on the CBC's *the fifth estate* (October 6, 2004), when Florida journalist Jean Heller got a hold of Soviet satellite photos showing no evidence of such a buildup, Cheney refused to talk to her. Cheney's photos were never released. When Bill Clinton became president, Dick Cheney became the CEO of the construction and oil services company Halliburton, and used his contacts inside the Pentagon and the State Department to dramatically boost both his own and the company's fortunes. In the five years he was Halliburton CEO, the company obtained US$2.3 billion in government contracts and another US$1.5 billion in taxpayer-ensured loans, almost double what it had made in the previous five years. When President Clinton declared an economic embargo on Iran in 1995, Halliburton set up an office in Tehran and did millions of dollars of business there. Others went to jail for trading with Iran but Cheney, one of the hawks now targeting Iran for invasion, called the embargo "a mistake."

As if this were not outrageous enough, his company had major contracts with Iraq during the embargo against that country, and made millions helping Saddam Hussein take advantage of the UN "oil for food" program to siphon off money both for personal use and to purchase weapons for his security forces. As secretary of defense in the administration of Bush, Sr., Dick Cheney helped to lead a coalition into war against Saddam. As vice president to Bush, Jr., he strongly endorsed the 2003 invasion of Iraq. As Halliburton CEO, however, he opposed the sanctions against Iraq (he called his country "sanction-happy" at an energy conference in 1996), and when he couldn't get them lifted, he went around them.

When he left Halliburton to become George W. Bush's running mate in 2000, Dick Cheney was paid US$20 million in stocks by the company. With its patron firmly ensconced in the White House, Halliburton obtained huge contracts to rebuild Iraq. In the fall of 2003, CBS News's *60 Minutes* confirmed the rumours swirling around the company and its patron: all of Halliburton's Iraq contracts were granted without bids, in violation of Pentagon rules that require competitive bidding. No other corporation, even those that were highly qualified, got the chance to bid for the contracts given to Halliburton. There was no fallout to either the Bush administration or the company in the wake of these revelations. Halliburton is now the seventh-biggest contractor for the Pentagon, up from thirty-seventh just four years ago.

## CONDOLEEZZA RICE, SECRETARY OF STATE

Unlike Dick Cheney, Condoleezza Rice did not start off as a neo-conservative. In fact, she was once a member of the Democratic Party, and her early books and academic papers do not reflect the views she would later espouse. Rice obtained a Ph.D. in international affairs from the University of Denver and subsequently taught political science at Stanford. She got her start in government in 1986 when she received a Council on Foreign Relations fellowship to serve on the strategic planning staff of the Joint Chiefs of Staff. Under George H. Bush, Rice was an assistant to the National Security Council on Soviet and East European Affairs, where she advocated a more restrained foreign policy strictly related to U.S. national issues. In those years, she became very close to the Bush family personally and was a frequent overnight guest.

Rice returned to Stanford as provost during the Clinton years. It was in this period that her views appear to have hardened, perhaps due to her connection with a number of corporate boards and foundations. Rice has served with many companies, including Transamerica, Charles Schwab, JPMorgan, Hewlett-Packard, Rand Corporation, and Chevron, which named an oil tanker after her. She was also a consultant to Chevron on Kazakhstan, where the company holds the largest concession of any of the international oil companies. Her new views were on display in a 1999 essay she wrote for *Foreign Affairs*, "Promoting the National Interest," in which she criticized the foreign policy of Bill Clinton as being de-linked from the national interest of the United States. "Foreign policy in a Republican administration will proceed from the firm ground of the national interest, not from the interests of an illusory international community." She said that U.S. foreign policy should not be constrained by international agreements like the Kyoto Protocol on climate change or the Comprehensive Test Ban Treaty. Instead, the United States should return to the core principle that "power matters." Instead of relying on "Wilsonian thought," that is, according to Rice, "exercising power legitimately only when doing so on behalf of someone else," she argued that when the United States focuses solely on pursuing its national interests, the rest of the world also benefits. She described this as a "second-order effect."

Rice was chosen to replace Colin Powell in George W. Bush's second term both because of her views and because she would espouse the hardline foreign policy Bush and Cheney advocate. Colin Powell, whom she replaced, had spent much of the second part of his term butting heads with Cheney and Rumsfeld over their aggressive Middle East policies and clearly no longer fit on the team. Rice has moved the State Department into full alignment with the neo-conservative foreign-policy vision and is housecleaning it to be sure of compliance up and down the line.

## STEPHEN J. HADLEY, NATIONAL SECURITY ADVISER

Stephen Hadley, Rice's replacement at the NSC, is a pro–nuclear weapons hardliner who was once a partner in a D.C. law firm representing major defence contractors such as Lockheed Martin and Boeing. Hadley advocates extending the role of nuclear weapons to include deterrence against weapons of mass destruction, including biological and chemical weapons. In the fall 1997 edition of the *Duke Journal of Comparative and International Law*, he wrote:

"One of the lessons other countries have drawn from the Gulf War is that no nation should even consider a confrontation with the United States military without having a weapon of mass destruction at its disposal."

When allegations arose regarding Rice's mishandling of the false report for which her department was responsible, which stated that Iraq was trying to buy uranium from Niger, Hadley, along with CIA director George Tenet, took the heat to protect her. In 2002, an operative now referred to by the CIA only as a "con man" reported that Saddam was about to make this purchase of uranium to build nuclear weapons. The rumour spread and the Bush administration sent retired diplomat Joseph C. Wilson to Niger to check it out. Wilson warned the White House that the story was "highly unlikely" but President Bush restated the story as fact in his 2003 State of the Union Address and pointed to it as a justification for going to war with Iraq. Rice came in for criticism because, by this time, Tenet had publicly admitted that the claim was incorrect (which led to his resignation). Hadley told the *Washington Post* in a story that ran July 23, 2003, that Rice had been unaware of the issue and that he should have remembered there was "some controversy" around the report. Nevertheless, weeks after the 2003 State of the Union Address, Hadley repeated the allegations that Saddam was seeking to buy uranium in a *Chicago Tribune* op-ed. He would soon be promoted. Meanwhile, Joseph Wilson was roundly punished by having his wife identified as a CIA agent, potentially putting her and Wilson in danger.

Working for Hadley at the NSC as a special assistant to the president's Global Democracy Strategy is the infamous **Elliott Abrams**. Abrams is the far-right Reagan operative who was indicted by the Iran-Contra prosecutor for intentionally deceiving Congress about the administration's role in supporting the Contras. Abrams is remembered for his volatile testimony at the hearings, where he defended death squads, dictators, and massacres. George H. Bush pardoned Abrams on Christmas Eve, 1992. In his new position, Abrams will oversee the Bush administration's promotion of "democracy and human rights" around the world.

## DONALD RUMSFELD, SECRETARY OF DEFENSE

Like Condoleezza Rice, Donald Rumsfeld has become more of a hawk with age (he is now in his mid-seventies). As a young congressman from Illinois in the 1960s, he was seen as a liberal Republican and supported civil rights. After serving in Congress for seven years, he left to join President Nixon's team and became President Ford's chief of staff and then secretary of defense. Rumsfeld then returned to private life. He sat on the board of a number of pharmaceutical companies and was the CEO of Fortune 500 giant G.D. Searle. (The big drug lobby gave historically high contributions to the Bush campaigns in 2000 and 2004.) He also sat on the board of the Swiss multinational Asea Brown Boveri, a key contractor in the controversial Three Gorges Dam in China. In 1983, Rumsfeld was appointed Ronald Reagan's special presidential envoy to the Middle East and helped "normalize" relationships with Iraq. His support for Saddam Hussein opened the door to overt and covert sales of poisonous chemicals and biological weapons to Iraq by American corporations. He also helped Bechtel secure a deal with Iraq to build a controversial oil pipeline.

When he returned to politics under George W. Bush, Rumsfeld was a full-blown neo-conservative. He had already allied himself publicly with the Project for the New American Century in advocating military intervention in the Middle East. He was on the board of several hawkish think-tanks including the Center for Security Policy, and chaired the Commission to Assess National Security Space Management and Organization, which called for the weaponization of space.

Rumsfeld's deputy and secretary of the navy, **Gordon England**, has extensive connections to American arms corporations, including Litton Industries, Honeywell, Combat Systems Group, and

General Dynamics, where he served as executive vice president for years. General Dynamics is the fourth-largest weapons supplier for the Pentagon and a leading producer of combat vessels for the navy. In 2004, the company obtained US$9.6 billion in defence contracts and gave US$1.42 million to the Bush campaign.

## JOHN D. NEGROPONTE, NATIONAL INTELLIGENCE DIRECTOR

After the 9/11 terrorist attacks, George Bush ordered an investigation of the various intelligence agencies and their failure to foresee the assault. The result was the Intelligence Reform and Terrorism Prevention Act, passed by Congress in late 2004, which established one director, John Negroponte, to oversee all fifteen U.S. intelligence agencies, including the CIA and the FBI. Tom Barry of the International Relations Center says that the real problem with intelligence before 9/11 was not any lack of coordination among agencies, but rather the administration's determination to take power away from the CIA and consolidate all intelligence under Rumsfeld and Cheney at the Pentagon. While human-rights observers over the years have charged the CIA with engineering coups against democratically elected governments, the neo-conservatives have criticized it from the right, calling it a haven for liberals, communists, and anti-American "internationalists." Barry says that for decades, the hawks have charged that the CIA has downplayed the national security threats posed by the Soviet Union, China, and the "rogue states" of Iraq, Iran, Cuba, North Korea, and Syria.

The neo-conservatives won two recent victories in their battle for control of the government's intelligence apparatus. The first, says Barry, was the appointment of **Porter Goss** to head the CIA and direct its "reform." Goss is a Republican Congressman from Florida, former chair of the House Intelligence Committee, and long-time ally of Vice President Cheney. Like some others, Goss has been rewarded for putting loyalty to the White House before other considerations. In his case, he refused to use his position with the House Intelligence Committee to confront the administration's lies about Iraq. The second conservative appointment of note was that of John Negroponte. These two appointments set the stage for the covert operations that have only recently started little by little to leak out to the press.

On January 23, 2005, the *Washington Post* reported that a new "Strategic Support Branch" of the Pentagon had been created without the knowledge of Congress to give Rumsfeld "broad authority" over clandestine operations abroad and to oversee "death squads" in Iraq and other countries harbouring terrorists. The *New York Times Magazine* called this development "The Salvadorization of Iraq" in a May 1, 2005, cover story. "There are far more Americans in Iraq today – some 140,000 troops in all," author Peter Maass wrote, "than there were in El Salvador, but U.S. soldiers are increasingly moving to a Salvador-style advisory role. In the process, they are backing up local forces that, like the military in El Salvador, do not shy away from violence."

John Negroponte should feel right at home. A career Foreign Service veteran, he has been an aide to Henry Kissinger and ambassador to the Philippines, Mexico, the United Nations, and most recently, Iraq. During the Reagan years, he served as ambassador to Honduras at a time when the U.S. embassy there served as the logistical centre for U.S. support of the war by the Contras against the democratically elected Sandinista government in Nicaragua. There, he played a key role in the U.S. strategy to support counterinsurgency and anti-dissident operations in Honduras as well as El Salvador and Guatemala. Under his watch, said the Council on Hemispheric Affairs, the Honduran military, and associated paramilitary squads, committed a multitude of human-rights abuses. In a 1995 four-part investigative report published by the *Baltimore Sun*, reporters Gary Cohn and Ginger Thompson revealed how the CIA-trained Battalion 316 in Honduras tortured and in some cases killed its captives, burying them afterward in unmarked graves. Former Honduran congressman Efrain Diaz told the *Sun* that the attitude of

Negroponte was one of "tolerance and silence." Reed Brody of Human Rights Watch said, "When Negroponte was ambassador in Honduras, he looked the other way when serious atrocities were committed." For its close co-operation with the Reagan administration, the Honduran government of the time was rewarded with a huge influx of U.S. military and economic aid.

## TOM DELAY, HOUSE MAJORITY LEADER

Tom DeLay is Senator Bill Frist's ally in the fight to take complete control of the Supreme Court from the secularists. He says that the federal court is "the left's last legislative body" and that the judiciary in America has "run amok." He has also threatened judges he doesn't like with congressional review.

DeLay was among the politicians who sought to exploit the tragic and bizarre case of Terry Schiavo. Schiavo was the Florida woman who lapsed into a coma after an accident in her home some fifteen years earlier. Although diagnosed as being in a "persistent vegetative state," she was kept on life-support at the insistence of her parents, and over the objections of her husband. The husband finally prevailed in the courts, and Terry Schiavo passed away. DeLay ordered a congressional investigation into the judges who refused to order the feeding tube to be reinserted and promised to change the laws so that the courts would no longer have the power to make such decisions.

Over the past four years, DeLay has become very powerful and has raised many millions of dollars for himself and other right-wing Republicans. He orchestrated congressional passage of the president's tax cuts, health-care cuts, Iraq war funding, and a bill banning "partial-birth" abortions.

DeLay – referred to around Capitol Hill as "The Hammer" – is also the best ally of the National Rifle Association. He has been instrumental in nearly all of the NRA's legislative battles over the last twenty years and in the aftermath of the 1999 Columbine massacre,

DeLay helped reduce the number of gun shows that were required to run federal background checks on customers and generally worked to ease regulations on the sale of guns. In 2000, he fought hard against BuyBack America, a Clinton administration program that paid local governments to buy back weapons from private owners. And, in 2005, he avoided a House vote on whether to renew the 1994 assault weapons ban, letting it expire. The NRA has rewarded him by giving US$46,000 to his campaigns.

Small wonder. This is a man who, when stopped from lighting a cigar in a government-owned building, said, "I am the federal government." In April 2005, "Guns and God" Tom DeLay was the featured speaker at the NRA's annual convention. Dressed in a tux and bow tie, and holding a flintlock rifle, DeLay declared to the delighted audience: "When a man is in trouble, or in a good fight, you want to have your friends around, preferably armed." Two days later, he told FOX News radio that his travails have left him feeling "closer to God."

On July 29, 2005, DeLay and the Senate voted to shield firearms manufacturers, dealers, and importers from lawsuits brought by victims of gun crimes, giving the industry broad immunity from municipalities, individuals, and law-enforcement agencies affected by shady gun dealers. This was pay-back to an industry that gave Republicans US$1.2 million in campaign donations in 2004 alone. Tom DeLay and his friends in the gun lobby appear to be unaffected by the fact that there are now more than 192 million privately owned firearms and over 30,000 gun deaths, including almost 3,000 children, every year in the United States.

DeLay is now in trouble. He is under investigation for a series of ethical violations, allegedly involving travel funds, corporate fundraising, and paying his wife and daughter from campaign committees. He is also facing potential indictment in Texas for a scheme to use corporate donations to mount a Republican take-over of the state legislature. Two of his associates have already been indicted in the case. But no one is counting him out. "I've never seen anyone play hardball like Tom DeLay," says Allan

Lichtman of American University in Washington. "People quake in their boots around him and he delivers. Everybody in the Republican Party owes Tom DeLay."

## JOHN ASHCROFT, FORMER ATTORNEY GENERAL

The right people were needed to bring about the systematic suspension of civil liberties that has accompanied the construction of the new American security state. George W. Bush and Dick Cheney found them. A group of men who would never have risen through a system based on merit and justice has worked tirelessly to remove the hard-earned rights of Americans and been rewarded for this with the top jobs in their fields.

Until he resigned in November 2004 (for health reasons), John Ashcroft was the leading architect and cheerleader for the USA Patriot Act. A former governor and senator from Missouri, Ashcroft was the perfect choice for the Bush team to lead the war on terror. He is a neo-conservative foreign-policy hawk (who received seven military deferments), a life-member of the National Rifle Association, and an evangelical Christian, who says, "You can legislate morality." He is anti-abortion and pro–death penalty. He opposed voluntary school desegregation when he was attorney general of Missouri. His world view is uncomplicated: "There are only two things you can find in the middle of the road – a moderate and a dead skunk," he says. Within months of Ashcroft becoming attorney general, reports Judy Bacharach (*Vanity Fair*, February 2004), most of the women and black attorneys left the department and were replaced by conservative white males. Ashcroft once brought his wife, Janet, in to speak to the women members of staff to honour Women's History Month. He introduced her as the woman who taught him how to put away the dishes. One of his first acts as attorney general was to circulate a memo banning two phrases common to departmental correspondence: "We are proud of the Justice Department" and "There is no higher calling than public service." Pride, said Ashcroft, citing the Bible, is a deadly sin, and the highest calling is to God. (In a speech to a fundamentalist South Carolina school in 1999, Ashcroft reflected, "Unique among nations, America recognized the source of our character as being godly and eternal, not being civic and temporal. And because we have understood that our source is eternal, America has been different. We have no King but Jesus.")

Barely two months after the terrorist attacks on New York, John Ashcroft sat his senior officials down and told them that the role of the department had been changed. It was no longer going to investigate crimes. Instead, it was going to prevent them before they happened. "If you are not up to this, you should leave now," he said. He and the president had already authorized the CIA to carry out rendition without case-by-case approval by the State or Justice departments (*New York Times*, March 6, 2005). It was Ashcroft's Orwellian idea to give the new anti-terrorism law the title USA Patriot Act. He was, in effect, capitalizing on the understandable fear of terrorism among the American people to initiate sweeping new powers of arrest and detention. He painted himself and his team in the executive branch as the true patriots and smeared anyone who dared to disagree. In a December 2001 speech to the Senate Judiciary Committee, Ashcroft said, "To those who pit Americans against immigrants, and citizens against non-citizens; to those who scare peace-loving people with phantoms of lost liberty, my message is this: Your tactics only aid terrorists – for they erode our national unity and diminish our resolve. They give ammunition to America's enemies, and pause to America's friends. They encourage people of good will to remain silent in the face of evil."

In August 2002, Ashcroft initiated a project called Operation TIPS (Terrorism Information and prevention System) to recruit and train several million volunteers (including postal workers, utility personnel, meter readers, truckers, train conductors, and cable technicians) to spy on their neighbours and customers and report any "suspicious" activity to authorities. The Boston *Globe* said that if successful, TIPS would create more spies in the United States than existed in East Germany. Thankfully, the program didn't fly with the American people.

## ALBERTO GONZALES, ATTORNEY GENERAL

It is hard to imagine anyone worse taking over for John Ashcroft, but Alberto Gonzales is just the candidate. Another self-described evangelical, Alberto is also an old friend of the Bush family. Before becoming attorney general, Gonzales was Governor George W. Bush's legal counsel (1995–97), then Texas secretary of state (1997–99), a Texas Supreme Court judge (1999–2001), and finally President George W. Bush's White House legal counsel (2001–05). He is also a good friend of big oil. Enron was the biggest contributor to Gonzales's Texas Supreme Court election, giving over US$100,000. In May 2000, Gonzales was author of a State Supreme Court opinion that handed the energy industry one of its biggest Texas legal victories in history (*New York Daily News*, February 2, 2002).

During his six years as Texas governor, Bush was known as the "Chief Executioner" because he approved the execution of 150 men and two women – a record unmatched by any other governor in modern American history. Alberto Gonzales, as his chief counsel, was responsible for writing a memo on the facts of each case and presenting them to the governor on the morning of the day scheduled for the execution. George Bush decided whether a defendant should live or die based on these memos. Texas court reporter Alan Berlow wrote an exposé for the July/August 2003 edition of *Atlantic Magazine*. "Gonzales repeatedly failed," he wrote, "to apprise the Governor of crucial issues in the cases at hand: ineffectual counsel, conflict of interest, mitigating evidence, even actual evidence of innocence." Berlow said that these memos caused Bush to approve executions on the most cursory of briefings. By leaving out vital information that might have cast doubt in the governor's mind (such as severe mental retardation or a violent and abusive childhood), Gonzales helped to make the decision to execute easy. Berlow writes: "The memoranda seemed attuned to a radically different posture, assumed by Bush from the earliest days of his administration – one in which he sought to minimize his sense of legal and moral responsibility for executions." In other words, Gonzales "enabled" George Bush to do what he was already determined to do.

Gonzales went a step further in the case of Irineo Tristan Montoya, a Mexican citizen on Texas's death row. The Mexican government strongly protested that the state had violated Tristan's rights under the Geneva Convention by failing to inform the Mexican consulate at the time of his arrest. (The Geneva Convention, ratified by the United States in 1969, ensures that foreign nationals accused of a crime are given access to legal counsel by a representative from their own country.) No problem, said Gonzales. He sent a memo to the U.S. State Department on behalf of Governor Bush asserting that the Geneva Convention does not apply to the State of Texas because Texas was not a signatory. Two days later, on June 18, 1997, Tristan was executed. (He was one of twenty-five foreign nationals on Texas's death row at the time.)

Alberto Gonzales, in his role as senior legal counsel to the president and now as attorney general, continues to be the White House "enabler," finding the arguments that permit Bush and company to do what they intend to do anyway. Five days after the terrorist attacks on New York and the Pentagon, Dick Cheney signalled the administration's intentions very clearly on MSNBC's *Meet the Press*. "The government has to work through, sort of, the dark side," he said. "A lot of what needs to be done here will have to be done quietly, without any discussion, using sources and methods that are available to our intelligence agencies, if we're going to be successful. That's the world these folks operate in, and so it's going to be vital for us to use any means at our disposal, basically, to achieve our objective." As Cofer Black, head of counterterrorism for the CIA, told a meeting of the Joint House and Senate Intelligence Committee on September 26, 2002, "All you need to know is that there was a 'before 9/11' and there was an 'after 9/11.' After 9/11, the gloves came off."

## MICHAEL CHERTOFF, SECRETARY OF THE DEPARTMENT OF HOMELAND SECURITY

The man who replaced Tom Ridge as the head of Homeland Security is the perfect partner for Gonzales. Michael Chertoff is, like Gonzales, a Harvard Law School graduate who earned his reputation for brutal and incisive cross-examination as special counsel to the Whitewater Commission investigation into Bill and Hillary Clinton's real-estate deals in Arkansas. Chertoff is a long-time member and activist with the Federalist Society, an association of right-wing lawyers and judicial reform activists dedicated to realigning the country's legal system to reflect a more conservative interpretation of the Constitution. As U.S. attorney general in New Jersey, he gained a reputation as a political attack dog for the Republican Party and was New Jersey's financial vice-chair for George W. Bush's 2000 campaign. As assistant attorney general from 2001–05, Chertoff worked closely with his boss John Ashcroft to implement the domestic war on terror and was considered by many to be equally responsible for the crackdown on civil liberties. In his 2003 book, *After: How America Confronted the September 12 Era*, author Steven Brill (founder of *The American Lawyer* journal) tells how Chertoff supervised the roundup of 750 Arabs and other Muslims on suspicion of immigration violations and held them without access to bonds or lawyers and without being charged with any crime for as long as three months. Not one of the detainees was indicted on terrorism-related crimes.

This, and Chertoff's coordination of a roundup of another five thousand Arab-Americans, led the Justice Department to issue a report calling the measures "indiscriminate and haphazard." Chertoff fought back, arguing in an op-ed to the *Weekly Standard* (December 2003) that Bush had avoided the kind of harsh measures used by other presidents in wartime. After all, he wrote, the president had not authorized the evacuation or preventive detention of American citizens based on ethnic heritage, such as the internment of Japanese-Americans during the Second World War, or "seized newspapers or banned them from the mails, as Lincoln did." All Bush did, Chertoff argued, was to follow the "customary and well-accepted practice of incapacitating enemy soldiers overseas." In another op-ed article, this time in the *Wall Street Journal* (June 2004), Chertoff wrote that the United States couldn't win the war against terrorism if "we fight in a legal fog, constantly speculating and litigating piecemeal about what the law might be. A murky legal climate only obscures our options and ham strings our forces" – an astounding statement for a former assistant attorney general.

Michael Chertoff believes that it is time for "the most creative legal thinking" about the role of the U.S. justice system in fighting a "war of extended duration." In a chilling understatement of the Bush administration's assault on the human rights and civil liberties of people around the world, he notes, "We are at a transition point in the evolution of legal doctrine to govern the armed conflict of terror."

## PAUL WOLFOWITZ, WORLD BANK PRESIDENT

The controversial decision to choose Paul Wolfowitz to head the World Bank came as a surprise to many. After all, Wolfowitz has no experience either in the world of poverty alleviation, the nominal role of the World Bank, or with the maintenance of global capital, which is its real role. But Paul Wolfowitz is the perfect man for this job. He embodies the Bush administration's unilateralism and contempt for international law. We can expect to see his neo-conservative views reflected in World Bank policies and applied, for example, to the conditions attached to World Bank loans in Third World countries.

Wolfowitz holds a Ph.D. from the University of Chicago and has been a neo-conservative for decades. In the 1970s, he was a leading hawk who helped put the country on a confrontational path with the Soviet Union and set the stage for the arms buildup under Ronald Reagan. As Dick Cheney's under secretary of defense in the George Bush, Sr., administration, Wolfowitz drafted a "defense policy guide" that is widely regarded as an early blueprint for the current administration's pre-emptive strike policy. A charter member of the Project for the New American Century, he was an early and vigorous proponent of the invasion of Iraq and was clearly linked to the Office of Special Plans, the Pentagon team considered by some in the American media to have originated the twisted intelligence on Iraq.

The World Bank is a key global institution that shapes the destiny of millions. It employs over eleven thousand people in sixty-five countries and hands out over US$20 billion a year to poor countries for development and aid. The World Bank has been criticized in recent years for pushing a corporate-led privatized model of development on applicants for aid. The model involves the privatization of essential and social services and has had the effect of deepening poverty in many countries. In the process of imposing U.S.–style market capitalism, the World Bank is reshaping whole societies. The Bank also promotes costly mega-projects that benefit transnational corporations. Several years ago, a top Treasury official told Congress that for every dollar the United States contributes to the World Bank, American companies receive back $1.30.

Recently, there have been some signs that the World Bank was listening to the rising chorus of opposition to its policies. However, by choosing as its new head Paul Wolfowitz, who is both an economic conservative and a foreign-policy neo-conservative, the Bush administration has signalled that neither the Bank's hardline market-orientation nor its lending policies will change. But there will also be dangerous new pressure on the Bank to promote the myopic, violent, and unilateralist policies of Washington's hawks.

And there may well be pressure to reroute development money for anti-terrorism systems.

## JOHN BOLTON, UNITED NATIONS AMBASSADOR

The Senate fight over George Bush's nomination of John Bolton to the UN post was one of the most bitter of all. In fact, his nomination was so controversial that Bush waited until the summer break when Congress was not sitting and on August 1, 2005, used a legislative loophole called a "recess opportunity" to confirm Bolton's appointment. "It is my opinion that John Bolton is the poster child of what someone in the diplomatic corps should not be," said fellow Republican, Senator George Voinovich. He added that if Bolton had worked for a major corporation, he would have been fired for his behaviour. This is because John Bolton is a hard-right ideologue who has spent his life denouncing the UN, all of its treaties and conventions, and all forms of multilateralism. He is also a strident "America First," pro–nuclear weapons neo-conservative who doesn't believe in graduated "carrot and stick" negotiations. "I don't do carrots," he likes to say. In his office, he displays a mock grenade with the label "To John Bolton, World's Greatest Reaganite."

John Bolton is another "chicken hawk" – a militarist who never went to war. A Yale-trained lawyer and Republican Party loyalist, Bolton was one of the "New Right Lawyers" who politicized the Reagan Justice Department. He was the assistant attorney general for George Bush, Sr., and under secretary of state for arms control and international security for Bush, Junior. In these positions, International Relations Center's Tom Barry reports, Bolton mounted a campaign to halt all international constraints on U.S. power and prerogative, fiercely opposing existing and proposed international treaties restricting land mines, enlisting child soldiers, biological weapons, nuclear-weapons testing, small-arms trade, and missile defence. He was among those who dismantled the

Anti-Ballistic Missile Treaty, blocked all efforts to add a verification clause to the biological weapons convention, and personally signed the letter abrogating Bill Clinton's adoption of the International Criminal Court (ICC), created to end immunity for those who commit genocide, war crimes, and crimes against humanity. In Congress, he worked with his mentor, Senator Jesse Helms, to make co-operation with the ICC illegal and organized a campaign to intimidate needy countries into agreeing never to take an American citizen to the ICC under threat of losing U.S. aid. Bolton opposed the use of international law to go after war criminal Augusto Pinochet, of Chile, saying, "Chileans made their choice, and have to live with it."

John Bolton has dismissed the United Nations for years. In a 1994 speech to the World Federalist Association, he said there is "no such thing as the United Nations" and added that if the UN headquarters in New York lost ten stories, it would not make a bit of difference. He believes the United States should stop its payments to the UN and deeply disagrees with Secretary General Kofi Annan's assertion that the United Nations is the sole source of legitimacy on the use of force. John Bolton is a strong proponent of American pre-emptive strikes and one of the leaders against the Comprehensive Test Ban Treaty, signed by President Clinton but never ratified because of Republican opposition.

In mid-2001, Bolton announced at the UN Conference on Illicit Trade in Small Arms and Light Weapons that Washington opposed any initiative to regulate trade in small arms or in non-military rifles because it would "abrogate the constitutional right of Americans to bear arms." Accompanying Bolton to the conference were members of the National Rifle Association.

Arch-conservative and evangelical Christian Senator Jesse Helms says, "John Bolton is the kind of man with whom I would want to stand at Armageddon." Others are less comfortable in his company. In March 2005, fifty-nine former U.S. diplomats sent a letter to the Senate stating that Bolton is the "wrong man" for this job. Among the signatories was Arthur A. Hartman, distinguished

Foreign Service officer, and former ambassador to both the Soviet Union and France, who served under presidents Nixon, Reagan, and Carter.

## ANN VENEMAN, EXECUTIVE DIRECTOR OF UNICEF

In May 2005, George Bush appointed his secretary of agriculture, Ann Veneman, to be the executive director of the United Nations Children's Fund, which works to protect the world's children and promote their rights globally. Her appointment set off alarm bells in the international community. There had been absolutely no warning: the United States just took it upon itself to appoint her and no other country objected. The People's Health Movement, an international coalition of grass-roots groups dedicated to the right of all to public health, decried this choice, saying the decision was "shrouded in secrecy" and had allowed no mechanism for individuals or NGOs in the health and children's rights movement to participate. The group pointed out that the United States and Somalia are the only two countries that have refused to join 189 others as signatories of the UN Convention on the Rights of the Child. "Given the U.S. practice of defunding UN agencies whose direction it disapproves (UNESCO, UNFPA, WHO, etc.), we can only imagine the pressures brought to bear on the Secretary General to name Ms. Veneman," said the People's Health Movement in an open "Letter of Concern."

Ann Veneman was a corporate lawyer for agribusiness for years and sat on the board of Calgene, the corporation that launched the first genetically engineered food in 1994, before becoming secretary of the California Department of Food and Agriculture. In that role, she became the bane of environmentalists, food and drug safety advocates, and family farmers for her unswerving support for agribusiness. She also sat on the steering committee of Farmers and Ranchers for Bush and became a formidable proponent of his policies in the farm community. Mark Ritchie of the Minneapolis-based

Institute for Agriculture and Trade Policy, an activist think-tank working to preserve food diversity and the family farm, said when Bush appointed Veneman to be his secretary of agriculture in his first term, that she was a "strictly pro-agribusiness, pro-pesticides company, pro-pharmaceutical company" appointment and warned, correctly, that she would lead a full frontal assault on food-safety standards and family farms.

Her appointment has reversed six decades of Unicef's proud humanitarian history, critics fear, and will prove disastrous to the world's children. As a negotiator of NAFTA, she helped consolidate neo-liberal polices that plunged millions of children into poverty. When Human Rights Watch sought her support for possible amendments to U.S. legislation to encode human rights and labour standards in trade agreements, she turned them down. It was on her watch as secretary of agriculture that the deregulation of food-safety standards took place and the practices that cause mad-cow disease went unchecked. She even refused to permit meatpackers to test cows in order to meet international export standards, because she was afraid that American consumers would demand similarly high levels of protection. The People's Health Movement warns that there are urgent issues facing the world's children right now, including: the right to basic food and shelter; the marketing of breast-milk substitutes; women's access to reproductive health and child spacing information and services; access to AIDS drugs; the privatization of water services; and the dumping of untested, genetically engineered foods into poor countries. A far-right conservative who will put profit for American corporations above the health and safety of the world's children is a disastrous choice to head Unicef.

## DAVID WILKINS, U.S. AMBASSADOR TO CANADA

The new U.S. ambassador to Canada will fit in very nicely with the extreme views of the Christian and conservative right in both countries as well as the big-business community. That the Bush administration would choose David Wilkins, a tax-cutting, corporate-friendly, fundamentalist Christian Republican from South Carolina to replace the unpopular Paul Cellucci shows just how far out of touch it is with the dominant values and political views of the Canadian people.

Wilkins is a fifty-eight-year-old lawyer who has been a member of the South Carolina legislature for twenty-four years and became speaker of the state House of Representatives a decade ago. He has been described as a "friend" of the Bush family through good times and bad. He delivered South Carolina for Bush, Sr., and Bush, Jr., three times, and capped the race for George W. against John McCain. He raised more than US$200,000 in that election, earning the coveted "Ranger" status in the Republican Party. Wilkins is a member of the First Baptist Church in Greenville, whose motto is "Faithful to our Savior Jesus, Conservative in our Beliefs." It is affiliated with the Southern Baptist Convention, a right-wing evangelical coalition that co-hosted the controversial April 25, 2005, broadcast to millions of fundamentalist Americans charging Democrats who oppose the hardline judicial nominees of the Bush White House with being "against people of faith."

Wilkins is also a hardline big-business proponent. In March 2005, Wilkins co-sponsored a controversial state tort reform bill to make it harder for citizens to sue business. Tort reform is one of the leading domestic "reform" goals of the Bush administration. When George W. Bush was governor of Texas, one of his first acts was to meet with corporate leaders in Texas to promise them a crackdown on "frivolous" lawsuits. He followed through with a series of laws insulating Texas corporations from lawsuits for reckless behaviour and stripping the rights of injured Texans who would have otherwise been eligible for protection. The consumer group TexasWatch said at the time that "these laws set back hard-fought consumer protection victories by decades, making it more difficult for injured workers and Texas families to hold irresponsible wrongdoers accountable." Bush went on to bring in similar laws at the federal level. Hailed by the big-business community in South Carolina for his work on "tort reform," Wilkins declared: "I always said the South Carolina House makes it our business to be pro-business and with the signing of this important legislation, that saying is even truer today."

Perhaps what is most distressing about David Wilkins is his admiration for a man who for decades stood for segregation and intolerance in the southern United States. Strom Thurmond led the fight against equality for blacks with a passion and a racist zeal unusual even for the Deep South of his day. He walked out of the Democratic Party when Truman desegregated the military, and in 1957, held the longest filibuster in Senate history in an attempt to defeat a key civil-rights bill. While it is true that Strom Thurmond abandoned his racist rhetoric in his later years, he never really apologized for the deep and abiding hatred he sowed and the harm he caused to generations of African-Americans.

In an October 8, 2001, speech to the Strom Thurmond Institute, David Wilkins, who served as Thurmond's campaign chairman in 1996, heaped praise on the late senator. Wilkins's enthusiasm makes the speech that got Senate Majority leader Trent Lott into so much trouble seem tame. (Speaking at Thurmond's hundredth birthday party in December 2003, Lott said that the country wouldn't have had "all these problems over the years" had it made the senator president.) Wilkins's speech, in contrast, was over-the-top in its praise for Thurmond, whom he described as "incredibly unique . . . the greatest statesman this state will ever produce . . . revered and respected like no one else in this state has been or ever will be . . . a living legend who'd get elected in South Carolina as long as he wanted to . . . a hero and patriot . . . beloved."

Wilkins ended his speech with the words: "There will never be another statesman in all of history who shares so strong a bond with his people, who is as connected to their past as he is to their present. . . . And God Bless America." For his comparatively mild, though certainly ill-advised remark, Trent Lott was forced to resign. David Wilkins has been sent to represent the American people in Canada.

## GROVER NORQUIST, AMERICANS FOR TAX REFORM

Rove is a close ally of the man who is widely regarded as the author of Bush's domestic agenda. Grover Norquist is the president of Americans for Tax Reform and the chief architect of the US$1.6-trillion tax-cut package enacted in the first Bush term of office. Americans for Tax Reform was established by President Ronald Reagan to build support for his tax cuts. Norquist ran it for Reagan and then transformed it from in-house organ to private-sector institution. He now works closely with about eight hundred state-based anti-tax groups to promote massive tax cuts at all levels of government. For these campaigns the organization gets funding from corporations such as Microsoft, Pfizer, AOL Time Warner, UPS, and Phillip Morris. It also gets support, politically and financially, from Karl Rove's massive mailing lists.

The *Nation* magazine reports that Grover Norquist has eclipsed older stalwarts on the far right such as Ed Feulner of the Heritage Foundation, David Keene of the American Conservative Union, and Paul Weyrich of the Free Congress Foundation to emerge as the "managing director of the hard-core right in Washington." Norquist first gained notoriety as the right-hand man to former speaker of the House Newt Gingrich. When Gingrich left in disgrace, Norquist survived to become an ally of Tom DeLay, House Majority leader. There is not an agency of government serving social, cultural, or environment goals that he would not abolish, from the Internal Revenue Service and the Food and Drug Administration to the Education Department and the National Endowment of the Arts. "My goal is to cut government in half in twenty-five years," he says regularly, "to get it down to the size where we can drown it in the bathtub."

Grover Norquist has played a pivotal role in building a solid alliance between the Fortune 500 corporate elite, the neo-conservatives, and the religious right. Roger Hickey of the Campaign for America's Future explains Norquist's strategy: "What he's managed to do is to chain the ideological conservatives together with the business guys, who have money, and to put that money to work in the service of the conservative movement." To cement this coalition, he organized the now-famous "Wednesday meetings" that regularly draw more than one hundred representatives of conservative groups to his office, including the National Rifle Association, the Christian Coalition, the Heritage Foundation, the White House, the Republican National Committee, leading Republicans in the House and Senate, corporate lobbyists, and selected reporters. Although he is not a Christian fundamentalist (he goes to church only "semi-regularly"), Norquist keeps in close touch with the Christian right, often speaking at Christian coalition events.

## STEPHEN L. JOHNSON, ENVIRONMENTAL PROTECTION AGENCY

Stephen Johnson is a twenty-four-year career biologist and pathologist with the Environmental Protection Agency who went along with the full dismantling of environmental regulations during George W. Bush's first term and supported the Bush retreat from the Kyoto Protocol. But his real claim to fame is that he is a strong supporter of pesticide testing on humans, a practice banned under the Clinton administration. In 2001, the Agency evaluated three studies from Dow Chemicals, Bayer Corporation, and the Gowan Company. The Bayer and Gowan studies were conducted in Third World countries, reports *Znet* journalist Gene C. Gerard (March 12, 2005), the Dow study in Nebraska. In the Nebraska study, human subjects were paid to take doses four times the level that the EPA knew produced adverse effects in animals. Subjects suffered numbness, headaches, nausea, vomiting, and stomach cramps. Although Dow's doctors determined that these symptoms were "possibly" or "probably" related to the chemical, in the final analysis of the study, Dow concluded, and the EPA concurred, that the pesticide did not pose any health risks.

All this work was being done in secret however, until April 7, 2005, when, during Johnson's nomination hearing before the Senate, another project came to light and hit the national media. Called the Children's Environmental Exposure Research Study, or CHEERS, the program paid poor families to test pesticide exposure on their infants. CHEERS was sponsored by the American Chemistry Council, whose members include Dow, ExxonMobil, and Monsanto, and which paid the EPA US$2.1 million to administer it. Poor families in Jacksonville, Florida, were offered US$970, a camcorder, a bib, and a T-shirt to participate in the tests by routinely exposing their babies to pesticides for two years. California senator Barbara Boxer called CHEERS "appalling, unethical, and immoral." Although he defended the project before the Senate, Johnson sent out a terse note the next day announcing its cancellation. On May 2, 2005, he was sworn in as the new head of the EPA.

# another
# path

*Finding Canada's Place in the World*

The world of geopolitics is in flux. Writer and philosopher John Ralston Saul believes that globalization – once presented as our inevitable Darwinian future but now understood as an experimental economic theory – is passing (*Harper's Magazine*, March 2004; see also *The Collapse of Globalization*, 2005). Much of it will remain, but much is being discarded as a failure. Saul says that the world is "transiting" eras, and is about to experience a time of intense disorder and contradictory tendencies.

At the centre of this transition are the four great questions of our time: how to deal with the proliferation of weapons, particularly nuclear weapons, and the stated intent of the Bush administration to weaponize space; how to deal with deepening global poverty and injustice, particularly in the Third World; how to end fundamentalist extremism, violence, and terrorism; and how to acknowledge and deal with the ecological limits of the earth, particularly climate change, and the coming energy and freshwater crises. The coalition that brought about the Bush Revolution has very clear answers for these four questions: aggressive escalation of the arms race so that the United States remains the sole uncontested superpower on Earth no matter what the cost to the American people; continued resistance to any other economic model for the world but its own model of corporate-led unregulated capitalism; refusal to consider any other model for confronting terrorism but more bombs, borders, and Bibles; and continued decimation of America's environmental legacy while allowing its own energy consumption to drive global warming.

Each of these four great questions, with a widening of the imagination, can be reframed as a question of security. Following 9/11, the Bush administration chose to define security in the narrowest possible terms. America, self-evidently, embodied good, and those opposed to America, obviously, were evil. The world was divided into good guys and bad guys, friends and foes. The task of defending America was essentially military – this, after all, was a war. It would be fought, therefore, through intelligence, by identifying terrorists by means of massive data collection, and by vigilantly defending the border. Scant allowance was made for the fact that poverty and injustice, rampant in our world, are the breeding ground for fundamentalism and violence. The challenge before the world community now, notwithstanding the blinkered vision of the present U.S. government, is to recast the notion of security to include the fundamental right to health and education, clean air and water, and peace and justice.

The heart of the deep integration debate is this: How will Canadians answer these great challenges? Will Canada take a different position from that taken by the U.S. administration? How much sovereign control will Canada have left at the end of the harmonization process now underway, or as it is envisaged by the Task Force on the Future of North America and the Canadian Council of Chief Executives? Are the answers of George Bush and his neo-conservative hawks to these questions the answers most Canadians would choose? Will Canada help or hinder the call of the global civil society and move to redefine security as the right of all peoples to economic, social, and environmental justice?

## GLOBAL SECURITY

The unprecedented proliferation of nuclear weapons and preparations for the weaponization of space, coupled with the "first strike" policy of the Bush administration, have set the stage for a new superpower conflict that threatens global security. American foreign policy now clearly rejects the constraints of collective security, the most effective vehicle for global security, in favour of unilateral use of force. Journalist and author Robert Kaplan argues that the alliance system of the latter half of the twentieth century is dead. "Warfare by committee as practised by NATO has simply become too cumbersome in an age that requires light and lethal strikes" (*Atlantic*, June 2005). The fissure started in Kosovo, escalated in Afghanistan, and became permanent by Iraq. The withdrawal of the most powerful country on Earth from the West's fragile consensus of collective security could well condemn it. One possible result might be a new superpower struggle.

Hardliners in the administration are sounding the alarm about the growing economic and military power of China, leading some to believe that the United States and Japan could soon be entangled in conflict with the world's most populous nation. Geoffrey York reports in the *Globe and Mail* (July 6, 2005) that ominous warnings about China's rapid military modernization and its voracious appetite for Western corporations are everywhere in the American and Japanese media. He notes in an article in the *New Republic* that China may become the first nation since the fall of the Soviet Union to seriously challenge the United States. In June 2005, in Singapore, Donald Rumsfeld sharply criticized the Chinese military buildup, predicting that China's new missiles could hit targets around the world. "Since no nation threatens China, one must wonder: Why this growing investment? Why the continuing large and expanding arms purchase?" he asked. The Washington *Times*, a right-wing daily with close links to the Pentagon, predicts that China could be ready to attack Taiwan in two years, and quotes a senior Pentagon official who likens modern China to Nazi Germany.

Benjamin Schwarz, national editor of *Atlantic*, writes that this is dangerous, self-fulfilling talk (June 2005). He reminds readers that the annual U.S. military budget is seventy-seven times bigger than the Chinese military budget in per capita terms, and comments that not all countries see the United States as a "benevolent hegemon." Both China and Russia saw the U.S. interventions in Kosovo and Iraq as a dangerous precedent. Consequently, Schwarz writes, they have formed an alliance for military co-operation and to conduct joint military exercises. "An interventionist global role may serve a number of American interests, but history has repeatedly shown that intervention by a dominant power accelerates the rise of other great powers and ensures their wariness, if not their hostility, toward it."

On May 19, 2005, a day after the *New York Times* reported that Bush had given his National Security Advisor a directive that, in effect, moved the United States closer to putting weapons in space, the *China Daily* published the Chinese government's response: "Space belongs to the commonwealth of all humanity. China opposes putting weapons into space." Until fairly recently, China relied on the 1967 Outer Space Treaty, which banned nuclear weapons and weapons of mass destruction in space. (Signed originally by the United States, the United Kingdom, and the Soviet Union, it has since been backed by most nations in the world.) However, in light of the Bush space offensive, while the strategy of the Chinese government is still to develop coalitions, in particular with Russia, to limit the way the United States uses space, it has nevertheless developed a "defensive" weapons policy and is building its own anti-satellite and space-weapons technology.

Russia is re-arming as well. In a November 17, 2004, speech to top-ranking commanders of the Russian armed forces, President Putin confirmed that Russia is "carrying out research and missile tests of state-of-the-art nuclear missile systems" and would "continue to build up firmly and insistently our armed forces, including the nuclear component." Russia still has 16,000 nuclear warheads left over from its peak of 45,000 in the mid-1980s, 7,200 of which are kept in a state of readiness for launch. (It is unreasonable to think that China and Russia are going to disarm while the United States continues its military buildup. In fact, both countries have said that if the United States puts weapons in space, their countries have no choice but to do the same. Yet the United States is defiant. Peter B. Teets, former president of Lockheed Martin, now under secretary of the U.S. Air Force, says, "Controlling the high ground of space is not limited to its protection of our own capabilities. It will also require us to think about denying the high ground to our adversaries; we are paving the road of 21st century warfare now. And others will soon follow.")

Many nations around the world are wary of these developments. The Union of Concerned Scientists warns of the "cooling" of U.S.–Russia relations and says that by neglecting opportunities to negotiate with North Korea, choosing instead to deploy weapons aimed at that country, the United States is undermining hope for peace. The International Atomic Energy Agency warns: "An atomic war draws near." The mayor of Hiroshima, Tadatoshi Akiba, says that the world "stands on the brink of hyper-proliferation" and warns of the "unspeakable violence and misery" that would follow nuclear war. The Canadian ambassador to Moscow, Christopher Westdal, says the world is in "a race with catastrophe" and that the very survival of humanity is at stake. In a March 8, 2005, presentation to the Parliamentary Review of Foreign Affairs and Defence, Canadian writer and nationalist Mel Hurtig summed up what these and many others have in common: "They all believe that recent and current American actions are leading to the breakdown of vitally important, long-standing bilateral and multilateral arms control agreements, leading to an accelerating, proliferating, and exceedingly dangerous arms race, the development of new weapons of mass destruction and the means for their delivery, and the ever-increasing possibility of an apocalyptic, catastrophic nuclear war."

The good news for the planet is the emergence of a massive civil society peace movement that brought out the biggest street protests in history in the run-up to the U.S. invasion of Iraq. This movement has had a profound effect on governments around the world, including in Canada, where it forced Prime Minister Martin to change his mind about joining the U.S. ballistic missile defence program. The International Relations Center predicts a new resolve by foreign nations, large and small, to confront U.S. initiatives that diverge from or intentionally undermine international law and multilateral rule. "Gradually, we can expect a more unified and clearly articulated counter-agenda by countervailing blocs of nations that insist on the importance of international treaties, reassert the primacy of diplomacy in settling security issues, and forge policy consensus around solutions that address the precarious state of the international economy and the impoverishment of many nations and communities."

## CANADA'S ROLE

This is a place where Canada could shine. It is unthinkable, given Canada's long history of promoting global security and disarmament, that it would be a party to the development of a system that is bleeding resources from health care, education, and environmental defence to build horrific new weapons of mass destruction. Because of its tendency to respond always to the U.S. agenda, Canada is missing the opportunity to assume a leadership role. The time is ripe for a country like Canada to present a different global vision and make nuclear disarmament and the abolition of all weapons of mass destruction the top priority of its defence and foreign policies.

Mel Hurtig calls on the Martin government to host a multilateral conference to produce a new treaty prohibiting all weapons in space and another prohibiting the unsupervised sale and distribution of all fissile (uranium and plutonium) materials. Through the United Nations, Canada should also lead a revitalized campaign for disarmament and for the destruction of all nuclear weapons. Former Canadian ambassador for disarmament Douglas Roche praises the Canadian government for being the first NATO country to sign on to the "The New Agenda," a thirteen-point plan to negotiate gradual nuclear disarmament with states that have nuclear weapons. Roche points out that compounding the nuclear risk is the threat of nuclear terrorism, which is growing day by day. It is estimated that forty nations now have the knowledge to produce nuclear weapons. The existence of an extensive illicit market for nuclear items shows up the inadequacy of the present export control system.

If Canada is to become a leader in the campaign for disarmament, it must first take on its own weapons industry. Canada is the seventh-largest arms producer in the world, with annual sales by its ten largest contractors in the $2.5-billion range. Most are subcontractors to the U.S. military, which means that Canada is directly complicit in America's wars. A Canadian company, for example, manufactures the bullets used by U.S. soldiers in Iraq. Project Ploughshares and the Canadian Council of Churches note that Canada's military export control system must be improved by returning the management of the program to Foreign Affairs from Trade where it now resides; subjecting military exports to the United States to the same export permit requirements that apply to military exports to any other destination; tightening up export controls to states that are in violation of UN Security Council sanctions; fully disclosing information on the "end-users" of Canadian military exports; and taking leadership in promoting effective, legally binding international standards for the control of international military trade.

The New Brunswick Federation of Labour, in a January 18, 2005, presentation to the Citizens' Inquiry on Canada–U.S. Relations, said that the war in Iraq clearly demonstrates that unilateral aggression and military might are not the way to stop terrorism or to promote world peace or good government. "Surely all countries have learned an important lesson. Either we utilize diplomacy and meaningful foreign aid, or resort to military force and aggression. Stronger military ties with the U.S. will only benefit the transnational corporations and entrepreneurs who stand to make money from a new and expanded arms race, not workers and average Canadians. Workers want jobs centred around peace and development, not star wars and military destruction." Like war itself, asserts the Federation, Canada–U.S. defence is about choices, and it rejects the C.D. Howe Institute's advice that Canada's role is to "keep the elephant fed and happy" as "neither acceptable nor sensible."

Nobel laureate John Polanyi says that Canadians are not generally comfortable with the aggressive military stance of the Bush administration because Canada is historically committed to the rule of international law. "This is the key to Canadian attitudes on both missile defence and the weaponization of space. One should not claim this as pure virtue," he writes in the *Globe and Mail* (May 17, 2005). "It's to be expected that the weak will favour law. It was not King John but the nobles who insisted on the Magna Carta (the nobles were right)." Essentially argues Polanyi, for each new weapon, there will always be an answer, and to each fear that gave rise to the weapon, a sequel. "The most obvious sequel will be the spread of the weapon into the hands of our opponents. Technological dominance cannot endure." As the Brazilian government has said, "One cannot worship at the altar of nuclear weapons and raise heresy charges against those who want to join the sect." Polanyi says the only global answer to this new arms race is restraint, but to have recourse to the restraint called law, one must acknowledge the supremacy of law. This is our global security challenge.

## SOCIAL SECURITY

Although economic globalization has been recently adopted by Europe, Canada, Japan, and some newly industrialized countries, it really has been a U.S.–driven initiative from its inception. Having outgrown their domestic market, American corporations sought new rules to limit the power of governments to legislate regulations, trade controls, and investment policies. They wanted a "level playing field" as they moved around the world in search of new business. Under the free-market doctrine known as the "Washington Consensus," countries around the world liberalized trade and foreign investment, deregulated their internal economies, privatized state services, and entered into head-to-head competition, lowering social standards for many millions of their citizens in order to survive. Economist Paul Krugman writes that the Washington Consensus "now defines not only the U.S. government, but all those institutions and networks of opinion leaders centred in the world's de facto capital – think tanks, politically sophisticated investment bankers, and world finance ministers – all those we meet in Washington and who collectively define the conventional wisdom of the moment." U.S.–based globalization has been the primary instrument used by corporate America to dismantle and deregulate nation-state authority around the world.

The World Bank and the IMF were enlisted to implement Structural Adjustment Programs in poor countries in order to gain access to local food, biodiversity, energy and minerals, and to privatize public services such as health care, education, and more recently, water services. In order to get relief from their growing debts to the rich North, poor countries had to adopt U.S.–style market liberalization in a cutthroat world in which many could not compete. Globalization was idealized as a "global village," in which all humanity enjoys the fruits of economic and social progress and freedom and democracy. In reality, writes Winnipeg *Free Press* columnist Frances Russell, globalization is code for the enforced "American Way" where everything is commodified and sold for a profit. Globalization is U.S. hegemony (July 8, 2005).

George Bush openly uses the rules of economic globalization to further his foreign policy as well as his war on terror. At the World Trade Organization Ministerial Meeting held in Doha,

Qatar, only two months after the terrorist attacks on the United States, then U.S. trade representative Robert Zoellick made it abundantly clear that a vote for a new round of negotiations would be seen by his government as a sign of support for the United States against terrorism. Conversely, a vote against the WTO would be a sign that the country in question was not an ally in the war on terror. The Bush administration sends clear signals to its allies about which countries they should trust and do business with. The definition of an "evil" country changes to suit U.S. economic and military interests. Bush and Cheney do business with dictatorships one day and invade them the next. Countries that go along with U.S. foreign policy are richly rewarded with lucrative contracts and trade deals. However, resistance to both the economic and military aspects of American-led globalization is growing everywhere, in ways peaceful and otherwise.

The economic legacy of the Washington Consensus has been devastating in many parts of the world. Its legacy in Latin America is unsustainable debt, feeble economic growth, and increased poverty. In 1980, 136 million Latin Americans suffered from poverty, 62 million of them from extreme poverty. By 2003, reports the United Nations Economic Commission on Latin America and the Caribbean, the number of Latin Americans living in poverty increased to 226 million, 100 million of them in extreme poverty. The *Economist* (November 6, 2003) expresses puzzlement that twenty years of liberalization have not narrowed the income gap in Latin America. Latin America's income gap is one of the widest in the world. (The greatest gap now belongs to the United States.) The richest tenth hold 48 per cent of the wealth, the poorest tenth, just 1.6 per cent. In Mexico, the number of people living in poverty has grown from 28 per cent in 1984 to 50 per cent in 2002, and those living in extreme poverty grew from 7 per cent to 20 per cent in the same years (2004 World Bank report, "Poverty in Mexico: An Assessment of Conditions, Trends and Government Strategies"). Even the Task Force on the Future of North America was forced to admit that the NAFTA promise of prosperity for Mexico has not been realized.

Having learned nothing from this experience, the United States (with strong support from the United Kingdom and Canada) has taken up the world call to "do something about Africa" and come up with the African Growth and Opportunity Act as its fundamental plan for the poorest continent on the planet. To become eligible for aid, countries must adopt a "market-based economy" that protects private-property rights; eliminate "barriers to United States trade and investment"; and establish an environment conducive to U.S. "foreign policy interests." The U.S. Agency for International Development, responsible for overseeing the implementation of the Act, has outsourced it to the Corporate Council of Africa, a lobby group representing most of the major corporations already operating (and plundering) in Africa, including Halliburton, ExxonMobil, Coca-Cola, General Motors, Starbucks, Boeing, Cargill, and Citigroup among others. George Monbiot of the *Guardian* (July 5, 2005) notes that the history of corporate involvement in Africa is one of forced labour, evictions, murder, wars, the under-costing of resources, tax evasion, and collusion with dictators.

Economic globalization has created a wealthy consumer class in much of Asia but has caused the majority to sink into deeper poverty. The *China Daily* (June 19, 2005) reported that the income gap in China, once almost non-existent save for the ruling party, continues to widen dramatically, with the top tenth owning 45 per cent of the wealth and the bottom tenth left with just 1.4 per cent. On the GINI measurement, an internationally recognized measure of income inequality, China is now "over the alarm level." Food First, an American organization working to eradicate hunger, reports that India's "economic miracle" has impacted only a "tiny fraction" of the population. Rural farmers and the urban poor are poorer than they have been in decades, and 223 million people do not have enough to eat. Farmer suicides haunt rural communities, often the legacy of the loss of seed ownership after they make deals with biotech companies like Monsanto.

Signs of the failure of globalization and U.S. hegemony abound. Successive attempts to launch a new round of negotiations at the World Trade Organization – the principal institutional vehicle used to enforce globalization – were rejected by angry Third World delegates in Seattle in 1999 and again in Cancun, Mexico, in 2003, and hopes are not high for the Sixth Ministerial meeting to be held in Hong Kong in December 2005. Little progress has been made on the key issue of agriculture and the services negotiations are "in crisis," according to the Global Services Coalition, the international lobby for the services industry. The Free Trade Area of the Americas, once considered NAFTA's unassailable heir, is all but dead, cut through the heart by Brazil's president, Lula da Silva. Its weaker cousin, CAFTA, the Central American Free Trade Agreement, intended to extend NAFTA to the poor countries of El Salvador, Nicaragua, Honduras, Guatemala, Costa Rica, and the Dominican Republic, barely survived a July 27, 2005, vote by the House of Representatives, where it passed by only three votes (214 to 211) and only after the president himself called in personal favours.

Latin America is, in fact, turning against U.S.–style market capitalism. A backlash was inevitable. Beginning with Venezuela in 1998, governments in Latin America's most important countries, including Brazil, Argentina, Uruguay, and Chile, have elected leftist governments with a very different model for the region. Mexicans could elect the popular leftist mayor of Mexico City, Andres Manuel López Obrador, as their next president in the 2006 federal election, much to Washington's chagrin. Citizens' movements in Bolivia, Ecuador, Nicaragua, Costa Rica, El Salvador, and several other smaller countries of Latin America have literally taken over the streets, demanding justice and basic public services. Indigenous peoples in the region are becoming mobilized across nation-state borders in their demand for more political power. "The free trade agenda is in very serious trouble in Latin America," Michael Shifter, vice president of the Washington-based policy group

Inter-American Dialogue, told the *New York Times* (June 30, 2005).

Riordan Roett, director of Latin American studies at Johns Hopkins University, says this is more than just a rejection of market capitalism. "It's almost a wholesale rejection of what people believe they were fed by the folks in Washington." Annette Hester, a foreign-affairs specialist at Laval University, writes in a *Globe and Mail* op-ed article ("The Eagle's Talons Loosen," June 13, 2005) that the failure of the U.S. government to get its way on a number of policy initiatives at the June 2005 meeting of the Organization of American States shows that trust is lacking in the relationship between the United States and the majority of its hemispheric neighbours. "The real story of the meeting," she writes, "is the decreasing ability of the United States to get its way."

Economic globalization was also dealt a blow in late May when first France, and then the Netherlands, voted against the new European Constitution, in spite of the fact that most leading newspapers in both countries were strong supporters. *Le Monde diplomatique* (June 1, 2005) said that the French vote was a "moment of hope for the peoples of Europe and nervousness for its political elites." Increasingly, the idea of one big Europe has been less about coming together to prevent future wars, its original dream, and more about "economic reform"– an ever-expanding free-market zone, the dismantling of the welfare state, lower corporate taxes, and business-friendly legislation. Luxembourg's prime minister, Jean-Claude Juncker, says that there are two deeply antagonistic visions of Europe. There are those who want "the big market and nothing but the big market – a high-level free-trade zone – and those that want a politically integrated Europe" (*Globe and Mail*, June 20, 2005). The *Guardian* (June 2, 2005) analyzed the vote by class and found that France's wealthy overwhelmingly voted for the Constitution and its poor, rural, and working class voted overwhelmingly against.

Alarmed newspaper journalists "have been behaving like entomologists," reports *Le Monde diplomatique*, "examining an insect they had long thought extinct," adding that, because most of them favoured the "yes" side, they are now incapable of understanding the scale of the rout. The citizens of France understood they were being asked to accept fierce competition within Europe among the producers of goods and services and among a set of social systems caught in a downward spiral. "The 'no' vote represents a setback to ultraliberals' attempts to impose, all over the world and in contempt of people's wishes, the economic monoculture laid down by the dogma of globalization." EU leaders admitted that their grand project is in tatters after an explosive June 19, 2005, summit. "People will tell you Europe is not in crisis," said Juncker. Don't believe them, he said: "It is in deep crisis."

The last five years have also witnessed the flowering of a civil-society movement to provide alternatives to economic globalization and the military might that keeps it in place. The World Social Forum was created as a symbolic and political counterweight to the World Economic Forum, where, every January, the CEOs of the world's thousand largest global corporations meet with heads of state in the village of Davos, Switzerland. While the World Economic Forum serves as an occasion for corporate and government elites to promote economic globalization, the World Social Forum, whose motto is "Another World Is Possible," brings literally thousands of grass-roots civil-society groups together to put forward alternative policies in the spheres of economics, international affairs, cultural diversity, human rights, social justice, and environmental stewardship. Organizers of the first meeting, held in Porto Alegre, Brazil, were overwhelmed by the attendance of 20,000 people. But that number seems modest when compared to the 2005 meeting, also held in Porto Alegre, which was attended by 150,000 activists, writers, and academics. Local, regional, and national Social Forums are also now held around the world.

## CANADA'S ROLE

The Martin Liberals appear to be untouched by this growing opposition to neo-liberal economic policies. Starting with the

Mulroney Conservatives, consecutive Canadian governments have increasingly not only adopted U.S. economic globalization policies at home and abroad, but taken an aggressive position to advance them. Canada is now a leading advocate for unregulated free trade at the WTO and in the Americas, where its policies are virtually indistinguishable from those of the United States. Canada was a strong proponent of the Multilateral Agreement on Investment, a proposed international treaty that would have given transnational companies huge new rights to challenge government authority in every sector of policy. (The MAI was defeated in 1997 by a coordinated international civil-society campaign.) Under the Chrétien and Martin Liberals, the Department of Foreign Affairs and International Trade has grown in power. DFAIT now vets all draft legislation for its implications on trade, creating what some call "policy chill." Canada's hard-earned reputation as a force for good in the world is tarnished now by its positions on human rights, food security, and the privatization of essential social services in the Third World.

Most Canadians don't know, for instance, that the Canadian government was the only country among fifty-three to vote against the human right to water at an April 26, 2002, meeting of a United Nations committee. Thirty-seven countries voted yes, fifteen abstained, but only Canada voted no. The official line from the Canadian government about this decision now is that "General Comment No. 15" – the first step toward a UN Convention on the Right to Water – contains a phrase on international obligations that might force Canada to share its water resources with other countries. Given Canada's careless inclusion of water in NAFTA and the lack of response by the federal government to the Great Lakes water diversion plan, it is pretty difficult to accept this reasoning. In any case, Ashfaq Khalfan, a human-rights lawyer with the UN Centre on Housing Rights and Evictions who helped draft General Comment No. 15, has written the Canadian government assuring it that any language that seems to imply a state obligation to share water could come out of any future documents. The Canadian government is standing firm in its opposition to the human right to water to the utter bafflement of the entire development community.

Similarly, Canada supports World Bank and IMF policies to privatize essential social and public services such as health care and water in developing countries, much to the distress of many Canadian aid and development groups. While it is naive to think the Martin Liberals are going to do an about-face on these questions in the near future, Canadians wanting to define security in a broader context are going to have to work hard to counter them. It is not overstating the case to say that these policies are killing people in poor countries. Canadian support for Structural Adjustment Programs must end and Canada must work as a force in the global community to reinstate essential public services around the world. This, of course, means fighting for them at home, and there is no more urgent domestic agenda for Canadians than preserving publicly funded health care. While all Canadians deplore the long waiting lists for certain surgeries, it is imperative that energies go into the fight to reduce these wait times and not into destroying medicare. Unless Canadians fight now and fight hard for public health, American health corporations are going to move into Canada. When this happens, there will no longer be American health care and Canadian health care: there will be North American health care built on the competitive model of unregulated competition.

Finally, Canadians must demand a review of trade policy in Canada and internationally. The U.S. government refuses to abide by the terms of NAFTA, and this gives Canada the opening to reopen the agreement and remove the most egregious provisions. At the very least, water must be exempted from NAFTA and all other trade agreements; Chapter 11, which allows corporations to sue governments, must be removed; and the energy provisions of the deal must be rewritten or deleted altogether. Canada needs to make a thorough assessment of what twenty years of neo-liberal policy and trade agreements have done to Canadians and to people around the world. Fundamental to this assessment should be a commitment to finally bring labour, social, and environmental groups into the process, instead of playing lip service to civil society while listening only to the big-business community. Above all, the right of each nation to develop and protect its own institutions and standards and to meet its development needs must be respected.

## HUMAN SECURITY

Fundamentalism, extremism, violence, and terrorism are on the rise. The horrific July 2005 bombings in London brought home the fact that vigilance cannot be weakened. The fight against terrorism is nowhere near won. Of course, the world community must take measures to protect innocent people from random acts of terror. But the same community must also ask why there are people who would kill like this, why they are prepared to give their own lives in the act of killing. The most important step is to be clear about the nature of the problem.

First, the current spate of terrorist attacks is not the result of a conflict between Muslims and Christians or between East and West, as it is so often characterized. The conflict that results in these attacks is between moderates and fundamentalists. Terrorists are not obeying some basic tenets of Islam; rather they have distorted the teachings of their religion. As Bonnie Diamond of the National Association of Women and the Law points out, the vast majority of Muslims do not choose radical Islam any more than the vast majority of Christians choose evangelical Christianity. These acts of violence have been committed by a tiny group of people and are contrary to the values and faith-based beliefs of the great majority of people around the world. The fact is there are fundamentalists in the West as well.

While it is true that Christian evangelicalism does not teach its followers to go out and kill, it does divide the world into sinners and believers and almost joyfully awaits the fate that will befall those who do not accept faith on their terms. What can be said of the sects of evangelical Christianity that believe that, at Armageddon, the entire population of Israel will be forced to choose between accepting Jesus Christ as their personal saviour or perishing in horrible ways, except that it, too, perpetrates violence? The same idea of choice between accepting Christ or perishing doesn't exist for Muslims, who are condemned by virtue of their faith.

Fundamentalist movements in both the Middle East and the United States work in mutually enforcing ways to resist peaceful solutions as they share a world view of absolutes. By adopting a Christian versus Muslim or West versus East analysis, society creates an atmosphere of "us versus them." For the vast majority of Muslims who are moderate, these are terrible times, and their sense of isolation in North America and Europe is growing. Omar Alghabra, president of the Canadian Arab Federation, wrote in a July 15, 2005, op-ed for the *Ottawa Citizen*, "It might be difficult for a non-Muslim, non-Arab to understand this insidious type of discrimination which is experienced on a daily basis: at border crossings, at the water coolers at work, in schools hallways, at social barbeques, or in encounters with law enforcement officers." Targeting a whole people is not the way to stop the spread of fundamentalism, which breeds violence. "If terrorism is going to create a divide, it should not be between Arabs and Muslims and the western world. It should be between peace-loving, law-abiding humans and the violent criminal elements of society."

Second, terrorism is not an act of war. It is a criminal act and must be treated as such. A war needs a clearly defined enemy. Characterizing terrorist acts as a "war on terror" allows the Bush administration to characterize whole countries and peoples as "evil." This is how Bush and Cheney got buy-in for the invasion of Iraq. They falsely connected Saddam Hussein to al-Qaeda and convinced the American people that they were at war with Iraq and invasion was just the next logical step. Timothy Garton Ash, professor of European studies at the University of Oxford, writes that there are three things necessary for a terrorist attack: hate (which has causes – some of which can be removed); mass migration and mass transit, enabling haters to roam freely among the hated; and "advances" in the technology of killing (*Globe and Mail*, July 9, 2005). Terrorism is not a single army that can be defeated, says Ash, it is a technique, a means to an end. The way to defeat it is not by being passive, but by being smart. If buses, subways, and buildings are the target, then what is needed is skilled policing at home, not more soldiering abroad.

Third, there are indeed "root causes" to some of the hate that fuels these crimes. It is possible and indeed imperative, to detest the crime and condemn and fight it effectively, while, at the same time, still seeking for ways to change the conditions that breed such hate. The Bush–Cheney team don't want to hear this, but the anger raging in so many poor and conflicted parts of the world can be traced directly to economic and military policies that have deliberately allowed some individuals, corporations, and countries to reap the wealth of the world while billions live in poverty and ecosystems crash. William Shulz, executive director of Amnesty International, reports that the gross product of all Arab countries together is less than that of Spain. One in five Arabs lives on less than US$2 a day. In Arab countries, unemployment averages around 20 per cent; in Egypt, it reaches 55 per cent, and in Saudi Arabia, nearly 60 per cent. In his 2004 book, *Tainted Legacy*, Shulz observes that millions of poor, unemployed young Arab men look "with sympathy" upon political and religious extremists. "If we define human rights in the broad sense of the word, i.e., the right to bed, board, health care, and education, the statistics in the Middle East are devastating. There are demonstrable ties between global violations of human rights and the onset and practice of terrorism." Leading U.S. experts on terror say the young London bombers fit the profile of a terrorist, reported Michael Valpy for the *Globe and Mail* (July 15, 2005): they may have been "home grown" as everyone likes to say, but they never felt part of British society. Rather they held strong personal and social grievances, which made them vulnerable to a message of violence.

Feminist scholars such as the Caribbean's Dr. Peggy Antrobus point out that when governments are forced to get out of the business of looking after the needs of their people, either because they are poor or because of Structural Adjustment programs, religious institutions often move in to fill the void. Naturally, they provide religious instruction along with food, education, and health care. Sometimes, they don't even provide much for the practical needs of the people to whom they minister. The *Times of London* reported on the infamous Pakistani religious school Darul Uloom Haqqania, near Peshawar, often referred to as the "University of Jihad," where vulnerable young people are exposed to fundamentalist and extremist teachings and trained to become a ready supply of soldiers and suicide bombers. Most of the students come from the poorest section of society and receive free education, lodging, and meals. However, conditions are deplorable and regularly condemned by human-rights groups as crowded and inhumane. The students are subjected to a regime as harsh as prison and many are put in chains and heavy iron fetters for any violation of the rules. Teaching is rudimentary: most instruction is on basic religious dogma. The youth are ill-prepared for any kind of work when they leave, except terrorism. Similar religious training in mosques is available to poor young men in Jamaica, another breeding ground for terrorism, where the message of injustice and the call for redistribution of wealth – a core message of terrorist indoctrination – is eagerly received.

Henry Giroux, American education scholar, says that the merging of religion and politics in both the East and the West has become the central problem of our time. Writing in the *Toronto Star* (July 24, 2005), Giroux reminds us that many Americans are also turning to religious groups to provide not only education and social services but also a sense of community and meaning – what he calls "the discourse of public morality, civil engagement and the ethical imperative of democracy." We must develop a "language of critique" argues Giroux, to counter the rabid individualism of market ideology. This means rooting out all those fundamentalisms

– market, political, religious, militaristic – so prevalent in American society today. "Collective security from poverty, illness, old age, unemployment and the loss of the most basic social provisions such as health care and a decent education have been replaced by market forces that view misfortune with disdain and welfare institutions as a poisonous reminder of Marxist orthodoxy." A deregulated, privatized, outsourced future is a bleak one. Giroux says the future has become the enemy. "As long as politics fails to provide a sense of meaning, purpose and dignity to people's lives, religious fundamentalists will step in and take up this task."

State-sponsored public services and education can help arm governments fighting these fanatics within their own borders. Bonnie Diamond of the National Association of Women and the Law says that people deprived of the legitimate ways of maintaining their dignity and security are easily turned to illegitimate actions. "You don't have the means to fight back with any sort of equal resources. All you have is the element of surprise, maybe a packet of dynamite, and the urge to have your people survive. If we don't go about levelling the playing field – redistributing resources and wealth in the world – I suspect that the danger we experience in New York or London will become a way of life."

The good news for humanity is that many governments seem to finally understand the need to broaden the definition of security if they are to counter terrorism. At a July 2005 Toronto conference of international security and emergency experts, from more than fifty countries, officials called for a dramatic rethinking of the global strategy on terrorism. Experts said that the world hasn't done a good enough job of understanding and tackling the "disenchantment that is the root cause" of terrorism. They argued that the morphing of al-Qaeda into a global movement that is increasingly attracting new recruits warrants a "challenge on the assumption of the war on terror." Former Scotland Yard anti-terror expert Peter Power told the *Ottawa Citizen* (July 11, 2005) that the West must embark on a new campaign for the hearts and minds of Muslims, especially the young. And it has to critically re-examine government policies to find out if they are feeding the fires of hatred in the Muslim world.

Power says that there is no point in trying to have a dialogue with al-Qaeda, "but we are in a long game and we've got to get into the Muslim communities, go to the mullahs, go to the teachers, go to the children, and understand what is happening." Power cited a concern of the conference that despite the "war on terror," hatred of the West – especially the United States – is growing and noted that a few months before, in a predominantly Muslim state of Nigeria, seventy-three of the one hundred baby boys born in one week at the state hospital were named Osama.

## CANADA'S ROLE

This is another opportunity for Canada to take a stand. There is clearly a new openness in the world to a fresh definition of security and a new way of understanding terrorism. Canada has taken leadership in this arena before. During the 1990s, reports Steven Staples of the Polaris Institute, Canada helped shape the post–Cold War environment by promoting the rule of international law. Canada was instrumental in the creation of both the International Criminal Court and the United Nations Landmines Treaty. Then Foreign Affairs Minister Lloyd Axworthy attempted to redefine security by promoting peacekeeping skills in the Canadian forces and developing the doctrine of human security, which places people and their human rights at the centre of security policy, rather than states. It was always hard slogging to try to get the United States to subscribe to this agenda, Staples notes, but it became impossible after George Bush was elected. He points to a post-9/11 Department of National Defense assessment of the global changes precipitated by the attacks that correctly predicted the shift back to traditional concepts of security and away from "championing poverty eradication and human rights." The report also correctly predicted that the rule of international law would be cast aside in the war on terror, adding, "The international system will be re-ordered into allies or enemies in the fight against terror."

The predictions made in the Department of National Defense report were chillingly accurate and the results of returning to the hard military solution are clear for all to see. The Bush administration, however, is not going to change course. On the contrary, only days after the terrorist bombings in London, the Pentagon announced a new strategy involving an expanded role for the U.S. military inside the United States. This has led civil liberties groups to worry that long-established barriers to military surveillance and combat operations would be eroded. Even the right-wing Cato Institute expressed concern. Gene Healey, a senior editor with the Institute, told the *Washington Post* (July 11, 2005), "The move toward a domestic intelligence capability by the military is troubling. The last time the military got heavily involved in domestic surveillance, during the Vietnam War era, military intelligence kept thousands of files on Americans guilty of nothing more than of opposing the war. I don't think we want to go down that road again."

The question for Canada is, once again, one of independence. Will Canada have the courage to reject the U.S. military strategy and lead the global community toward a redefinition of the threat to personal security? If it is true that U.S. hegemony is making the world more violent and less stable, does Canada not have an obligation to take a different path? Roch Tasse of the International Civil Liberties Monitoring Group, adding his voice to that of many groups in Canada, has urged a rollback of the new laws in Canada that threaten the civil liberties of Canadians. "Canada's response to terrorism," he says, "must be rooted in the rule of law, with an emphasis on international law and the use of multilateral institutions, including the Criminal Court; in democratic development and good governance; in respect for human rights and civil liberties; and ultimately in social justice and eradication of poverty as the only way to truly confront terrorism."

Inter Pares, a Canadian organization working to promote international social justice, agrees. In its November 2004 paper,

"Rethinking Development," the group expressed concern about the breakdown in the rule of international law. Yes, there are outlaws, rogue states, and military forces, says Inter Pares. But these elements are operating outside the law and are, therefore, lawless when they conduct their campaigns. "But these forces are not responsible for protecting and sustaining the rule of law; to the contrary, they are committed to undermining and overturning it. It is the state that is charged with defending the rule of law. When the legitimate actors of the state overturn law to seek out the lawless, the lawless win and the rule of law loses, and with it, the rights of citizens everywhere." The deterioration of the international rule of law since 9/11 has been a major victory for all those who seek anarchy as the landscape out of which to construct an authoritarian future, says the report. Times of extreme global militarism such as the one we are currently experiencing form the perfect terrain for "demagogues, warlords, dictators, and crime bosses, whose power is reinforced by illicit wealth and the impunity they secure in lawless times." Inter Pares expresses no surprise that within this continuum, intolerant and cruelly repressive fundamentalisms – religious and ideological – easily breed, grow, and dominate.

Any reconfiguring of the notion of security from terror must take into account the issue of social security as well. Canada disgraced itself at the July 2005 G-8 meeting in Scotland when the Martin government refused to meet its previous commitment to spend 0.7 per cent of its GDP on international aid. Although Canada has one of the most robust economies in the world, says Gerry Barr, president of the Canadian Council for International Co-operation, its commitment is one of the lowest among OECD countries. For every hundred dollars the economy produces, only twenty-six cents goes to overseas development. It will be hard for Canada to "punch above its weight" as it has done in the past, if it continues to break such minimal promises, says Barr.

The connection between terrorism and Third World poverty was put in sharp relief when George Bush, in a break from the

G-8 meeting in Scotland, commented on the "contrast" between the suicide bombers and the gathering of world leaders. Here they were trying to solve world poverty, he declared, while others were bent on destruction. However, the British-based World Development Movement summed up the thoughts of the civil-society movement on the G-8 meeting in a July 8, 2005, press release: "The final G8 communiqué is an insult to the hundreds of thousands of campaigners who listened in good faith to the world leaders' claim that they were willing to seriously address poverty in Africa. More importantly, it is a disaster for the world's poor. The agreements on trade, debt, aid, and climate change are nowhere near sufficient to tackle the global poverty and environmental crisis we face. We are furious but not surprised. Calling on the G8 to Make Poverty History this year was always a brave attempt to put aside 30 years of knowledge of G8 failures and suspend our disbelief at the notion that the countries responsible for causing so much poverty could become the solution." John Hilary, with the group War on Want, added: "Bob Geldoff may be content with crumbs from the table of his rich political friends, but we did not come to Gleneagles as beggars. We came to demand justice for the world's poor. We didn't get it."

## ECOLOGICAL SECURITY

If anything is going to limit the supposedly infinite possibilities of economic globalization, it will be the earth itself. Humanity has destroyed more forests, wetlands, and wild spaces in the last hundred years than in all of history. The highly regarded journal *Science* reports that recent extinction rates are one hundred to one thousand times higher than before humans existed. Moreover, it says, with the exponential extinction rate now being experienced, that number could increase to between one thousand and ten thousand times by the end of the century. Smithsonian Institution biologist Jonathan Coddington predicts a "biodiversity deficit" within this century, as a result of which species and ecosystems will be destroyed at rates faster than Nature can create new ones. Eighty per cent of the oceans' large fish are gone. The United Nations Environment Program reports that only one-fifth of the planet is still covered with sustainable forests, and few of those are protected by governments. Over half of the world's wetlands have been lost over the last century. In Asia alone, more than five thousand square kilometres are destroyed every year to make way for industrialization.

And greenhouse-gas emissions are due to reach double pre-industrial levels by 2080, enough to lead to an increase in warming similar to the increase that ended the ice age. Simon Retallack and Peter Bunyard describe the implications of global warming in a 2003 special edition of the *Ecologist*: "With higher temperatures, there is more energy driving the earth's climatic systems, which in turn causes more violent weather events. Severe storms, floods, droughts, dust storms, sea surges, crumbling coastlines, salt water intrusion of groundwater, failing crops, dying forests, the inundation of low-lying islands, and the spread of endemic diseases such as malaria, dengue fever, and schistosomiasis is in the cards if the consumption of fossil fuels is not phased out. . . . Agriculture world-wide would face severe disruption and economies would tumble. There would be millions of environmental refugees – people fleeing from the intruding seas, or equally from the deserts they have left in their wake after stripping the land of its vegetation."

Phasing out fossil-fuel use would require a different model for the earth than the current model of unrestricted, unregulated growth. Even if humanity does not voluntarily phase out fossil fuels, it is soon going to be facing major limitations due to coming energy shortages. Similarly, the world is running out of fresh water, as economic globalization, industrialization, and urbanization draw down the existing stock. To fuel its "economic miracle," China is diverting water from the vast wheat fields in the north, destroying surface water and depleting aquifers. Four hundred of the country's six hundred northern cities are facing severe water shortages, as is over half the population.

The tragic truth is that the world is running out of clean water. With every passing day, our demand for fresh water outpaces its availability, and thousands more people are put at risk. Per-capita water use doubles every twenty years. And we will add another 2.6 billion people to the earth in the next quarter century. Technology and advanced sanitation systems in the global North have allowed people to use – and waste – far more water than they need, while lack of funding for sanitation in the Third World ensures that 90 per cent of the sewage and waste water is poured untreated into waterways. The legacy of factory farming, flood irrigation, the construction of massive dams, toxic dumping, wetlands and forest destruction, and urban and industrial pollution has damaged the earth's surface water so badly that we are now mining underground water reserves far faster than nature can replenish them. Ancient aquifers are either being drained or destroyed by pollution.

As a result, the earth is beginning to resemble an apple that is drying up on the inside, with brown spots on an otherwise healthy-looking skin. Scientists call these areas "hot stains" and want us to understand that these parts of the world are not undergoing cyclical drought but are actually running out of water. They include the Middle East, twenty-two countries in Africa, all of Northern China, huge parts of India, Australia, the Mexican Valley, including Mexico City, which is literally sinking into the ground it stands on, and the southwestern United Sates.

Finally, the model of unlimited growth is destroying food and biological diversity in the name of science and profit. Genetically engineered foods are contaminating local seeds and crops, invading wild species, and destroying biodiversity. Transnational corporations, using the intellectual property rights imposed through the WTO, are plundering the biological heritage of the Third World. Indian activist and physicist Vandana Shiva compares it to the conquest and colonization of the New World by European powers five hundred years ago. In her 1997 book, *Biopiracy: The Plunder of Nature and Knowledge*, Dr. Shiva writes: "The assumption of 'empty lands' – terra nullus – of Columbus's time, is now being expanded to 'empty life,' seeds and medicinal plants. The takeover of native resources during colonization was justified on the ground that indigenous people did not 'improve' their land. The same logic is now used to appropriate biodiversity from the original owners and innovators by defining their seeds, medicinal plants, and medical knowledge as nature, as non-science, and treating the tools of genetic engineering as the yardstick of 'improvement.'"

Five hundred years ago, says Shiva, it was enough to be a non-Christian culture to lose all claims and rights. Now it is enough to be a non-Western culture with a distinctive world view and diverse knowledge systems to lose all rights and claims. Just as people's humanity was blanked out then, their intellect is blanked out now. Patents and genetic engineering are being used to carve out new colonies. "The land, the forests, the rivers, the oceans, and the atmosphere have all been colonized, eroded, and polluted. Capital now has to look for new colonies to invade and exploit for its further accumulation. These new colonies are, in my view, the interior spaces of the bodies of women, plants, and animals," Shiva writes.

If nothing else will do it, surely these stunning realities will wake up a sleeping elite. Right now, the system of economic globalization and the ecological limits of the earth are on a collision course. The only way to cope with current and impending ecological crises is to change our economic systems and political models and build new ones around the requirements of the natural world. Richard Heinberg teaches sustainable ecology at New College in Santa Rosa, California. He has been warning about what he calls the "petroleum plateau" for several years and describes two paths to deal with the coming energy crisis: Plan War and Plan Powerdown. By merely maintaining its current course, says Heinberg, the world is heading toward Plan War, in which some parts of the world will start to run out of energy sources before others. Those with military might will use their wealth and power to protect supplies for themselves, wasting precious resources that could have been used for conservation. Plan Powerdown calls for an international effort toward conservation and co-operation in reducing non-essential energy use. This course will need political will at the highest level if it is to be implemented. Alternative-energy sources that are not currently competitive with fossil fuels would have to be subsidized, and the use of fossil fuels taxed to encourage conservation. Economic processes would have to be localized and downsized.

## CANADA'S ROLE

While Heinberg is referring only to energy, there is little question that the world is on a "Plan War" footing environmentally. What is clearly needed is "Plan Rejuvenation" for the earth, and many Canadians would be thrilled to see their country lead or join such a campaign. But this would require Canada to address its own shortcomings.

First and perhaps foremost, Canada must abandon the Smart Regulation initiative and commit itself to a regime of rules and standards to ensure the safety of Canada's food and drug supply, as well as clean air and water for generations to come. Cathy Holtslander of Beyond Factory Farming says that regulations are the "nuts and bolts" of sovereignty and are designed to create fairness, protect people's health and safety, and set limits on unacceptable behaviour. To give them up is to give up the right to self-determination. All of the policies now being drafted that would undermine the safety of Canada's food supply, seeds, and drugs must be abandoned and the Precautionary Principle must be placed at the centre of the rules governing these sectors. The National Farmers Union says that Canadians need a publicly funded, publicly controlled plant-breeding system to protect their food supply. Shiv Chopra says simply that Canada must immediately rid the food supply of hormones, antibiotics, GMOs, rendered protein, and pesticides.

Canada also must do better in honouring its Kyoto commitment, which also means that Environment Canada must abandon its Smart Regulation–inspired "Framework" project and return to its role as the most important protector of Canada's ecosystem. It is a mistake of monumental proportions for the department to exchange its monitoring and enforcement role for a voluntary "partnership" with big business, including, or perhaps especially, with the energy sector. Plans for the Mackenzie Valley pipeline should be scrapped and a moratorium placed on further development of the Alberta tar sands while a full assessment is made of both the environmental impacts of tar-sands development and the political and economic ramifications of American control of these resources. A fixation with the energy and military needs of the United States has limited Canada's vision and potential.

As Sierra Club of Canada's Elizabeth May says, "Canada has a place in the world distinct from our proximity to the United States. Our geographical placement alongside the declining and decaying empire to the South has the magnetic force of economic clout, but the True North for Canada is to the pole. Our destiny lies far more in our planetary role as a Circumpolar nation. We must increasingly make common cause with the other Arctic Nations. We must be a voice for radical reductions in North American dependency on fossil fuels, or we risk losing ice cover at the North Pole altogether. We risk losing the polar bear, the permafrost, the Peary Caribou, the way of life of the traditional peoples, the Dene, the Inuit, the Gwitchen – indeed we risk destroying life on Earth. We cannot have our SUVs and polar bears too."

Similarly, Canada must take action to protect its freshwater supplies and this must happen soon. Canada needs a National Water Policy, which would include an exemption for water from NAFTA and all other present and future trade and investment treaties; recognition of the human right to water; binding rules to stop corporations and factory farms from abusing fresh water; a moratorium on all new diversions from the Great Lakes and other shared boundary waters; a prohibition against the privatization of public water; and rules to protect Canada's groundwater sources. The Boundary Waters Treaty must be altered to include all waters of the Great Lakes Basin, including groundwater and tributaries; to strengthen bi-national control over use and diversion of the Lakes; to adopt ecological integrity and the Precautionary Principle as the cornerstones of the Treaty; and to establish the priority of that agreement in the event of conflicts with international trade agreements. If the United States does not want to enter into these kinds of negotiations, Canada should reassert its sovereign right to its own energy resources and withhold or reduce energy exports.

Finally, to become eligible to take international environmental leadership, Canada must clean up the disgraceful practices of its mining industry in other countries. Canada is the world's leading mineral exploration nation and the leading supplier of capital for the mining industry worldwide. MiningWatch Canada reports that 64 per cent of the world's mining companies are based in Canada, and Canadian companies have an interest in a portfolio of almost 2,800 mineral properties located outside of Canada. Almost half of the $12.7 billion in equity financing raised for mineral exploration and development projects every year is for companies listed on Canadian stock exchanges. "The expansion of Canadian mining overseas has been accompanied by some of the world's worst environmental disasters, the forced relocation of Indigenous Peoples, and numerous human rights abuses," says the watchdog group. The irresponsible mining practices of Canadian companies are facilitated by the government's financial policies. Tax credits and subsidies enabling the write-off of foreign exploration and development expenses against income and corporate tax are some of the most generous in the world.

The Export Development Corporation provides export credits, loans, and political risk insurance, with no human-rights framework, no disclosure, and ineffective environmental regulation. Canadian stock exchanges have no environmental or human-rights requirements. Says MiningWatch, "Action is needed to hold Canadian mining companies and the Canadian government to account. Mining companies are too often the 'ugly Canadian' in their complicity in human rights abuses and environmental disasters when they operate abroad." In fact, a broad-based coalition of human rights and environmental groups, unions, and Canadian churches have been urging the Canadian government to adopt binding human rights, labour, and environmental standards for Canadian corporations – including mining companies – operating overseas. At issue, explains John Lewis of KAIROS, the Canadian Ecumenical Justice Initiative, is the existing Canadian government approach of encouraging voluntary compliance with such standards. This approach, Lewis argues, has demonstrably failed. The Canadian government must hold Canadian corporations accountable for their actions in other countries, and government, financial, and political support should be conditional on compliance with tough international standards. The coalition is also urging Canada to adopt legislation that would make it possible for people from other countries to sue Canadian corporations in Canadian courts for alleged "violations of the laws of nations."

How the government of Canada answers these great questions of our time will depend on whose counsel it seeks. So far, it is listening almost exclusively to the Canadian Council of Chief Executives and its think-tank allies. The Canadian Council of Chief Executives does not speak for Canada. It speaks for the interests of its members, many of which are branch plants of American corporations. It is past time for the Martin government to seek the counsel of other sectors in society. Civil-society organizations concerned with human rights, health care, social justice, poverty, working people, education, international development, cultural diversity, conservation, and the environment would have a very different set of priorities. They would tell the prime minister that they want to be good neighbours and help secure safe borders. But they would warn him to back away from this process of deep integration with the Bush administration and get on with the job he was elected to do – protecting the lives and livelihoods of Canadians.

Joining the Bush Revolution would be a terrible mistake for Canada in this time of "transiting eras." A better choice would be to seek out and work with the many millions of Americans who are equally appalled at their government and the triumvirate that brought George Bush to power. They are hard at work forming an effective opposition to the Bush administration and need support in building a different base for a future North America.

They are achieving some remarkable successes. Bush's social-security reform is deeply unpopular and may not succeed. Both sides of the House are fighting back against the power of the big drug companies. A bill that would permit the import of cheaper drugs from countries like Canada, co-sponsored by a Democrat, Senator Byron Dorgan, and a Republican, Senator Olympia Snowe, is making its way through Congress despite opposition from the White House. On July 21, 2005, the House handed Bush his first defeat in his efforts to preserve the broad powers of the USA Patriot Act when it voted to place a time limit on the FBI's ability to seize library and bookstore records for terrorism investigations. Moderate Republicans joined Democrats to prevent the Bush administration from bringing in legislation to end the right of filibuster when the Democrats were using the practice to hold up judicial nominations. And George Bush has been forced by the international community to adopt a more respectful tone with North Korea in order to get that country back to the nuclear-weapons negotiating table. In addition, partly because of the growing unpopularity of the costly military disaster in Iraq, polls show that George Bush is finally losing support at home.

This is not a call to put up borders around Canada. Nor is it an announcement of presumed moral superiority with respect to our neighbours. The world has some very serious problems that need to be addressed. Canada must decide if it is going to forge deeper economic, foreign policy, social, and resource ties with the world's superpower under its most aggressive government in modern history, or if it is going to stand with moderate countries and people around the world to form a counterweight. The world will take note of what Canada decides.

# index